HOTEL CRONSTADT
10 R
PARIS

D0039622

PARIS

ENCOUNTER

— Paris Shuttle —
33 1 53 39 18 18.

CATHERINE LE NEVEZ

Paris Encounter
1st edition – May 2007

Published by Lonely Planet Publications Pty Ltd
ABN 36 005 607 983

Australia	Head Office, Locked Bag 1, Footscray, Vic 3011
	☎ 03 8379 8000 fax 03 8379 8111
	talk2us@lonelyplanet.com.au
USA	150 Linden St, Oakland, CA 94607
	☎ 510 893 8555
	toll free 800 275 8555
	fax 510 893 8572
	info@lonelyplanet.com
UK	72–82 Rosebery Avenue, Clerkenwell, London EC1R 4RW
	☎ 020 7841 9000 fax 020 7841 9001
	go@lonelyplanet.co.uk

This title was commissioned in Lonely Planet's London office and produced by: **Commissioning Editors** Amanda Canning, Judith Bamber **Coordinating Editor** Sasha Baskett **Coordinating Cartographer** Corey Hutchison **Layout Designer** Pablo Gastar **Assisting Editors** Laura Stansfeld, Melissa Faulkner **Assisting Cartographer** Valentina Kremenchutskaya, Daniel Fennessy **Assisting Layout Designer** Wibowo Rusli **Managing Editor** Bruce Evans **Managing Cartographer** Mark Griffiths **Cover Designer** Jennifer Smith **Project Manager** Sarah Sloane **Series Designers** Nic Lehman, Wendy Wright **Thanks to** Stephanie Pearson, Sally Darmody, Celia Wood, Kate McDonald, Imogen Bannister, Laura Jane, Quentin Frayne, Paul Piaia, Vivek Wagle, Michelle Glynn

ISBN 978 1 74059 748 7

Printed through Colorcraft Ltd, Hong Kong.
Printed in China.

Acknowledgement Paris Metro Map © 2006 RATP.

HOW TO USE THIS BOOK

Colour-Coding & Maps

Colour-coding is used for symbols on maps and in the text that they relate to (eg all eating venues on the maps and in the text are given a green fork symbol). Each neighbourhood also gets its own colour, and this is used down the edge of the page and throughout that neighbourhood section.

Shaded yellow areas on the maps are to denote 'areas of interest' – be that for historical significance, attractive architecture or a strip that's good for bars or restaurants. We'd encourage you to head to these areas and just start exploring!

Prices

Multiple prices listed with reviews (eg €10/5 or €10/5/20) indicate adult/child, adult/concession or adult/child/family.

CATHERINE LE NEVEZ

Catherine first lived in Paris aged four and has been returning at every opportunity since, completing her Doctorate of Creative Arts in Writing, Masters in Professional Writing, and postgraduate qualifications in editing and publishing along the way. After revisiting her favourite Parisian haunts and uncovering new ones, she wrote this book in a tiny (but charming) garret under the eaves of a crumbling building in the Sentier quarter in the city's heart.

Catherine's writing on Paris includes Lonely Planet's *Citiescape Paris* book, and newspaper and radio reportage covering the city's literary scene. Elsewhere in France, Catherine has written for Lonely Planet's *France* and *Provence & the Côte d'Azur* guidebooks, and Lonely Planet online accommodation reviews for the Bordeaux and Provence regions, as well as for Nice and Marseille, for which she's also authored Lonely Planet European City Break guides. Wanderlust aside, Paris remains her favourite city on earth.

CATHERINE'S THANKS

Merci beaucoup to the innumerable Parisians who offered insights and inspiration. At Lonely Planet, cheers to Amanda Canning, Mark Griffiths and Sasha Baskett, and to Judith Bamber for entrusting me with this gig. And *merci surtout* to my brother for his resident's knowledge and my parents for instilling in me my lifelong love of Paris.

Our Readers Many thanks to the travellers who wrote to us with helpful hints, useful advice and interesting anecdotes. Trevor Angel, Bianca Barbaro, A Benda, Ann Curthoys, John Docker, My le Ducharme, Margaret Frey, Barry Goldsmith, Tina Hagger, Linda Harper, Sharnie Huth, Sarah Jameson, Christopher Packham, Tom & Mary Rothschild, Dean Wanless, Shao Wei.

Photographs p42, p78, p86, p112, p157, p159 by Catherine Le Nevez; p24 by Destination Events. All other photographs by Lonely Planet Images, and by Barbara Van Zanten p4, p189, p193, p194; Jonathan Smith p6, p62, p83, p96, p131, p152, p160, p161, p191; Carole Martin p6; Jan Stromme p6; Kevin Levesque p8; Ann Cecil p10, p13, p16, p32, p67, p171; Dennis Johnson p12, p118, p174; John Hay p15, p39, p127, p188; Jean-Bernard Carillet p17, p45, p64, p66, p69, p124, p151, p168, p178, p179, p187, p190, p195, p196; Witold Skrypczak p19; Bruce Yuan-Yue Bi p21, p76, p93; John Elk III p22, p26, p30, p60, p73, p123; Sally Dillon p23; Olivier Cirendini p25; Pascale Beroujon p28; Stephen Saks p29, p165; Dennis Jones p30; Martin Moos p30, p54, p80, p120, p128, p184; Anne C Dowie p34; Wayne Walton p44; Greg Gawlowski p52; Bill Wassman p58, p98; Veronica Garbutt p70; Glenn Beanland p77, p138; Greg Elms p82, p163, p192; Richard Nebesky p85, p90, p97, p199; Izzet Keribar p91; Richard I'Anson p94; Manfred Gottschalk p100; Neil Setchfield p106, p115, p167, p182; Bethune Carmichael p107; Juliet Coombe p109, p146, p170, p180, p185; Christine Osborne p135, p148; David Tomlinson p175; Elliot Daniel p183; Mark Honan p186. **Cover photograph** Centre Pompidou, Cozzi Guido/4Corners Images.
All images are copyright of the photographers unless otherwise indicated. Many of the images in this guide are available for licensing from **Lonely Planet Images:** www.lonelyplanetimages.com.

Gargoyles on the Cathédrale de Notre Dame de Paris (p135) overlook the Seine

CONTENTS

THE AUTHOR	**03**
THIS IS PARIS	**07**
HIGHLIGHTS	**08**
PARIS DIARY	**23**
ITINERARIES	**29**
QUARTERS	**34**
>INVALIDES & EIFFEL TOWER	38
>ARC DE TRIOMPHE, CHAMPS-ÉLYSÉES & GRANDS BOULEVARDS	48
>LOUVRE & LES HALLES	72
>MONTMARTRE	88
>BELLEVILLE & SURROUNDS	102
>MARAIS & BASTILLE	114
>THE ISLANDS	134
>LATIN QUARTER, ST-GERMAIN DES PRÉS & MONTPARNASSE	142
FURTHER AFIELD	**169**
SNAPSHOTS	**174**
BACKGROUND	**199**
DIRECTORY	**209**
INDEX	**223**

THIS IS PARIS

France's romanticised capital is one of the world's major metropolises, yet it retains an intimate air. Hidden among Paris' icons is a maze of cobblestone backstreets. And, with an almost total absence of high-rises, the *quartiers* (quarters) making up central Paris resemble a collection of villages.

There is, of course, no shortage of icons. Paris has more recognisable monuments than any other city. Landmarks such as the Art Nouveau Eiffel Tower, the stained-glass Notre Dame and the dove-white domes of Sacré-Cœur all depict the city timelessly. Just as iconic are lamplit bridges reflecting in the Seine and wicker chairs lining the terraces of *belle époque* brasseries. And striking additions, such as the Musée du Quai Branly, contribute to the city's contemporary cachet.

Paris' grandeur abounds along its sweeping boulevards, and in its superb *haute cuisine* restaurants and luxurious fashion houses. It's evident in the astonishing array of museums, including the inimitable Louvre.

But it's a stroll in the quarters' narrow backstreets that will take you into the city's heart. Above the screech of scooters and sirens you might hear the tinkling of a piano from an open apartment window, a DJ spinning a set in a bar, or sax players practising on church steps. Or maybe you'll inhale the aroma of baguettes baking at a *boulangerie*, coffee grinding at a corner café, scorched rubber rising through vents from the metro, or perfume wafting from chic city dwellers. Perhaps you'll be lured by offbeat boutiques, centuries-old passageways or an empty table at a cosy, candlelit bistro. Open-air street market stalls spilling over with flowers and fresh produce, and flea markets filled with antiques, are just as enticing.

For all its impressive icons, it's this village life that gives the city its prevailing charm. *This* is Paris.

Top left Coffee break on rue Mouffetard (p162), Latin Quarter **Top right** Romance in the grounds in front of Basilique du Sacré-Cœur (p90), Montmartre **Bottom** Shops on rue Cler (p45), Invalides

>1 See the City of Light at night from the Eiffel Tower 10
>2 Browse the shelves of a legendary
   Paris bookshop 12
>3 Enjoy a picnic in Paris' most popular park 13
>4 Marvel at Monet's *Waterlilies* in the
   Musée de l'Orangerie 14
>5 Take a romantic stroll along the Promenade
   Plantée 15
>6 Amble the enchanting backstreets of Montmartre 16
>7 Watch Paris float past from a boat on the Seine 17
>8 Navigate your way around the labyrinthine Louvre 18
>9 Pay homage to the departed at Cimetière
   du Père Lachaise 20
>10 Contemplate modern art and architecture
    at the Centre Pompidou 22

Eiffel Tower (p39)

HIGHLIGHTS

>1 EIFFEL TOWER

SEE THE CITY OF LIGHT AT NIGHT FROM THE EIFFEL TOWER

The second-most mesmerising view of this city by night is from the tip of the city's iconic spire, with its 360-degree views over Paris. (The most mesmerising night-time view is from an aeroplane – preferably one that is landing.)

About 250 million people have ascended the tower to date. Most visit its three platforms (57m, 115m and 276m) in daytime hours, when, on a clear day, views from the top extend up to 60km. Far fewer visitors make the pilgrimage after sunset. Although you're unlikely to have it to yourself, come nightfall the queues are significantly shorter, and the illuminated boulevards and floodlit monuments spread out before you to provide an impossibly romantic perspective of the city.

Gustave Eiffel constructed the tower initially as a temporary exhibit for the Exposition Universelle (World Fair) in 1889. Until the completion of Manhattan's Chrysler Building in 1930, it remained the world's tallest structure, at 320m (varying by up to 15cm when its 7000 tonnes of iron and 2.5 million rivets expand in warm weather and contract when it's cold). Its immense popularity assured its

survival beyond the World Fair and its elegant architectural design became a striking fixture of the city's skyline.

Each night, the tower's twin searchlight beacons beam an 80km radius around the city (look up from the top platform to see the 6000-watt lamps). And every hour, for 10 minutes on the hour, the entire tower sparkles with 20,000 gold-toned lights. It took 25 mountain climbers five months to install the bulbs, and the glittering, diamond-like effect when viewed from within the tower is dazzling.

Night-time at the top can be breezy – bring a jacket.

To prolong the panoramas (and the romance), book dinner at one of the tower's restaurants: Altitude 95, on the 1st level; or Le Jules Verne, the rarefied 2nd-level restaurant, accessed by private lift (see p46).

See also p39, and p42 for an insider's view.

LA VILLE LUMINÈRE

Paris was dubbed *la Ville Lumière* (the City of Light) in the 19th century, when it was the first continental European city to install gas lamps along its streets — although some believe the nickname derives from the soft light captured by the Impressionists' paintings. Either way, it endures as a fitting description of the shimmering city.

>2 SHAKESPEARE & CO
BROWSE THE SHELVES OF A LEGENDARY PARIS BOOKSHOP

A kind of spell descends as you enter this cluttered, charming bookshop. Situated across from Notre Dame, its enchanting nooks and crannies overflow with new and secondhand English-language books. Amid handpainted quotations and a wishing well, a miniature staircase leads to an atticlike reading library. Next to the children's books is a 'mirror of love', where people leave messages for friends and strangers, and recount finding love between the shop's shelves.

The bookshop is the stuff of legends. The original shop (12 rue l'Odeon; it was closed by the Nazis in 1941) was run by Sylvia Beach and became the meeting point for Hemingway's 'Lost Generation'. Beach published James Joyce's *Ulysses* there in 1922, when no-one else would. In 1951 George Whitman opened the present incarnation, attracting a Beat Poet clientele. Scores of authors have since passed through its doors. George is now aged in his 90s, and his daughter, Sylvia Beach Whitman, maintains Shakespeare & Co's serendipitous magic.

See also p158.

>3 JARDIN DU LUXEMBOURG

ENJOY A PICNIC IN PARIS' MOST POPULAR PARK

The merest ray of sunshine is enough to draw apartment-dwelling Parisians outdoors to soak up the sun while indulging in a picnic of fresh produce and fine cheeses, crusty, still-warm baguettes, and, of course, wine.

You'll see locals picnicking everywhere: in parks, on bridges and by the side of the Seine. The Luxembourg Gardens have a special place in the hearts of Parisians.

Napoleon dedicated the gardens to the children of Paris, and many residents spent their childhood prodding little wooden sail boats with long sticks on the octagonal pond, watching marionettes perform Punch & Judy–type shows, and riding the *carrousel* (merry-go-round) or ponies.

All those activities are still here today, as well as a modern playground and sporting and games venues. But above all, the gardens are still a place to unwind – and to dine.

The elegantly manicured lawns are off-limits apart from a small wedge on the southern boundary.

Otherwise, do as the Parisians do, and corral a metal chair and find your own favourite part of the park.

See also p149.

>4 MONET'S WATERLILIES

MARVEL AT MONET'S *WATERLILIES* IN THE MUSÉE DE L'ORANGERIE

After six-and-a-half years of renovations, the Musée de l'Orangerie finally reopened in 2006 to again showcase its prized cycle of eight of Monet's enormous *Nymphéas (Waterlilies)*, conceived by Monet specifically for this building.

The museum's renovations hit a wall – literally – when workers encountered a stone fortification built by Charles IX to enclose his palace and the Tuileries Gardens, where the museum, originally the palace's greenhouse and its only remaining structure, is located. Monet's masterpieces were protected in temperature-controlled glass cases while the reconstruction worked around the wall.

Today, the *Waterlilies* wrap around two skylit oval rooms on the museum's upper level. Elliptical benches in the centre of each room offer a meditative spot to reflect on their ethereal shades of pink, violet and wintergreen, making the lilies appear as if they're floating on the canvas.

An unforeseen bonus: part of the historic rediscovered wall is also on display.

See p76 for more on the Musée de l'Orangerie. More of Monet's water lilies can be seen at Musée Marmottan (see the boxed text, p55). To see the real-life lilies, head further afield to Monet's former house and gardens at Giverny (p172).

>5 PROMENADE PLANTÉE

TAKE A ROMANTIC STROLL ALONG THE PROMENADE PLANTÉE

Climbing the stairs from av Daumesnil in the busy Bastille brings you out on top of this former railway viaduct, which has been transformed into one of Paris' most serene – and romantic – places to stroll.

Planted with a profusion of cherry trees, maples, rose bushes and fragrant lavender, the Promenade Plantée the world's first elevated park – is a haven of tranquillity, which feels far from the madding crowds below. Four storeys above ground, its walking path offers views over the surrounding *quartiers* as well as intimate glimpses of wrought-iron balconies and rooftops including an Art Deco police station crowned by a dozen marble torsos.

Lovers young and old embrace on benches as joggers, parents with prams, and amblers pass by.

At the end of the viaduct, the Promenade Plantée continues at ground level almost to the *Périphérique,* a total distance of 4.5km. If you're not ready to return to the urban jungle just yet, there are signs directing you east to the nearby woods, the Bois de Vincennes (see the boxed text, p122).

See also p121.

HIGHLIGHTS

>6 MONTMARTRE

AMBLE THE ENCHANTING BACKSTREETS OF MONTMARTRE

Montmartre's slinking streets, steep staircases lined with crooked ivy-clad buildings, pretty little parks and squares all have fairytale charm. It's a wonderful place for a wander, especially early morning or midweek when the tourists are few.

From the Abbesses metro station (renovated in 2006, it was origi-nally designed by Hector Guimard, and is the only metro in Paris with its original Beaux Arts glass roof), wend your way north past rue des Trois Frères, dotted with outdoor cafés, to the Dalí Espace Montmar-tre (p91), a homage to just one of the legendary painters who set up their easels on place du Tertre (today it's the domain of portrait artists). Further north, the Musée de Montmartre (p91) transports you to the windmill-filled village of days gone by. Montmartre's two surviving windmills, Moulin de la Gallette and Moulin Radet, are just west of rue Girardon.

Presiding over Montmartre to the east, the Roman-Byzantine ba-silica Sacré-Cœur (p90) has panoramas over Paris from its front steps, and you can climb its 234 spiralling steps to the dome for more views.

On your way down, you can cut through the terraced gardens to square Willette and continue east to the colourful Château Rouge area, which is overflowing with North African market stalls and eclectic shops and bars.

>7 THE SEINE

WATCH PARIS FLOAT PAST FROM A BOAT ON THE SEINE

Looking at a riverboat plying the Seine, you might be tempted to give a boat ride a wide berth. With all those camera-wielding tourists, no self-respecting Parisian would be caught dead on one (or at least admit to it).

But once you're aboard, gently gliding past monuments, parks and elegant Haussmannian buildings along Paris' most beautiful boulevard of all, any reservations ebb away.

The Seine's sightseeing boats are colloquially called Bateaux Mouches (literally 'fly boats', though the name originates from the Mouche area of Lyon). In fact, while 'Bateaux Mouches' refers specifically to the original and still best-known operator, there's a raft of other companies offering cruises, including the hop-on, hop-off Batobus, which travels between the Jardin des Plantes and the Eiffel Tower, making a total of eight stops.

A number of operators also run leisurely lunch and dinner cruises with on-board chefs and well-stocked wine holds.

And the locals may yet embrace travelling on the Seine if long-mooted plans for a 24km, 35-stop Métro Fluvial (metro boat) go ahead.

See also p218.

>8 THE LOUVRE

NAVIGATE YOUR WAY AROUND THE LABYRINTHINE LOUVRE

The Louvre's sheer size strikes fear into the hearts of even the most dedicated museum-goers. The world's largest museum spans a whopping 700m along the Seine and it's estimated it would take nine months just to glance at every piece of art here.

And it keeps getting bigger. Constructed as a fortress by Philippe-Auguste in the early 13th century, the Palais du Louvre was rebuilt in the mid-16th century as a royal residence, and in 1793 the Revolutionary Convention turned it into the country's first national museum. The 'Grand Louvre' project inaugurated by the late President Mitterrand in 1989 doubled the museum's exhibition space. New and renovated galleries have opened in recent years devoted to paintings and *objets d'art*. In all, some 35,000 works are now on display.

As if that weren't daunting enough, the hype around Dan Brown's *The Da Vinci Code* (which was partly set in the museum, which was also used as a shooting location for the film), has seen a further surge of visitors and raised expectations even higher.

But (if you plan ahead a bit) the Louvre doesn't disappoint.

The star attraction, Da Vinci's *La Joconde* (*Mona Lisa;* see the boxed text, p79), now resides – albeit behind a wooden railing and thick bulletproof glass – in the newly renovated, glass-roofed Salle des Etats on the 1st floor. The rest of the rambling palace houses a veritable treasure trove of priceless art and artefacts, dating from antiquity (such as the *Venus de Milo,* pictured opposite) to the 19th century.

Save time by purchasing your ticket beforehand. Tickets are available from the museum's website, the ticket agencies Fnac or Virgin Megastore (see p215), or the ticket machines in the Carrousel du Louvre. Alternatively, the Paris Museum Pass (p215) is valid here. To avoid the queues at the pyramid (the main entrance), enter via the Carrousel du Louvre at 99 rue de Rivoli, or follow the

> ### CULTURAL RESPITE
> Take time out from admiring the Louvre's lavish collections with a cocktail or classic café fare looking out over the glass pyramid from the terrace of Café Marly (p82).

Musée du Louvre exit from the Palais Royal-Musée du Louvre metro station. Museum tickets are valid for the whole day, so you can take a break any time.

Once inside, it helps to rough out an itinerary based around what you most want to see before you set off down the endless corridors. Pick up a free English-language map, which includes floor plans, from the information desk in the centre of the Hall Napoléon. For serious fans, the museum's bookshop sells extensive guides (up to 475 pages long). A guided tour (available in English) is a great, info-packed option to make the most of your visit. Otherwise, multi-language audio-guides can help you self-navigate.

See also p77.

>9 CIMETIÈRE DU PÈRE LACHAISE

PAY HOMAGE TO THE DEPARTED AT CIMETIÈRE DU PÈRE LACHAISE

Paris is a collection of villages, and this 48-hectare cemetery of cobbled lanes and elaborate tombs the size of small houses qualifies as one in its own right.

The cemetery was founded in 1804, and initially attracted few funerals because of its distance from the city centre. The authorities' response was to exhume famous remains and resettle them here. The marketing ploy worked and Père Lachaise has been the city's most fashionable final address ever since.

With a population (as it were) of one million, among the cemetery's celebrity residents are the composer Chopin; writers Molière, Apollinaire, Balzac, Proust, Wilde, Gertrude Stein (and Alice B Toklas) and Colette; artists Delacroix, Pissarro, Seurat and Modigliani; singers Édith Piaf and rock god Jim Morrison; and 12th-century lovers Abélard and Héloïse, who in 1817 were disinterred and reburied here together beneath a neogothic tombstone.

Long-standing traditions at Père Lachaise include leaving love letters on Abélard and Héloïse's crypt, red roses on Édith Piaf's grave, and lipstick kisses on Oscar Wilde's tomb, which is topped with a naked winged angel. The angel was formerly well-endowed, which was apparently deemed so obscene that the offending section was lopped off and used by the cemetery director as a paperweight.

Another raunchy resting place is that of Victor Noir, pseudonym of the journalist Yvan Salman, who was shot and killed in 1870 by Pierre Bonaparte, great-nephew of Napoleon, at the age of just 22. According to legend, a woman who strokes Noir's amply proportioned bronze effigy will quickly fall pregnant. The enthusiastic response by would-be mothers led to the statue being literally worn down, and a fence was constructed around his grave, though subsequent protests by Parisian women have since seen it removed.

But the most venerated tomb belongs to the Doors' Jim Morrison, who died in Paris in 1971 (although conspiracy theorists believe he's alive and well and living it up away from the spotlight). Prior to complaints from Morrison's family, fans regularly took drugs, drank

beer and had sex atop his grave. The family's protests resulted in a crackdown which has seen the beer bottles, graffiti and discarded evidence of intimacy cleaned up, a security guard permanently posted to watch out for misbehaving fans and even a special leaflet outlining a code of conduct for homages to the poet/singer. Given his wild lifestyle, you can't help but wonder if Morrison isn't finding the new arrangements rather boring.

Maps indicating the location of noteworthy graves are posted around the cemetery, but it's worth purchasing a detailed map from one of the nearby newsstands.

See also p103.

>10 CENTRE POMPIDOU

CONTEMPLATE MODERN ART AND ARCHITECTURE AT THE CENTRE POMPIDOU

Fresh from a facelift, the building housing Paris' premier cultural centre is so iconic that you could spend hours looking at it without ever going inside.

Architects Renzo Piano and Richard Rogers' bold design – with plumbing, pipes and air vents forming part of the external façade – caused a *scandale* when the centre opened in 1977. Especially when viewed from a distance, such as from the Sacré-Cœur or Parc de Belleville, the centre's primary-coloured, boxlike form amid a sea of muted-grey Parisian rooftops makes it look like a child's Meccano set abandoned on someone's very elegant living room rug.

Cultural offerings include a ground-level open space, hosting temporary exhibitions; the Bibliothèque Publique d'Information (BPI; public library); and cinemas and entertainment venues. But the most compelling reason to enter is the Musée National d'Art Moderne (MNAM), which includes works by the Surrealists and Cubists, a fabulous Matisse collection, pop art and contemporary creations.

The Centre Pompidou is just six storeys high, but because of Paris' low-rise cityscape, the views from the roof (reached by external escalators enclosed in tubes) are superb. Views also unfold from the 6th-floor temporary exhibition space and from the restaurant, Georges (p83).

See also p73.

>PARIS DIARY

Pomp and ceremony have been part and parcel of Parisian culture for centuries. A vast array of cultural and sporting events animate the French capital, and no matter what time of year you visit, you're bound to encounter the city's festive spirit. Extensive events listings appear weekly in the publications *Pariscope* and *L'Officiel des Spectacles,* and the colourful entertainment magazine *Zurban*. All are in French but easily navigable and available from kiosks, newsagents and bookshops each Wednesday. Listings also appear under the 'What's On' section of the tourist office's website (www.parisinfo.com). See p216 for a list of public holidays.

Tour de France (p26)

PARIS DIARY

JANUARY

Grande Parade de Paris
www.parisparade.com
Paris' New Year's Day parade originated in Montmartre but these days it takes place in different venues from year to year – which might be anywhere from under the Eiffel Tower (pictured right) to along the Grands Boulevards. Check the website to see where it'll be while you're here.

FEBRUARY

Paris, Capitale de la Creation
www.pariscapitaledelacreation.com
Prêt-à-Porter (ready-to-wear fashion salons, held in January/February and September) joins forces with trade shows dealing with all aspects of fashion and interior design.

Chinese New Year
www.paris.fr
Dragon parades and lanternlit festivities are held in late January/early February in Paris' main Chinese districts: the 13e (see p154) and the 3e.

MARCH

Banlieues Bleues
www.banlieuesbleues.org
Paris' suburbs swing to the tunes of jazz, blues, world, soul, funk and R & B during the 'Suburban Blues' festival; it's held over five weeks in March and April in the suburbs of Paris, such as St-Denis, just north of the inner city, with big-name talent taking to the stages and streets.

APRIL

Marathon International de Paris

www.parismarathon.com

On your marks... The Paris International Marathon, in early April, starts on the av des Champs-Élysées, 8e, and finishes on av Foch, in the 16e.

Foire du Trône

www.foiredutrone.com in French

This giant funfair's 350 attractions spread over 10 hectares from the pelouse de Reuilly at the Bois de Vincennes for eight weeks during April/May.

MAY

Internationaux de France de Tennis

www.frenchopen.org

The only Grand Slam played on clay (and the most elusive slam for many champs), the glamorous French Open tennis tournament hits up from late May to mid-June at Stade Roland Garros, situated at the southern edge of the leafy Bois de Boulogne (p57) in the 16e.

JUNE

Gay Pride March

www.gaypride.fr in French

Bright floats and costumes parade (pictured opposite) through the Marais to Bastille.

La Course des Garçons de Café

www.paris.fr

Waiters and waitresses race through central Paris balancing a glass and bottle on a tray.

Paris Jazz Festival

www.parcfloraldeparis.com

Free jazz concerts held in the park every Saturday and Sunday afternoon in June and July.

PARIS DIARY

JULY

La Goutte d'Or en Fête
www.gouttedorenfete.org
Catch the vibe of this week-long world-music festival incorporating raï, reggae, rap and more, held in the multicultural 18e from around late June to early July.

Bastille Day (14 July)
Paris marks France's national day with flag-waving fanfare. Festivities kick off at 10am with a military and fire-brigade parade along av des Champs-Élysées. At 11pm, fireworks light up the sky above the Champ de Mars.

Tour de France
www.letour.fr
This prestigious cycling event's final stage culminates with a race up av des Champs-Élysées on the third or fourth Sunday of July.

Paris Plage
www.paris.fr
From mid-July to mid-August, landlocked Parisians lounge on Paris Beach (pictured above), which extends east along the Seine from the quai des Tuileries. Lined with sun beds and plastic palms, and even trucked-in sand in some parts, the 'beach' stays open late.

AUGUST

Paris Cinéma
www.pariscinema.org
Despite being a relatively recent arrival on the cinematic scene, this two-week festival in late July/early August has become a fixture on Parisians' annual calendar; a wonderful array of rare and restored films are screened in selected cinemas across the city.

SEPTEMBER

Festival d'Automne
www.festival-automne.com
The tourist hordes leave and Paris gets cultural during the 'Autumn Festival' of arts, with city-wide exhibitions, music, dance and theatre from mid-September to December.

European Heritage Days
www.journeesdupatrimoine.culture.fr
During the third weekend in September, step inside otherwise off-limits Parisian buildings such as government ministries and the Palais de Élysée (French President's residence).

OCTOBER

Nuit Blanche
www.paris.fr
For one 'White Night', museums across town stay open till the *very* wee hours.

Fête des Vendages de Montmartre
www.fetedesvendangesdemontmartre.com
The minuscule Close du Montmartre vineyard celebrates its harvest on the second weekend in October.

Foire Internationale d'Art Contemporain
www.fiac-online.com
Get your fill of avant-garde art at this five-day contemporary art fair held in late October.

NOVEMBER

Mois de la Photo
www.mep-fr.org

'Photography month' sees more than 60 exhibitions (some free) set up in galleries, museums and cultural centres throughout Paris, with many top-name photographers in attendance.

Fête du Beaujolais
www.beaujolaisgourmand.com

On the third Thursday in November, Parisians debate the merits of the Beaujolais vintage over a glass or bottle in cafés and bars throughout town.

DECEMBER

Patinoire de l'Hôtel de Ville
www.paris.fr

From early December to early March, twirl on the free outdoor ice-skating rink (pictured above) in front of Paris' town hall. Skate hire costs €5.

New Year's Eve
www.paris.fr

Join in the revelry at blvd St-Michel (5e), place de la Bastille (11e), the Eiffel Tower (7e) and especially the av des Champs-Élysées (8e).

ITINERARIES

TWO DAYS

On the first day, kick off at place de la Concorde (p56), drop into the Musée de l'Orangerie (p76) to see Monet's *Waterlilies,* and then continue to the Musée d'Orsay (p43) for more Monet and the breathtaking collection of other impressionist masters. Next, wander west along the river to the Eiffel Tower (p39), and catch a Batobus (p219) through the heart of the city to the Jardin des Plantes (p148). Poke around the Latin Quarter and St-Germain des Prés (p142), perhaps making a stop at a quintessential Paris café, before settling in for dinner (p160) and drinks (p164) and then strolling over the lamplit bridges to your accommodation.

The next day, visit Notre Dame (p135) and beautiful Ste-Chapelle (p139), tackle the Musée du Louvre (p77) and amble through the Jardin des Tuileries (p73) along the av des Champs-Élysées (p52) to the Arc de Triomphe (p52). Cross town via the Église de la Madeleine (p53) to the Centre Pompidou (p22), for avant-garde art and architecture, then experience quirky backstreet shopping in the Marais (p122) before capping the night off in the Marais' bars (p130).

THREE DAYS

On your third day, wind your way through the cobbled streets of the artists' enclave Montmartre (p88) up to Sacré-Cœur (p90), then head to the spirited quarter of Belleville (p102), perhaps taking a local-led walking tour (p103) to learn about the area's history and multicultural makeup. Hop on a canal cruise (p218) along Canal St-Martin (p103) and then check out the legendary tombs at Cimetière du Père Lachaise (p103) before making your way back to Montmartre for a dinner-and-cabaret spectacle (p98).

FOUR DAYS

With four days you'll also have time to make a foray further afield to the gilded palace of Versailles (p170), to the gardens planted and painted by Monet at his house in Giverny (p172), or to sip champagne on the drink's home soil in the city of Reims (p173). Alternatively, check out

---

Top left Catacombes (p146) **Top right** Cathédrale de Notre Dame de Paris (p135) **Bottom** Canal St-Martin (p103) **Previous page** Finding your way on the metro

the skyscrapers at La Défense (see the boxed text, p53), or ramble in one of the city's two forests (Bois de Boulogne, see the boxed text, p57; Bois de Vincennes, see the boxed text, p122). For an evening of grandeur, take in an opera or ballet (p194) – or if you haven't yet had the chance, ascend the Eiffel Tower at night (p10) for glittering views of the City of Light.

RAINY DAY

Buy a chic, handmade Parisian umbrella at Alexandra Sojfer (p155) or a cheap one at any of chain store Monoprix's branches, then scout out the ornate covered *passages* (arcades; see p192). If you're game, you can escape the rain below ground in the eerie skull- and bone-lined catacombs (p146). Plan an afternoon in the city's myriad museums and galleries (see p178) before holing up in a café (p195), or cosying up at a jazz club (p197).

ON A BUDGET

Soak up the atmosphere of the street markets (p184), and take a stroll along the Promenade Plantée (p15), before browsing bookshops (p182) on the bohemian left bank. Feast on a crêpe at Chez Nicos (p160) on

Musée d'Orsay (p43)

historic rue Mouffetard (see the boxed text, p162), and stop in for a drink at the street's lively bars. Pick up half-price tickets (p215) for a concert or theatre production, and hit the city's free museums (p178). If you're here on the first Sunday of the month, you can also catch the national museums for free.

ON A SUNDAY

Yes it's Sunday, so most of the shops are shut, but not Paris' sprawling flea markets (p184), such as the Marché aux Puces de St-Ouen (p92), where you can also catch entertainers performing *chansons* (songs) over lunch at Chez Louisette (p99). Otherwise, enjoy a languid brunch (select a dining spot from the Eat sections of the Quarters), then grab a delicious Berthillon ice cream (see the boxed text, p140) and stroll around Île St-Louis (p134), before watching Parisians at play in the Jardin du Luxembourg (p149). Make your dinner plans (p180) early in the day to avoid being caught short, as many restaurants close.

>1 Invalides & Eiffel Tower	38
>2 Arc de Triomphe, Champs-Élysées & Grands Boulevards	48
>3 Louvre & Les Halles	72
>4 Montmartre	88
>5 Belleville & Surrounds	102
>6 Marais & Bastille	114
>7 The Islands	134
>8 Latin Quarter, St-Germain des Prés & Montparnasse	142

Ice-cream shop, Île St-Louis (p140)

QUARTERS

The good news for anyone coming to Paris for a good time, not a long time, is that the city's compact size, mostly flat terrain and superb metro system make it easy to cover a lot of ground during even the most fleeting visit.

Central Paris spans 9.5km north–south by 11km east–west. It's split into 20 *arrondissements*, which spiral clockwise in the shape of a snailshell from the centre to the *Périphérique* (ring road). *Arrondissement* numbers (1er, 2e etc) form an essential part of all Parisian addresses, particularly since there's often more than one street by the same name, and are included throughout this book. Overlapping these administrative boundaries are Paris' villagelike *quartiers* (quarters). The following chapter pieces the main quarters together in eight interlocked sections.

The Invalides and Eiffel Tower area boasts some of the city's most majestic monuments and museums. To its north, more major icons and swank shops line the Arc de Triomphe, Champs-Élysées and Grands Boulevards precinct. On the river's right bank, the postmodern Centre Pompidou; the mecca of all museums, the Louvre; and the city's former ancient wholesale markets turned modern shopping mall make up the Louvre and Les Halles area. Uphill, past sexy, seedy Pigalle, is the age-old artists' hangout, Montmartre, capped by the white Byzantine domes of Sacré-Cœur. Heading east from Montmartre brings you to the rapidly gentrifying area of Belleville and Surrounds, which incorporates Cimetière du Père Lachaise and hip Canal St-Martin, and is lined by offbeat fashion designers' digs and arty cafés. South of here, towards the Seine, you'll find the funky boutiques and bars of the Marais and Bastille. Within the river itself sit the city's two islands: Île de la Cité, guarded by Notre Dame's Gothic gargoyles; and the intimate, exclusive Île St-Louis. The Seine's left bank shelters the student cafés and chic shops of the Latin Quarter, St-Germain des Prés and Montparnasse.

In and around these quarters are several fascinating detours worth the trip.

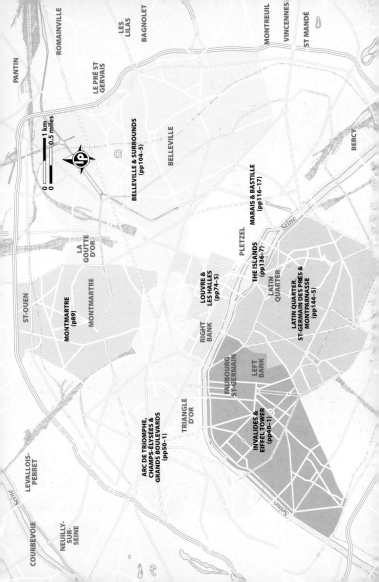

PANTIN

ROMAINVILLE

LES LILAS

BAGNOLET

LE PRÉ ST GERVAIS

MONTREUIL

VINCENNES

ST MANDÉ

COURBEVOIE

NEUILLY-SUR-SEINE

LEVALLOIS-PERRET

ST-OUEN

LA GOUTTE D'OR

BELLEVILLE & SURROUNDS
(pp104–5)

BELLEVILLE

Seine

BERCY

MONTMARTRE (p89)

MONTMARTRE

PLETZEL

MARAIS & BASTILLE
(pp116–17)

LOUVRE &
LES HALLES
(pp74–5)

THE ISLANDS
(pp136–7)

Seine

ARC DE TRIOMPHE,
CHAMPS-ÉLYSÉES &
GRANDS BOULEVARDS
(pp50–1)

RIGHT
BANK

LATIN
QUARTER

LATIN QUARTER,
ST-GERMAIN DES PRÉS &
MONTPARNASSE
(pp144–5)

TRIANGLE
D'OR

FAUBOURG
ST-GERMAIN

LEFT
BANK

INVALIDES &
EIFFEL TOWER
(pp40–1)

Seine

1 km
0.5 miles
0
0

>INVALIDES & EIFFEL TOWER

Stretching west along the Seine's southern bank, the broad boulevards and imposing architecture of the Invalides and Eiffel Tower quarter are Paris at its most bombastic.

This is where you can get up close and personal with the city's symbolic tower, and promenade through the sprawling grounds of the Hôtel des Invalides, the 17th-century war veterans' residence which includes a military museum and Napoleon's tomb. It's where you'll find the private mansion housing the Musée Rodin, and its tranquil rose gardens filled with Rodin's sculptures including *The Thinker*. And it's where you can eye the Musée d'Orsay's incredible impressionist paintings, and peer out over Paris through this historic former railway station's giant glass clockface.

But time hasn't entirely stood still in this *grande dame* of a quarter: 2006 saw the opening of the cantilevered black-and-burgundy boxlike buildings containing the Musée du Quai Branly, designed by Jean Nouvel, which showcases indigenous art.

INVALIDES & EIFFEL TOWER

👁 SEE
Ballon Eutelsat 1 A6
Église du Dôme 2 F3
Eiffel Tower 3 C2
Hôtel
des Invalides 4 F3
Musée de l'Armée 5 F2
Musée des Égouts
de Paris.........................6 E1
Musée d'Orsay..............7 H2
Musée du Quai Branly....8 D1
Musée Rodin 9 F3

Tombeau
de Napoléon 1er..........(see 2)

🍴 EAT
Altitude 95 ....(see 11)
L'Arpège 10 G3
Le Jules Verne 11 C2
Les Deux Abeilles 12 D1
Les Ombres.................(see 8)
Restaurant
Musée d'Orsay.............(see 7)
Rue Cler 13 E2

🍸 DRINK
Café Branly ....(see 8)
Café des Hauteurs ....(see 7)

⭐ PLAY
La Pagode....................14 F3

Please see over for map

👁 SEE

Art, architecture and amazing views abound in this quarter. Several boat cruises along the Seine depart from near the Eiffel Tower; see p219.

👁 BALLON EUTELSAT

☎ 01 44 26 20 00; www.aeroparis.com in French; Parc André Citroën, 2 rue de la Montagne de la Fage, 15e; admission Mon-Fri €10/5, Sat & Sun €12/6; 🕑 9am-9.30pm summer, to 5.30pm winter; Ⓜ Balard or Lourmel

Drift up and up but not away – this helium-filled balloon remains tethered to the ground as it lifts you 150m into the air for panoramas of Paris and the Seine. Confirm ahead as the balloon doesn't ascend in windy conditions.

👁 EIFFEL TOWER

☎ 01 44 11 23 23; www.tour-eiffel.fr; Champ de Mars, 7e; lift 1st fl € 4.20/2.30, 2nd fl € 7.70/4.20, 3rd fl €11/6, stairs €3.80/3; 🕑 lifts 9am-12.45am mid-Jun–Aug (final ascension to top 11pm, to other levels midnight), 9.30am-11.45pm Sep–mid-Jun (final ascension to top 10.30pm, to other levels 11pm), stairs 9am-12.30am mid-Jun–Aug (final admittance midnight), 9.30am-6.30pm Sep–mid-Jun (final admittance 6pm); Ⓜ Champ de Mars-Tour Eiffel or Bir Hakeim; &

Lifts yo-yo up and down the north and west pillars of Paris' signature

Eiffel Tower from rue St-Dominique

tower, with its three viewing platforms affording fabulous views of its Art Nouveau ironwork as well as the cityscape. If you're feeling athletic, you can take the south pillar's stairs – some 1665 of them – as far as the 2nd floor. There's wheelchair access to the 1st and 2nd floors. See also p10.

Florence Bernard
Agent d'Accueil (lift operator, ticketing and information), Eiffel Tower

How many times do you drive the lift up and down the tower each day yourself? Twenty times up and 20 times down between the ground and 2nd floor; 40 times up and 40 times down between the 2nd and 3rd floor. **Favourite view from the tower?** The Louvre pyramid. It's a game for me – 'Can I find it today?' – because it's hard to see, not like Tour Montparnasse. **Funniest thing you heard a tourist say?** When they look out over Paris and say, 'Where is the Eiffel Tower – I can't see it!'. They get so distracted they forget they're inside it. **Number of people who propose at the top?** In summer sometimes two or three in one hour! **Most famous lift visitor** Mick Jagger. Sometimes we make a private lift for kings or presidents, but singers and actors and their bodyguards get in the lift with everyone else.

◉ HÔTEL DES INVALIDES

☎ 01 44 42 37 72; www.invalides.org; Esplanade des Invalides, 7e; admission €7.50/5.50; ☽ 10am-6pm Apr-Sep, to 5pm Oct-Mar, closed 1st Mon of month Ⓜ Invalides; ♿

Built in the 1670s to provide housing for 4000 *invalides* (infirm veterans), this immense complex screens sobering wartime footage at its **Musée de l'Armée** (Military Museum), with weapon, flag and medal displays. The **Église du Dôme**, which is visible throughout the city, receives its name for its gilded dome. Underneath it, Napoleon's remains lie in the **Tombeau de Napoléon 1er** (Napoleon I's Tomb).

◉ MUSÉE DES ÉGOUTS DE PARIS

☎ 01 53 68 27 81; opposite 93 Quai d'Orsay, 7e; admission €4/3.20; ☽ 11am-6pm Sat-Wed May-Sep, to 5pm Sat-Wed Oct-Apr, closed last 3 weeks Jan; Ⓜ Alma-Marceau

Aim to visit in the afternoon, as one whiff of this working-sewer museum will surely put you off lunch. Raw sewage runs beneath your feet along 480m of subterranean tunnels, with exhibits demonstrating the development of Paris' waste-water disposal system.

◉ MUSÉE D'ORSAY

☎ 01 40 49 48 14; www.musee-orsay .fr; 62 rue de Lille, 7e; all-day ticket €7.50/5.50, entry after 4.15pm Tue, Wed & Fri-Sun & after 8pm Thu €5.50; ☽ 9.30am-6pm Tue-Sun, to 9.45pm Thu; Ⓜ Musée d'Orsay or Solférino; ♿

Resplendently housed in a former train station from the 1900s, this national museum traces art from the 1840s to 1914, spanning the impressionist, postimpressionist and Art Nouveau movements. Cézanne, Van Gogh (including *Starry Night*), Seurat and Matisse dazzle on the skylit upper level. Also on display are masterpieces

---

WHAT GOES UP…

… must come down, including the Eiffel Tower's glass-panelled double-decker lifts – but only when automated safety mechanisms give the lifts the green light, literally.

If you're nervous about trusting machinery to scale the tower's heights, you'll be relieved to know that the tower's lift load bearings are monitored by computer.

If too many people board the lift, a red light comes on and the doors are automatically prevented from closing, and the lift is immobilised and unable to leave.

Still wary? Lift operator Florence Bernard (opposite) assures visitors she 'wouldn't do this job if it wasn't safe'.

Musée Rodin

by Monet, Pissarro, Renoir, Sisley, Degas and Manet.

◎ MUSÉE DU QUAI BRANLY

☎ 01 56 61 70 00; www.quaibranly.fr; 37 quai Branly, 7e; admission €8.50/6, temporary exhibitions additional €8.50/6; ☾ 10am-6.30pm Tue-Sun, to 9.30pm Thu; Ⓜ Alma-Marceau or Bir Hakeim; ♿

Raked ramps lead through this urban-industrial building to darkened, mesh-encased rooms, which form a sharp contrast to the indigenous art and artefacts from Africa, Oceania, Asia and the Americas displayed here, and the 'music box' screening indigenous musical celebrations. The on-site café (p47) and restaurant, Les Ombres (p46), both have ringside Eiffel views.

◎ MUSÉE RODIN

☎ 01 44 18 61 10; www.musee-rodin .fr; 77 rue de Varenne, 7e; admission €7/5, garden only €1; ☾ 9.30am-5.45pm, garden to 6.45pm Tue-Sun Apr-Sep, 9.30am-4.45pm Tue-Sun Oct-Mar; Ⓜ Varenne; ♿

This museum's rose-clambered garden, home to Rodin's bronze sculptures including *The Thinker* and *Balzac*, is one of the most peaceful places in Paris. Along with the marble monument to love, *The Kiss*, the 18th-century mansion's interior proves that

Courtyard at Hôtel des Invalides (p43)

Rodin's talents weren't limited to sculpture alone, with sketches, paintings and engravings, and works by his student/model/muse, Camille Claudel, also on display here.

🛍 SHOP

Most of the quarter's museums – though fortunately not the Musée des Égouts de Paris – sell high-quality souvenirs (*souvenirs* is the French word for 'memories'), including art books, postcards, prints, and other items such as scarves imprinted with classic works of art.

🍴 EAT

The sprawling lawns under the Eiffel Tower are a scenic spot for a picnic. The best place to pick up picnic fare is **rue Cler** (7e; ⏰ 7am or 8am to 7pm Tue-Sat, 8am-noon Sun; Ⓜ École Militaire), which buzzes with local shoppers, especially on weekends.

🍴 L'ARPÈGE

Gastronomic €€€€
☎ 01 47 05 09 06 84; rue de Varenne, 7e; ⏰ lunch & dinner Mon-Fri; Ⓜ Varenne
Acclaimed chef Alain Passard specialises in seafood, such as crayfish with caviar cream sauce, and inspired desserts, such as tomatoes

STAYING ON TRACK

Throughout central Paris, the very efficient metro (underground rail) network has 372 stations (373 when the new Olympiades station opens), which are spaced an average of 500m apart. If you get lost, track down the nearest metro station, where large-scale maps of the immediate district are generally posted outside the entrance at street level. Hopping on a metro will easily connect you back to where you planned to be. See p212 for ticket info.

stuffed with a veritable orchard of a dozen dried and fresh fruits, and served with aniseed ice cream. Book at least two weeks ahead.

LE JULES VERNE
Gastronomic   €€€€
☎ 01 45 55 61 44; fax 01 47 05 29 41; Champ de Mars, 7e; ☾ lunch & dinner; Ⓜ Champ de Mars-Tour Eiffel or Bir Hakeim
Book way ahead to dine on Alain Reix's Michelin-starred cuisine in moody black surrounds on the Eif-

fel Tower's 2nd level, accessed by private lift. For something less rarefied, **Altitude 95** (☎ 01 45 55 20 04; fax 01 47 05 94 40) on the 1st level serves lunch and dinner daily, along with Seine views from its bay windows.

LES DEUX ABEILLES
Salon de Thé   €
☎ 01 45 55 64 04; 189 rue de l'Université, 7e; ☾ 9am-7pm Mon-Sat; Ⓜ Alma-Marceau or Bir Hakeim
Around the corner from the Musée du Quai Branly, the faded floral wallpaper and even the somewhat stuffy service make this tearoom a charmingly old-fashioned stop for authentic baked treats such as *clafoutis aux cerises* (cherry flan), Madeline cakes, and quiche.

LES OMBRES
Gastronomic   €€€
☎ 01 47 53 68 00; www.lesombres -restaurant.com; 27 quai Branly, 7e; ☾ lunch & dinner; Ⓜ Alma-Marceau or Bir Hakeim
Paris not only gained a new museum in the Musée du Quai Branly,

JE SUIS VÉGÉTARIEN

Exclusively vegetarian eateries are almost unheard of in Paris, and while some traditional places do have vegetarian dishes, the French love of chicken and meat stocks can make these a dicey proposition. Aquatarians (ie fish eaters), however, will be fine, with fish or seafood a mainstay on most menus. One of the best bets for vegetarians is Paris' burgeoning array of North African, Middle Eastern, Indian and Asian restaurants, which all have at least some meatless dishes on the menu. See p198 for where to find mondial eateries.

AS TIME GOES BY

In 1962, Orson Welles filmed Kafka's *The Trial* in the then-abandoned railway station now housing the Musée d'Orsay (p43).

Time literally ticks by before your eyes when you're at the museum's **Café des Hauteurs** (☼ 10.30am-5pm, to 9pm Thu). You can take a tea break looking right through the former station's massive glass clockface across Paris.

Time has scarcely changed the **Restaurant Musée d'Orsay** (☼ lunch Tue-Sun, dinner Thu; restaurant tearoom 3.30-5.30pm Tue, Wed & Fri-Sun), the museum's – and formerly the train station's – restaurant. An Art Nouveau showpiece of ceiling frescoes, chandeliers and sage-green furniture, it serves inexpensive cold buffets and lunch *menus* (from €14.90) as well as an excellent children's *menu* (€7.15).

it also gained this steel-and-glass-roofed 5th-floor restaurant. Named *les ombres* (the shadows) for the patterns cast by the Eiffel Tower's webbed ironwork, the dramatic views are complemented by Arnaud Busquet's creations such as pan-seared tuna with sesame seeds and onion rings, or lamb with zucchini ravioli and gingerbread.

Y DRINK

Y CAFÉ BRANLY
Café & Salon de Thé
☎ 01 56 61 70 00; www.quaibranly
.fr; 27 quai Branly; ☼ lunch noon-3pm,
tearoom from 3pm until museum closing;
Ⓜ Alma-Marceau or Bir Hakeim
Drink in Eiffel Tower views while sipping an espresso or wine on the terrace of the Musée du Quai Branly's café, amid reflecting pools and gardens. Lunches, such as a *tartine Parisienne* of Parisian ham, Emmen-

tal cheese, tomatoes and mustard-butter, offer a light alternative (for your wallet too) to dining in style upstairs at Les Ombres (opposite).

★ PLAY

This stately quarter doesn't rock after dark, but night owls will find plenty of options nearby just north of the river (see p68) and east in Montparnasse (p167).

▣ LA PAGODE *Cinema*
☎ 01 45 55 48 48; 57bis rue de Babylone; ☼ vary; Ⓜ St-François Xavier
Set in fairytale gardens, this 19th-century Japanese pagoda was converted into a cinema in the 1930s. Its ceiling is held up by scaffolding, with plastic to stop the roof leaking, but the Ministry of Culture has now safeguarded its role as a venue for arthouse and classic films.

>ARC DE TRIOMPHE, CHAMPS-ÉLYSÉES & GRANDS BOULEVARDS

Pomp and grandeur reigns in the Arc de Triomphe, Champs-Élysées and Grands Boulevards quarter. This is where Baron Haussmann famously reinvented the Parisian cityscape. Haussmann's commanding reformation revolves around the soaring Arc de Triomphe, from which 12 avenues radiate like spokes on a wheel. Of them, the most celebrated (and the scene of Paris' major celebrations) is the Champs-Élysées, which forms part of the *Axe Historique*. Nowadays, this 'Grand Axis' stretches from La Défense through the vast place de la Concorde and beyond. Nearby, nine grand boulevards, flanked by fashionable department stores, stand on the site of the old city ramparts.

The quarter's splendour extends to its dining scene, with some of France's finest *haute cuisine* chefs established here; its couture scene, with the likes of Chanel, Dior, Lacroix and Yves Saint Laurent in residence; and cultural venues, including the Garnier opera house and the striking Palais de Tokyo located in the area.

ARC DE TRIOMPHE, CHAMPS-ÉLYSÉES & GRANDS BOULEVARDS

🌐 SEE

Arc de Triomphe **1** B3
Av des
Champs-Élysées **2** D3
Église
de la Madeleine **3** F3
Galerie Musée
Baccarat **4** B4
Jardins du Trocadéro **5** B5
Maison de Balzac **6** A6
Musée d'Art Moderne
de la Ville de Paris **7** C4
Musée de la Marine **8** A5
Musée de l'Homme **9** A5
Musée du Parfum **10** G3
Musée Galliera de la
Mode de la Ville
de Paris **11** C4
Musée Grévin **12** H3
Musée Guimet
des Arts Asiatiques **13** B4
Palais de Chaillot **14** B5
Palais de Tokyo **15** C4
Place de la Concorde ...**16** E4
Place Vendôme **17** F4
Théâtre-Musée
des Capucines **18** F3

🏠 SHOP

Chanel **19** D4
Chloé **20** E3
Chloé **21** D4
Christian Dior **22** D4
Christian Lacroix **23** E3

Commes
des Garçons **24** E3
Drugstore Publicis **25** C3
Eres **26** C3
Fauchon **27** F3
Fromagerie
Alléosse **28** C2
Galerie Vivienne **29** H4
Galeries Lafayette **30** G3
Givenchy **31** C4
Guerlain **32** D3
Hermès **33** F3
Jean-Paul Gaultier **34** C3
La Maison
de la Truffe **35** F3
La Maison du Miel **36** F3
Lancel **37** C3
Lanvin **38** F4
Le Printemps **39** F3
Louis Vuitton **40** C3
Passage
des Panoramas **41** H3
Passage Jouffroy **42** H3
Passage Verdeau **43** H3
Séphora **44** C3
Thierry Mugler **45** D4
Virgin Megastore **46** D3
Yves Saint Laurent **47** E4

🍽 EAT

Alain Ducasse
au Plaza Athénée **48** C4
Aux Lyonnais **49** H3
Guy Savoy **50** B2

Le Bistrot
du Sommelier **51** E3
Le Cristal Room   (see 4)
Le Roi du Pot
au Feu **52** F3
Maison Prunier **53** B3
Musée du Vin
Restaurant **54** A6
Pierre Gagnaire **55** C3
Spoon, Food
& Wine **56** D4
Taillevent **57** C3

🍷 DRINK

Bar Hemingway **58** F4
Harry's New York
Bar **59** G4
Hédiard **60** F3
Ladurée **61** C3

⭐ PLAY

Crazy Horse **62** C4
Le Baron **63** C4
Le Lido **64** C3
Le Limonaire **65** H3
Le Pulp **66** H3
Le Queen **67** C3
L'Olympia **68** F3
Palais Garnier **69** G3
Tryptique **70** H4

Please see over for map

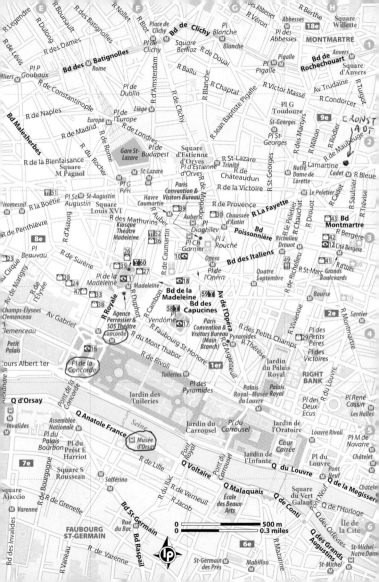

◉ SEE

◉ ARC DE TRIOMPHE

☎ 01 55 37 73 77; www.monum.fr; place Charles de Gaulle, 8e; viewing platform €8/6; ⏲ 10am-11pm Apr-Sep, to 10.30pm Oct-Mar; Ⓜ Charles de Gaulle–Étoile

If anything rivals the tower as the symbol of Paris, it's this magnificent, 1836-built monument to Napoleon's victory at Austerlitz in 1805. Staircases lead beneath the traffic-choked boulevards to the intricately carved triumphal arch, which stands a proud 50m high in the centre of the Étoile (star) roundabout. Climbing another 284 steps brings you to the top

for views swooping down the Champs-Élysées.

◉ AV DES CHAMPS-ÉLYSÉES

Ⓜ Charles de Gaulle–Étoile, George V, Franklin D Roosevelt or Champs-Élysées Clemenceau

No trip to Paris is complete without strolling this elegant, tree-shaded avenue lined with luxury shops. Named for the Elysian Fields ('heaven' in Greek mythology), the Champs-Élysées is beamed around the world each July, when Tour de France cyclists undertake their last mad dash to the finish line. This is also where Paris turns out for both organised and impromptu celebrations.

Arc de Triomphe and Av des Champs-Élysées

WORTH THE TRIP

The futuristic glass-and-chrome skyline of the La Défense business district makes you half expect a spaceship to dock on its vast concrete concourses.

Just northwest of the *Périphérique* (ring road), La Défense's 100-plus skyscrapers are an insight into what all of Paris might have looked like by now had developers got their way. Mostly comprised of office buildings, the standout structure is the white Carrara marble and grey granite **Grande Arche** (☎ 01 49 07 27 27; www.grandearche.com in French; 1 parvis de la Défense; admission €7.50/6; ☺ 10am-8pm Apr-Sep, to 7pm Oct-Mar; Ⓜ La Défense Grande Arche), designed by Danish architect Johan-Otto von Sprekelsen and inaugurated on 14 July 1989. A glass lift takes you to a gallery (with unlikely temporary exhibitions such as a September 11 retrospective – not what you want to see at the top of a 110m building), and a rooftop overlooking the Grand Axis.

Adjacent to the arch is a contemporary art garden with sculptures and murals, including works by Miró and César.

Architectural aficionados will find the **Espace Histoire** (History Space; ☎ 01 47 74 84 24; www.ladefense.fr in French; 15 place de la Défense; admission free; ☺ 10am-6pm Mon-Sat Apr-Sep, 9.30am-5.30pm Mon-Sat Oct-Mar; Ⓜ La Défense Grande Arche) fascinating for its drawings, architectural plans and scale models, including projects that were never built.

At the same premises, the Espace Info-Défense has maps outlining walking tours through this very un-Parisian part of Paris.

⊙ ÉGLISE DE LA MADELEINE

☎ 01 44 51 69 00; www.eglise
-lamadeleine.com in French; place
de la Madeleine, 8e; ☺ 10am-7pm;
Ⓜ Madeleine

Styled outwardly like an austere Greek temple, with 52 Corinthian columns, the interior of the Church of St Mary Magdalene is ornately decorated with gilt, marble and frescoes. The organ – one of the city's largest – is set above the main entrance on the southern side and played during Mass on Sundays.

⊙ GALERIE MUSÉE BACCARAT

☎ 01 40 22 11 00; www.baccarat.fr;
11 place des Etats-Unis, 16e; admission
€7/3.50; ☺ 10am-6.30pm Mon & Wed-
Sat; Ⓜ Iéna; ♿

Showcasing services designed for illustrious dining tables over the centuries, this crystal museum is at home in its striking new rococo-style premises in the ritzy 16e. It is also home to an on-site restaurant, Le Cristal Room (p65).

ARC DE TRIOMPHE, CHAMPS-ÉLYSÉES & GRANDS BOULEVARDS

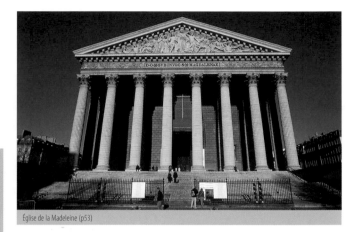
Église de la Madeleine (p53)

◉ JARDINS DU TROCADÉRO
Ⓜ Trocadéro; ♿
These fountained gardens are dramatically floodlit at night.

◉ MAISON DE BALZAC
☎ 01 55 74 41 80; www.balzac.paris .fr in French; 47 rue Raynouard, 16e; admission free, temporary exhibitions extra; ⏱ 10am-6pm Tue-Sun; Ⓜ Passy or Kennedy Radio France
Nonliterary junkies can cross this one off their lists, but Balzac fans will be fascinated by the prolific French novelist's little cottage (rented in his housekeeper's name to avoid his creditors), where he wrote for 18-hour days, fuelled by 'torrents' of coffee, from 1840 to 1847.

◉ MUSÉE D'ART MODERNE DE LA VILLE DE PARIS
☎ 01 53 67 40 00; www.mam.paris.fr in French; 11 av du Président Wilson, 16e; admission €5/2.50, temporary exhibits extra; ⏱ 10am-6pm Tue & Thu-Sun, to 10pm Wed; Ⓜ Iéna; ♿
Housed in the Electricity Pavilion from the 1937 Exposition Universelle (World Fair), the Modern Art Museum of the City of Paris spans virtually every major artistic movement of the 20th and nascent 21st centuries: Fauvism, cubism, Dadaism, surrealism, the School of Paris, expressionism, abstractionism and so on by artists including Matisse, Picasso, Braque, Soutine, Modigliani and Chagall.

☾ MUSÉE DU PARFUM
☎ 01 47 42 04 56; www.fragonard.com;
9 rue Scribe, 2e; admission free; ☾ 9am-
5.30pm Mon-Sat, 9.30am-3.30pm Sun
mid-Mar–Oct, 9am-5.30pm Mon-Sat
Nov–mid-Mar; Ⓜ Opéra

The secrets of perfume-making are
revealed at this museum run by
Grasse-based *parfumerie* Frago-
nard. Its essences are sold mainly to
factories, so you're unlikely to rec-
ognise the scents, but you can, of
course, buy them here cheaply. Just
south, at 39 blvd des Capucines,
2e, its annexe, the **Théâtre-Musée des
Capucines** (admission free; ☾ 9am-5.30pm
Mon-Sat), concentrates on bottles,
including Bohemian crystal.

☾ MUSÉE GALLIERA DE LA MODE DE LA VILLE DE PARIS
☎ 01 56 52 86 00; www.galliera.paris.fr;
10 av Pierre 1er de Serbie, 16e; admission
€7/5.50; ☾ 10am-6pm Tue-Sun; Ⓜ Iéna

This Italianate villa and its luxuriant gardens are a fitting backdrop
for Paris' fashion museum, which
has more than 100,000 garments
and accessories in its collection.

☾ MUSÉE GRÉVIN
☎ 01 47 70 85 05; www.grevin.com;
10 blvd Montmartre, 9e; admission
€17/15.50; ☾ 10am-6.30pm Mon-Fri, to
7pm Sat & Sun; Ⓜ Grands Boulevards; ♿

You'll see billboards for the Musée
Grévin plastered all over metro

WORTH THE TRIP

Given Paris' surfeit of art, the secluded location of the **Musée Marmottan** (☎ 01 44 96 50
33; www.marmottan.com; 2 rue Louis Boilly, 16e; admission €7/4.50; ☾ 10am-6pm
Tue-Sun; Ⓜ La Muette; ♿), in the Duke of Valmy's former hunting lodge, two blocks
east of the Bois de Boulogne (p57), makes it a relatively little visited gem.

The Marmottan houses the world's largest collection of Claude Monet's works, including
his *Impression: Sunrise,* which gave rise to the name of the impressionist movement. On
the upper levels are numerous works by the impressionist master, along with paintings by
Gauguin, Sisley, Pissarro, Renoir, Degas and Manet. Downstairs are paintings from Monet's
spectacular *Waterlilies* series.

In the same far-flung part of town are two quirky museums worth a peek: the intriguing
Musée de la Contrefaçon (Counterfeiting Museum; ☎ 01 56 26 14 00; www.mu
seedelacontrefacon.com; 16 rue de la Faisanderie, 16e; admission €4/3; ☾ 2-5.30pm
Tue-Sun), where you can spot the difference between a range of real items from fakes (or at
least try); and the **Musée du Stylo et de l'Écriture** (Pen & Penmanship Museum; ☎ 06
07 94 13 21; 3 rue Guy de Maupassant, 16e; admission €2/1; ☾ 2-6pm Sun, other days
by appointment; Ⓜ Avenue Henri Martin or Rue de la Pompe), which has an astonishing
collection of writing utensils.

QUARTERS

ARC DE TRIOMPHE, CHAMPS-ÉLYSÉES & GRANDS BOULEVARDS

stations, and its 300-odd wax figures, including vintage Hollywood stars, do have a kitsch charm, but it's hard to justify the whopping admission charge.

☉ MUSÉE GUIMET DES ARTS ASIATIQUES

☎ 01 56 52 53 00; www.museeguimet .fr; 6 place d'Iéna, 16e; admission €7/5; ☯ Musée Guimet des Arts Asiatiques 10am-6pm Wed-Mon, Japanese Gardens 1-5pm Wed-Mon; Ⓜ Iéna; ♿

France's leading museum of Asian art incorporates sculptures, paintings and *objets d'art* from Afghanistan, India, Nepal, Pakistan, Tibet, Cambodia, China, Japan and Korea. Buddhist art is displayed at the nearby annexe **Galeries du Panthéon Bouddhique du Japon et de la Chine** (Buddhist Pantheon Galleries of Japan & China; 19 av Iéna; ☯ 9.45am-5.45pm Wed-Mon). Afterwards, zen out in the Galeries' tranquil Japanese gardens.

☉ PALAIS DE CHAILLOT

Ⓜ Trocadéro; ♿

The terrace between the two wings of the Palais de Chaillot offers a stunning view of the river, the Eiffel Tower and the Jardins du Trocadéro (p54). The Palais' western wing incorporates two worthwhile museums: the **Musée de l'Homme** (Museum of Mankind; www.mnhn.fr in French; admission

€7/5; ☯ 9.45am-5.15pm Mon, Wed-Fri, 10am-6.30pm Sat & Sun), featuring ethnographical exhibits; and the **Musée de la Marine** (Maritime Museum; www.musee-marine.fr; admission €9/7; ☯ 10am-6pm Wed-Mon).

☉ PALAIS DE TOKYO

☎ 01 47 23 38 86; www.palaisdetokyo .com; 13 av du Président Wilson, 16e; admission €6/4.50; ☯ noon-midnight Tue-Sun; Ⓜ Iéna; ♿

The Tokyo Palace, created for the 1937 Exposition Universelle, opened in 2002 as a contemporary art space, and is Paris' only museum to stay open until midnight. There's no permanent collection; instead its shell-like interior of polished concrete and steel is the stark backdrop for rotating art installations. DJs often hit the decks at night.

☉ PLACE DE LA CONCORDE

Ⓜ Concorde; ♿

Paris spreads around you, with views of the Eiffel Tower, the Seine and along the Champs-Élysées, when you stand in the city's largest square, laid out in 1775. In the centre is the 3300-year-old pink granite obelisk, which was a gift from Egypt in 1831.

☉ PLACE VENDÔME

Ⓜ Tuileries or Opéra; ♿

In 1796 Napoleon married Josephine in building No 3 of this

WORTH THE TRIP

On Paris' western edge, the rambling woods of Bois de Boulogne (pull-out map, A4) encompass charming chateau gardens, sports venues, and playgrounds for kids and kids at heart.

Midsummer days are idyllic for boating on Lac Inférieur, the largest of the wood's lakes and ponds. **Row boats** (☾ noon-6pm Mon-Fri, 10am-7pm Sat & Sun mid-Apr–mid-Oct; Ⓜ Avenue Henri Martin) cost around €9 per hour.

Irises, roses and waterlilies splash colour across the lush **Parc de Bagatelle** (☾ 8am-8pm Mon-Fri, 9am-8pm Sat & Sun May-Aug, 8am-7pm Mon-Fri, 9am-7pm Sat & Sun Sep-Apr) in the woods' northwestern corner, surrounding the 1775-built **Château de Bagatelle** (☎ 01 40 67 97 00; route de Sèvres à Neuilly, 16e; admission €3/1.50; ☾ 9am-6pm Apr-Sep, to 5pm Oct-Mar), while plants, flowers and trees mentioned in Shakespearian plays flourish in the poetic Jardin Shakespeare.

Every Parisian kid is familiar with the **Jardin d'Acclimatation** (☎ 01 40 67 90 82; www.jardindacclimatation.fr in French; av du Mahatma Gandhi; admission €2.70/1.35; ☾ 10am-7pm Jun-Sep, to 6pm Oct-May; Ⓜ Les Sablons), an amusement park filled with rides and entertainment for tots. A little narrow-gauge train (€1.35 one-way) runs to the park from Porte Maillot.

In 2009 the Jardin d'Acclimatation will be home to the new contemporary art centre, Fondation Louis Vuitton Pour la Création, situated in a giant glass 'cloud'-like building designed by Frank Gehry.

At the woods' southern end, the Stade Roland Garros is home of the French Open tennis tournament as well as its museum, the **Tenniseum-Musée de Roland Garros** (☎ 01 47 43 48 48; www.rolandgarros.com; 2 av Gordon Bennett, 16e; admission €7.5/4, with stadium tour €15/10; ☾ 10am-6pm Wed & Fri-Sun; Ⓜ Porte d'Auteuil). The museum has more than 200 hours of footage, including player interviews. Book ahead for stadium tours; English-language tours usually depart at 11am. Nearby, punters can take a flutter at two horse-racing tracks: the Hippodrome de Longchamp for flat races and the Hippodrome d'Auteuil for steeplechases.

Horse-drawn carriages, which cost around €20 per ride, are a pricey but not impractical way to get around the Bois de Boulogne's 845 hectares — you'll find the carriages lined up in the woods' busier spots. Or you can spin through the woods on a bike. **Paris Cycles** (☎ 01 47 47 76 50; per hr €5; ☾ 10am-sunset daily mid-Apr–mid-Oct, 10am-sunset Wed, Sat & Sun mid-Oct–mid-Apr) rents wheels from a couple of locations: across from the Porte Sablons entrance to the Jardin d'Acclimatation, and at the northern end of Lac Inférieur.

(Note that after dark — and occasionally during the day in more remote corners — the Bois de Boulogne is a favourite with prostitutes of all persuasions.)

Place de la Concorde (p56)

octagonal 'square'. Its colonnades now shelter some of the city's most fashionable boutiques, as well as the drop-dead-posh Hôtel Ritz. The square's 43.5m bronze-and-stone column commemorates Napoleon's battle at Austerlitz, with bas-reliefs illustrating his subsequent victories, and a crowning statue depicting the great (little) leader as a Roman emperor.

SHOP

CHLOÉ *Fashion*

☎ 01 47 23 74 12; www.chloe.com in French; 44 av Montaigne, 8e; ⏱ 9am-7pm Mon-Sat; Ⓜ George V
Stella McCartney and co's sassy low-rider jeans and high-waisted dresses have given street cred to this 1956-established Parisian label. There's another boutique at 54 rue du Faubourg St-Honoré, 8e.

🅰 DRUGSTORE PUBLICIS
Department Store
☎ **01 44 43 79 00; www.publicisdrug store.com; 131 av des Champs-Élysées; Ⓜ Charles de Gaulle–Étoile**
An institution since 1958, this revamped former haunt of Serge Gainsbourg (see the boxed text, p147) and Catherine Deneuve now incorporates a glassed-in café (with wi-fi), *épicerie,* pharmacy and newsagent (all open from 8am to 2am); and a wine *cave* (cellar), cigar bar and beauty salon (all open from 11am to 11.30pm).

🅰 ERES *Fashion*
☎ **01 47 42 28 82; www.eres.fr; 2 rue Tronchet, 8e; ⏱ 10am-7pm Mon-Sat; Ⓜ Madeleine**
Before you and your suntan oil hit Paris Plage (p26), shimmy into a swimsuit from this beachwear boutique, which is shielded by full-length frosted-glass windows. In addition to shapely one-pieces

and bikinis (with tops and bottoms sold separately), Eres also does its own line of lingerie.

🅰 FAUCHON *Food & Drink*
☎ **01 47 42 60 11; 26-30 place de la Madeleine, 8e; ⏱ 8.30am-7pm Mon-Sat; Ⓜ Madeleine**
Many a lavish Parisian dinner party has been catered for by this famous pair of shops, which are fronted by elaborate revolving window displays such as pyramids of pastel-coloured macaroons. Inside you can buy beautifully wrapped delicacies such as pâté de foie gras and jams. A dozen smaller outlets are located throughout the city.

🅰 FROMAGERIE ALLÉOSSE
Food & Drink
☎ **01 46 22 50 45; 13 rue Poncelet, 17e; ⏱ 9am-1pm & 4-7pm Tue-Sat, 9am-1pm Sun; Ⓜ Ternes**
There are cheese shops… and then there is this temple to cheese. This

PLACE DE LA MADELEINE
Tantalising fine-food and gourmet shops garland the Église de la Madeleine (p53) on and around place de la Madeleine (F3).
For a fabulous photo op of place de la Concorde's obelisk and the Invalides' gold dome, head to the grand staircase on the church's southern side. To the east, the colourful **flower market** (⏱ 8am-7.30pm Tue-Sun) has been trading here since 1832. Exquisite *belle époque* tiling can be seen, for the cost of loose change, below ground in the adjacent public toilet.
While in the area, pick up half-price, same-day theatre and concert tickets at the Kiosque Théâtre Madeleine (see p216).

fromagerie is sectioned into five main categories: *fromage de chèvre* (goat's milk cheese), *fromage à pâte persillée* (veined or blue cheese), *fromage à pâte molle* (soft cheese), *fromage à pâte demi-dure* (semi-hard cheese), and *fromage à pâte dure* (hard cheese).

🏠 GALERIES LAFAYETTE
Department Store
☎ 01 42 82 34 56; www.galerieslafayette.com; 40 blvd Haussmann, 9e; ⏰ 9.30am-7.30pm Mon-Wed, Fri & Sat, to 9pm Thu; Ⓜ Auber or Chaussée d'Antin

Beneath a stained-glass dome, this opulent department store stocks innumerable fashion labels and stages free catwalk shows at 3pm Friday (bookings ☎ 01 42 82 30 25). The rooftop café has stunning views of the city. A footbridge leads to its adjoining premises, and there's also a separate homewares store, Lafayette Maison, at 35 blvd Haussmann.

🏠 GUERLAIN *Perfume*
☎ 01 45 62 52 57; www.guerlain.com; 68 av des Champs-Élysées, 8e; ⏰ boutique 10.30am-8pm Mon-Sat, 3-7pm Sun, spa 9am-7pm Mon-Wed, to 8pm Thu-Sat; Ⓜ Franklin D Roosevelt

This 1912 *parfumerie* just got more beautiful after a makeover of

Galeries Lafayette

ARCADES PROJECT

Embark on your own 'arcades project' (see p192) in some of the city's most beautiful remaining covered passages.

Galerie Vivienne (6 rue Vivienne to 4 rue des Petits Champs, 2e) Jewellery, designer fashion, children's toys and books; there's a sumptuous café at the rue Vivienne entrance.

Passage des Panoramas (off rue Vivienne, 2e) Antiques, old postcards and stamps.

Passage du Grand Cerf (Map pp74-5, G3;145 rue St-Denis to 10 rue Dussoubs, 2e) Contemporary jewellery, funky fashion, eccentric hats and stylish lighting.

Passage Jouffroy & Passage Verdeau (10-12 blvd Montmartre, 9e) Doll houses, film memorabilia, antique cameras, antiquarian books and postcards.

glistening toffee- and caramel-coloured mosaic tiles. You can shop for perfumes (including the namesake of the shop's address, the distinctive gold-and-pink-packaged Champs-Élysées), or take a decadent beauty treatment at the heavenly spa.

🅐 LA MAISON DE LA TRUFFE
Food & Drink

☎ 01 42 65 53 22; www.maison-de-la-truffe.com in French; 19 place de la Madeleine, 8e; 🕑 shop 9am-9pm Mon-Sat, eating area 11am-9pm Mon-Sat; Ⓜ Madeleine

Prized 'black diamond' truffles (which can be cooked) from Provence and other parts of France and elusive Italian white truffles (always eaten raw) are available at this 'house of truffles'; the truffles cost almost literally their own weight in gold. You can also taste the rare fungi in the small on-site eating area.

🅐 LA MAISON DU MIEL
Food & Drink

☎ 01 47 42 26 70; 24 rue Vignon, 9e; 🕑 9.15am-7pm Mon-Sat; Ⓜ Madeleine

More than 40 varieties of honey gleam on the shelves of this 1898-established 'honey house'.

🅐 LANCEL *Accessories*

☎ 01 56 89 15 70; www.lancel.com; 127 av des Champs-Élysées; 🕑 10.30am-8pm Mon-Sat; Ⓜ Charles de Gaulle–Étoile

With its metallic-silver handbags dangling from the ceiling and open racks of luscious totes, this handbag purveyor is stealing thunder from its neighbour Louis Vuitton.

🅐 LANVIN *Perfume & Fashion*

☎ 01 44 71 33 33; www.lanvin.com; women's boutique 22 rue du Faubourg St Honoré, 8e, men's boutique 15 rue du Faubourg St Honoré, 8e; 🕑 10am-7pm Mon-Sat; Ⓜ Concorde

Everything old is new again since Alber Elbaz took up the reins of

ARC DE TRIOMPHE, CHAMPS-ÉLYSÉES & GRANDS BOULEVARDS

Galerie Vivienne (p61)

this languishing perfume/couture house. The women's store is designed like a 1900s apartment, with black satin sofas, old timber wardrobes, and oversize mirrors resting on the floor. Beautifully cuffed shirts are tailor-made at the men's boutique, and the company's signature perfume,

Arpège, is back on every fashionista's Christmas list.

LE PRINTEMPS
Department Store
☎ 01 42 82 50 00; www.printemps.com;
64 blvd Haussmann, 9e; ⏰ 9.35am-
7pm Mon-Wed, Fri & Sat, to 10pm Thu;
Ⓜ Havre Caumartin

One of Paris' most spectacular *grands magasins* (department stores), Le Printemps' fashion, accessories and homewares span three neighbouring buildings. Free fashion shows take place under the 7th-floor cupola at 10am Tuesday.

SÉPHORA *Perfume*
☎ 01 53 93 22 50; www.sephora .com; 70 av des Champs-Élysées, 8e; 🕑 10am-1am Mon-Sat, noon-1am Sun; Ⓜ Franklin D Roosevelt
Shopaholics have limited options late at night, but at *perfumerie* Séphora's mothership you can spray, sniff and buy more than 12,000 fragrances until 1am.

LUXURY LABELS
Parisian shopping is at its ritziest in and around the Triangle d'Or (Gold Triangle), home to following famous flagship stores:
Chanel 40-42 av Montaigne, 8e
Christian Dior 30 av Montaigne, 8e
Christian Lacroix 26 av Montaigne, 8e
Commes des Garçons 54 rue du Faubourg St-Honoré, 8e
Givenchy 8 av Georges V, 8e
Hermès 24 rue du Faubourg St-Honoré, 8e
Jean-Paul Gaultier 44 av George V, 8e
Louis Vuitton 101 av des Champs Élysées, 8e
Thierry Mugler 49 av Montaigne, 8e
Yves Saint Laurent 38 rue du Faubourg St-Honoré, 8e

VIRGIN MEGASTORE *Music*
☎ 01 49 53 50 00; www.virginmega.fr in French; 52-60 av des Champs-Élysées, 8e; 🕑 10am-midnight Mon-Sat, noon-midnight Sun; Ⓜ Franklin D Roosevelt
The music retailer itself needs no introduction, but this is one of Virgin's handiest branches for buying event tickets – see p215.

🍴 EAT
ALAIN DUCASSE AU PLAZA ATHÉNÉE *Gastronomic* €€€€
☎ 01 53 67 65 00; www.alainducasse .com; Hôtel Plaza Athénée, 25 av de Montaigne, 8e; 🕑 lunch Thu & Fri, dinner Mon-Fri, closed mid-Jul–mid-Aug & mid-Dec–end Dec; Ⓜ Alma Marceau
Seated beneath 10,000 crystal shards glittering from the ceiling's chandeliers, dine on Iranian caviar with langoustines and a 'geometric' chocolate ensemble of textures and flavours, while sipping vintages from the 47-page wine list and being attended to by charcoal-suited waiters – and brace yourself for the bill.

AUX LYONNAIS *Lyonais* €€
☎ 01 42 96 65 04; www.alainducasse .fr; 32 rue St-Marc, 2e; 🕑 lunch & dinner Tue-Fri; Ⓜ Richelieu Drouot
Now under Alain Ducasse's ever-expanding umbrella, this authentic

QUARTERS

ARC DE TRIOMPHE, CHAMPS-ÉLYSÉES & GRANDS BOULEVARDS

Alain Ducasse au Plaza Athénée (p63)

Art Nouveau venue turns out Lyonais cuisine, such as frogs' legs, free-range poultry, and plenty of pork and porcine products. You'll still need to book, but you could eat here for the best part of a week for the cost of one meal at Ducasse's Plaza Athénée digs (p63).

🍴 GUY SAVOY
Gastronomic €€€€

☎ 01 43 80 40 61; www.guysavoy .com; 18 rue Troyon, 17e; ⏰ lunch Tue-Fri, dinner Tue-Sat; Ⓜ Charles de Gaulle–Étoile

Chef extraordinaire Guy Savoy's artichoke soup served with layered brioche of black truffles and wild mushrooms is a legend

in its own time, but his poached blue lobster, shelled and roasted and served with puréed carrot seasoned with star anise, is fast becoming another Savoy classic. For dessert, take the melt-in-your-mouth chocolate cake layered with praline and chicory cream.

🍴 LE BISTROT DU SOMMELIER
Gastronomic €€€€

☎ 01 42 65 24 85; www.bistrotdusom melier.com; 97 blvd Haussmann, 8e; ⏰ lunch & dinner Mon-Fri; Ⓜ St-Augustin

If you like *haute cuisine* with your wine (rather than the other way around), this brainchild of star sommelier Philippe Faure-Brac offers superb degustation menus with pre-paired wines. French wines figure strongly, but there are also top international drops.

LE CRISTAL ROOM
Gastronomic €€€€

☎ 01 40 22 11 10; ☼ lunch & dinner Mon-Sat; Ⓜ Iéna

Located at the Galerie Musée Baccarat (p53), Le Cristal Room features interiors conceived by the ubiquitous Philippe Starck. The restaurant drips with chandeliers, and elegant diners who booked their table many months ahead.

LE ROI DU POT AU FEU
French €€

☎ 01 47 42 37 10; 34 rue Vignon, 9e; ☼ lunch & dinner Mon-Sat; Ⓜ Havre Caumartin

This homey 1930s bistro is a charming alternative to the quarter's *très* elegant eateries. True to its name, it dishes up wonderful hotpots, with the herb-infused stock served as an entrée, and the beef and root vegetables as the main, as well as classic desserts like crème caramel. There are no bookings; just turn up.

MAISON PRUNIER
Gastronomic €€€€

☎ 01 44 17 35 85; www.prunier.com in French; 16 av Victor Hugo, 16e; ☼ lunch & dinner Mon-Sat; Ⓜ Charles de Gaulle–Étoile

A 1925 Art Deco treasure, the highlight of the erstwhile Prunier is the *maison*'s own brand of caviar. It also specialises in seafood of all varieties as well as vodkas. For a moveable feast, you can buy the house caviar at the on-site boutique.

PIERRE GAGNAIRE
Gastronomic €€€€

☎ 01 58 36 12 50; www.pierre-gag naire.com in French; 6 rue Balzac, 8e; ☼ lunch & dinner Mon-Fri, dinner Sun; Ⓜ Charles de Gaulle–Étoile

Pierre Gagnaire puts vigour into classic French cuisine without dabbling in fusion fads (there's no bubblegum-flavoured ice cream here). All of his dishes are works of art, visually and culinarily, and his signature *le grand dessert Pierre Gagnaire* is a time-honoured masterpiece.

WINING & DINING
You don't just get a regional or full gourmet menu at the excellent **Musée du Vin restaurant** (☎ 01 45 25 63 26; www.museeduvinparis.com; rue des Eaux, 5 square Charles Dickens, 16e; ☼ 10am-6pm Tue-Sun; Ⓜ Passy). You also get free entry to the attached Paris Wine Museum (usually €8), which has viticulture displays and – the best part – a free glass of wine at the end of your visit.

🍽 SPOON, FOOD & WINE
Fusion   €€€€

☎ 01 40 76 34 44; www.spoon.tm.fr; 14 rue de Marignan, 8e; ☺ lunch & dinner Mon-Fri; Ⓜ Franklin D Roosevelt

Alaine Ducasse and Philippe Starck teamed up to create the concept-driven Spoon (Food & Wine being the subtitle), and the partnership has spawned six Spoons worldwide to date. The 'modular' menu lets you mix and match mains and sauces. Spoon's super-slick ambience is enhanced by touches such as notepads and pencils on tables, hot towels, and 37 international editions of *Elle* to leaf through.

🍽 TAILLEVENT
Gastronomic   €€€€

☎ 01 44 95 15 01; www.taillevent.com; 15 rue Lamennais, 8e; ☺ lunch & dinner Mon-Fri; Ⓜ Charles de Gaulle–Étoile

Since opening its doors in 1946, Taillevent, situated in a gracious mid-19th-century townhouse, has been one of Paris' most highly regarded restaurants. Now under the stewardship of chef Alain Solivérès, one of the best options to experience Solivérès' Basque influences is via the lunch tasting *menu* (€70).

🍸 DRINK
🍸 BAR HEMINGWAY   Bar

☎ 01 43 16 30 30; www.ritzparis.com; Hôtel Ritz Paris, 15 place Vendôme, 1er; ☺ 6.30pm-2am Mon-Sat; Ⓜ Concorde or Madeleine

The drinks are tall, the prices taller and the stories taller still – legend has it that Hemingway himself, wielding a machine gun, helped liberate this timber-panelled, leather-upholstered bar during WWII, and was then put in charge. Today the Ritz's showpiece is awash with photos taken by Papa and has the best martinis in town. Dress to impress.

Spoon, Food & Wine

Cafés on Av des Champs-Élysées

☕ HARRY'S NEW YORK BAR
Bar

☎ 01 42 61 71 14; www.harrys-bar.fr; 5 rue Daunou, 2e; ☾ bar 10.30am-4am, piano bar 10pm-2am Mon-Fri, to 3am Mon-Sat; Ⓜ Opéra

The larger-than-life presences of Hemingway and F Scott Fitzgerald linger at this mahogany-panelled beauty of a bar. The venue's great gift to the world was the Bloody Mary, invented here in 1921 following the advent of canned tomato juice. (Harry's also invented the Blue Lagoon in 1960, but we'll forgive them for that.)

The basement piano bar knocks out Sinatra-style tunes.

☕ HÉDIARD
Salon de Thé

☎ 01 43 12 88 88; www.hediard.fr; 21 place de la Madeleine, 8e; ☾ 9am-10pm Mon-Sat; Ⓜ Madeleine

Since 1880 this gourmet emporium has sold exotic teas and luxury goods (such as cherry tomatoes for €30 per kilogram) in open barrows here at its original location. The upstairs tearoom/restaurant serves sumptuous brunches: try for a window seat overlooking place de la Madeleine. A number of branches exist elsewhere in Paris and internationally.

▼ LADURÉE
Salon de Thé
☎ 01 40 75 08 75; www.laduree.fr; 75 av des Champs-Élysées, 8e; ⏰ restaurant 7.30am-12.30am, shop 7.30am-11pm; Ⓜ George V
Graced by a pistachio-coloured, gilded portico, Ladurée's house speciality macaroons can be taken away or nibbled over a cup of tea in the tearoom. There's a handful of other outlets in Paris and a couple further afield, including one at Harrods in London.

⭐ PLAY
⭐ BALLET DE L'OPÉRA NATIONAL DE PARIS *Ballet*
☎ 01 72 29 35 35; www.opera-de-paris.fr in French
France's premier ballet company performs at the Palais Garnier

(p71), as well as the Opéra Bastille (p133). The website lists the upcoming season's program, which includes classic ballets (eg *Coppélia* and *Giselle*) as well as new works.

⭐ CRAZY HORSE *Cabaret*
☎ 01 47 23 32 32; www.lecrazyhorseparis.com; 12 av George V, 8e; Ⓜ Alma Marceau
The un-dressing rooms of Paris' most risqué cabaret raised eyebrows when they appeared in Woody Allen's 1965 film, *What's New Pussycat?*. If you don't want a fancy dinner or champagne or both with premium seating, you can pay from €50 for a seat at the bar plus two drinks (€35 plus one drink if you're under 26) without a reservation.

⭐ LE BARON *Club*
☎ 01 47 20 04 01; www.clublebaron.com; 6 av Marceau, 8e; ⏰ 10pm-5am; Ⓜ Alma Marceau

CREATURES OF THE NIGHT
Paris does cafés and bars brilliantly, but when it comes to clubbing, it's certainly no Berlin. Partying in the French capital veers from swigging champagne on the Champs-Élysées to trekking out to the suburbs for a dance party.

The biggest late-night scene at the moment is salsa (and zouk, which blends African and Latin American dance rhythms); R & B and hip-hop get less of a run. Electronica, laced with funk and groove, remains alternative rather than mainstream, with DJs tending to have short stints in a venue – look out for flyers in shops.

Admission generally costs around €15 including a drink.

Le Limonaire

Ensconced in a former brothel, this hipper-than-thou club, frequented by an endless list of celebs, is renowned for its formidable door policy. Try to look as famous as possible.

⭐ LE LIDO *Cabaret*

☎ 01 40 76 56 10; www.lido.fr; 116bis av des Champs-Élysées, 8e; Ⓜ George V
In 1946, a newly liberated Paris embraced the opening of this sparkling cabaret venue on the Champs-Élysées, and the lavish

sets, towering feather head-dresses, sequined gowns and synchronised dancing still dazzle the crowds today.

⭐ LE LIMONAIRE *Chansons*

☎ 01 45 23 33 33; 18 cité Bergère; admission free; ⏰ 6pm-midnight Tue-Sun; Ⓜ Grands Boulevards
Traditional *chansons* enthral audiences at this perfect little Parisian wine bar, which is tucked far away from the glitz and glamour of the quarter's big-name venues.

QUARTERS

ARC DE TRIOMPHE, CHAMPS-ÉLYSÉES & GRANDS BOULEVARDS

⭐ LE PULP *Gay & Lesbian*
☎ 01 40 26 01 93; www.pulp-paris
.com; 25 blvd Poissonière, 2e; admission
free to €10; 🕙 midnight-6am Thu-Sun;
Ⓜ Grands Boulevards

Paris' premier lesbian club
welcomes a mixed crowd on
Thursdays (provided boys are accompanied by girls), when leading
DJs hit the decks.

⭐ LE QUEEN *Gay & Lesbian*
☎ 01 53 89 08 90; www.queen.fr; 102 av
des Champs-Élysées, 8e; admission €10-
20; 🕙 11pm-6am; Ⓜ George V

This *grande dame* is now as popular
with a straight crowd as it is with
its namesake clientele, although

Monday's feverish disco nights are
still prime dancing queen territory.

⭐ L'OLYMPIA *Live Music*
☎ 08 92 68 33 68; www.olympiahall
.com; 28 blvd des Capucines, 9e; tickets
from €20; 🕙 box office noon-7pm Mon-
Fri; Ⓜ Opéra

Opened in 1888 by the founder of
the Moulin Rouge, this hallowed
concert hall's list of past performers
include Hallyday, Hendrix and Piaf,
who gave one of her final performances here, as well as Jeff Buckley,
who considered his 'Live at the
Olympia' his best-ever gig. The
website lists upcoming performances and takes online bookings.

Palais Garnier

CLUBBING IN PARIS: BEFORE & AFTER *Annabel Hart*

Seasoned Parisian clubbers, who tend to have a finely tuned sense of the absurd, divide their night out into three main parts. First, *la before,* usually drinks in a bar that has a DJ playing. Next they head to a club for *la soirée,* which rarely kicks off before 1am or 2am. When the party continues (or begins) at around 5am and goes until midday, it's called *l'after*. Often, however, the before and the after blend into one without any real 'during'. Meanwhile *'after d'afters'* are increasingly held in bars and clubs on Sunday afternoons and evenings, with a mix of strung-out clubbers kicking on and people out for a relaxed party that doesn't take place in the middle of the night. Go figure.

⭐ **PALAIS GARNIER**
Opera House

☎ 08 92 89 90 90, tours 01 41 10 08 10; tours http://visites.operadeparis .fr, library www.bnf.fr; place de l'Opéra, 9e; tours €7/4, library €11/6; 🕐 tours 11.30am & 2.30pm Jul & Aug, 11.30am Sat & Sun Sep-Jun, library 10am-5pm Sep-Jun, to 6pm Jul & Aug; Ⓜ Opéra

The mythological phantom of the opera lurked in this grand opera house – one of only two designed by Charles Garnier (the other is in Toulon). A performance here is unforgettable – see p215 for ticket booking agencies. Otherwise, you can take a guided tour, or visit the attached research library/museum, which includes a self-guided behind-the-scenes stickybeak provided there's no matinee or rehearsal taking place.

⭐ **TRIPTIQUE** *Club*

☎ 01 40 28 05 55; www.letryptique .com; 142 rue Montmartre, 2e; admission from €5; 🕐 9pm-2am Sun-Wed, to 5am Thu-Sat; Ⓜ Grand Boulevards

This dungeon-like club is a rare breed for the inner city, offering electro, hip hop and funk until dawn on weekends from a wicked sound system, and regular jazz and live acts in the huge stone rooms.

>LOUVRE & LES HALLES

Carving its triumphal way through the city, Paris' Grand Axis passes through the elegant Tuileries Gardens and the Arc de Triomphe du Carrousel before it reaches IM Pei's glass pyramid at the entrance to world's largest museum, the Louvre. Clustered around this art lovers' Holy Grail are many smaller museums and galleries.

Shoppers crowd along rue de Rivoli, which has beautiful cloisters along its western end, and congregate within Les Halles – the underground mall that supplanted the city's ancient marketplace. The original markets' spirit lives on in Les Halles' lively backstreets, such as rue Montorgueil.

The bright-blue-and-red Centre Pompidou (colloquially referred to as 'Beaubourg' due to its location) attracts art aficionados with its amazing hoard of modern art. Outside, place Georges Pompidou is a hub for buskers, and the adjacent place Igor Stravinsky's mechanical fountains are a riot of colourful skeletons, dragons and similarly outlandish creations.

LOUVRE & LES HALLES

◉ SEE
Arc de Triomphe
du Carrousel 1 C4
Centre Pompidou 2 H5
Jardin des Tuileries 3 B4
Jardin du Palais Royal 4 E3
Jeu de Paume 5 A3
Musée de la Mode
et du Textile .... (see 7)
Musée de la Publicité.. (see 7)
Musée de l'Orangerie..... 6 A4
Musée des Arts
Décoratifs 7 C4
Musée du Louvre............ 8 D5
Tour St-Jacques 9 G6

⌂ SHOP
agnès b Children's
Shop 10 F4
agnès b Men's Shop 11 F4

agnès b Women's
Shop 12 F4
Carrousel du Louvre 13 D4
Colette........................... 14 C3
Forum des Halles 15 G4
Galerie Véro Dodat 16 E4
Kenzo............................. 17 F5
Vache & Cow.................. 18 G5

🍴 EAT
Au Pied de Cochon 19 F4
Au Rocher
de Cancale 20 G3
Café Marly 21 D4
Comptoir
de la Gastronomie........ 22 F3
Georges .... (see 2)
Le Grand Véfour 23 E3
L'Escargot 24 G4
Stohrer 25 G3

🍷 DRINK
Angélina........................ 26 B3
Kong 27 F5
Le Tambour 28 F3

★ PLAY
Comédie Française
Salle Richelieu............... 29 D4
Comédie Française
Studio Théâtre 30 D4
Forum des Images..... (see 15)
Le Baiser Salé 31 G5
Le Duc des Lombards ... 32 G5
Sunset & Sunside 33 G5

Please see over for map

SEE

ARC DE TRIOMPHE DU CARROUSEL

place du Carrousel, 1er; M Palais Royal–Musée du Louvre; &
Although smaller than Paris' most famous Arc de Triomphe, this 1805 triumphal arch, located in the Jardin du Carrousel at the eastern end of the Tuileries, is more ornate. It's adorned with eight pink marble pillars, each topped with a statue of a soldier in Napoleon's army.

CENTRE POMPIDOU

☎ **01 44 78 12 33; www.centrepom pidou.fr; place Georges Pompidou, 4e; Musée National d'Art Moderne (MNAM) €10/8;** ☼ **MNAM 11am-9pm Wed-Mon, library noon-10pm Mon & Wed-Fri, 11am-10pm Sat & Sun; M Rambuteau;** &
The highlight of this groundbreaking 1970s cultural centre is the extraordinary Musée National d'Art Moderne (MNAM; National Museum of Modern Art), which picks up roughly where the Musée d'Orsay leaves off, housing the national collection of art from 1905 on (some 50,000 pieces). See also p22.

Centre Pompidou

JARDIN DES TUILERIES

☎ **01 40 20 90 43;** ☼ **7am-9pm late Mar-late Sep, 7.30am-7.30pm late Sep-late Mar; M Tuileries or Concorde;** &
Bisected by the Axe Historique, these 28-hectare formal gardens are where Parisians paraded their finery in the 17th century. Now a Unesco World Heritage Site, the paths, ponds and merry-go-round are as enchanting as ever for a stroll.

UNDER WRAPS

The scaffolding- and plastic-encased structure rising above rue de Rivoli just north of place du Châtelet isn't, mercifully, a newfangled apartment building set to blight the cityscape, but the **Tour St-Jacques** – a 52m Flamboyant Gothic belltower constructed in 1523. The tower's renovations are due to wrap up by 2010.

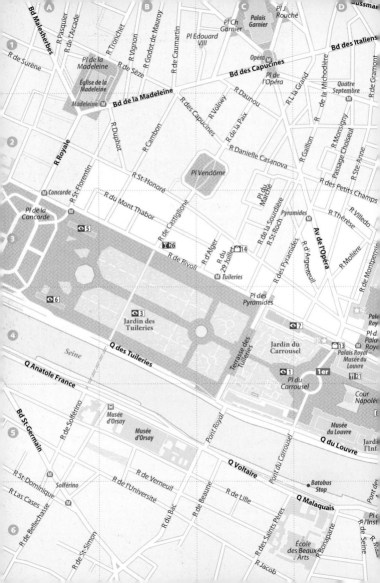

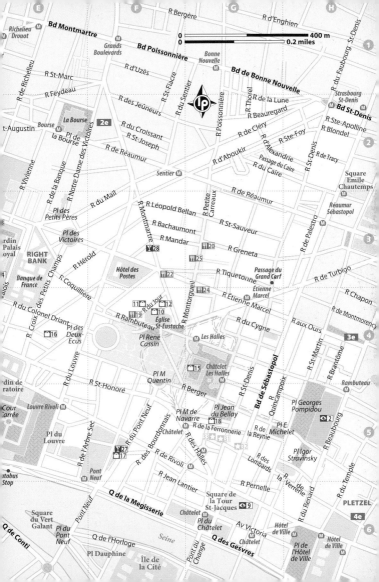

Jardin des Tuileries (p73)

toy soldiers. The black-and-white striped columns at the southern end were installed by sculptor Daniel Buren in 1986, creating a public outcry that temporarily halted construction.

JEU DE PAUME
☎ 01 47 03 12 52; www.jeudepaume .org; 1 place de la Concorde; admission €6/3; ☼ noon-9pm Tue, to 7pm Wed-Fri, 10am-7pm Sat & Sun; Ⓜ Concorde
In the northwestern corner of the Jardin des Tuileries, this former tennis court is now France's national photography centre, and features rotating exhibitions from the world of images. A second site is located in the Hôtel de Sully (see p115). Combination tickets for the two museums cost €8/4.

MUSÉE DE L'ORANGERIE
☎ 01 42 97 49 21; www.musee -orangerie.fr; Jardin des Tuileries, 1er; ☼ 12.30-7pm Wed, Thu, Sat-Mon, 12.30-9pm Fri; Ⓜ Concorde; ♿
Monet's *Waterlilies* take pride of place in this freshly renovated, light-filled museum, but you'll also find the astonishing collections of Jean Walter and Paul Guillaume, which include additional works by Monet and many by Sisley, Renoir, Cézanne, Gauguin, Picasso, Matisse, Modigliani; the collection also includes Derain's *Arlequin & Pierrot*. See also p14.

JARDIN DU PALAIS ROYAL
place du Palais Royal, 1er; ☼ 7am-10.15pm Apr & May, to 11pm Jun-Aug, to 9.30pm Sep, 7.30am-8.30pm Oct-Mar; Ⓜ Palais Royal–Musée du Louvre; ♿
This lovely park is just north of the Palais Royal, where a young Louis XIV once resided (and which now houses government buildings). The park is flanked by two arcades, which house shops selling old-fashioned items such as lead

◙ MUSÉE DU LOUVRE

☎ 01 40 20 53 17; www.louvre.fr; place du Louvre, 1er; permanent collections/permanent collections & temporary exhibits €8.50/13; ⊙ 9am-6pm Mon, Thu, Sat & Sun, 9am-9.45pm Wed & Fri; Ⓜ Palais Royal–Musée du Louvre; ♿

Mona aside, the *pièces de résistance* of this national vault of art and artefacts include the crown jewels of Louis XV, the *Venus de Milo* and Michelangelo's *The Dying Slave*. There's also dazzling Oriental, Egyptian, Greek and Roman antiquities. For the lowdown on navigating the labyrinthine Louvre, see p18.

◙ OTHER PALAIS DU LOUVRE MUSEUMS

☎ 01 44 55 57 50; www.ucad.fr in French; 107 rue de Rivoli, 1er; admission for all 3 museums €6/4.50; ⊙ 11am-6pm Tue, Thu & Fri, to 9pm Wed, 10am-6pm Sat & Sun; Ⓜ Palais Royal–Musée du Louvre; ♿

Not content with being the largest museum in the world, the Louvre

Musée du Louvre

Clémence Lutz
Documentary maker, The Louvre

What's your job? I work with directors and producers to make programs for television, and also record archival footage for future documentaries and to keep a historical memory. **Best thing about working here?** To be alone in the rooms when the museum's closed. You can be alone with *La Joconde (Mona Lisa)* – it's crazy. **Favourite piece of art here?** Vermeer's *La Dentellière (The Lacemaker)*. **Insider tips?** Les Peintures du Nord is a quiet place for a moment of contemplation. The Cour Khorsabad in the Mesopotamia section could be in antiquity. You don't have to eat at the food court; the prices are similar at the Café Richelieu, which has a terrace; or the Café Denon. **Other art favourites?** Beaubourg (MNAM, Centre Pompidou; p73), Musée Delacroix (p151), and the galleries in the Marais.

THE DA VINCI ENIGMA

In late 2006 Canadian scientists used infrared technology to peer through paint layers of Da Vinci's *Mona Lisa;* confirming her identity as mother-of-five Lisa Gherardini, wife of Florentine merchant Francesco de Giocondo (hence the alternative name *La Joconde,* meaning de Giocondo).

Contradicting Dan Brown's theory that the enigmatic portrait represents a man *and* a woman, they also discovered her dress was covered in a transparent gauze veil typically worn in early 16th-century Italy by pregnant or new mothers; it's surmised that the work was painted to commemorate the birth of her second son, around 1503, when she was aged about 24.

shelters three additional museums in its Rohan Wing: the **Musée des Arts Décoratifs**, featuring furniture, ceramics and glassware; the **Musée de la Publicité**, displaying advertising including posters dating from the 13th century; and the **Musée de la Mode et du Textile**, showcasing couture and fabrics.

🛍 SHOP

For fashion basics as well as sporting goods, the eastern end of the rue de Rivoli is rife with chain stores, while the backstreets house quirkier boutiques.

🛍 AGNÈS B *Fashion*
☎ 01 45 08 56 56; www.agnesb.fr; 6 rue du Jour, 1er; ☼ 10.30am-8pm Mon-Sat; Ⓜ Les Halles
Another Parisian label that has become a global empire, agnès b is synonymous with durable basics such as well-cut jackets, body-hugging shirts and fine-knit

cardigans, plus quirky items such as artist-designed humanitarian T-shirts. As well as the women's shop, there's also a nearby men's shop (3 rue du Jour, 1er), and children's shop (2 rue du Jour, 1er).

🛍 CARROUSEL DU LOUVRE *Shopping Centre*
☎ 01 43 16 47 10; www.carrouseldulouvre.com; 99 rue de Rivoli, 1er; ☼ 11am-8pm; Ⓜ Palais Royal–Musée du Louvre
IM Pei's inverted glass pyramid is the focal point of this underground shopping centre's upmarket shops and restaurants.

🛍 COLETTE *Fashion*
☎ 01 55 35 33 90; www.colette.fr; 213 rue St-Honoré, 1er; ☼ 10.30am-7.30pm Mon-Sat; Ⓜ Tuileries
There's no sign – two sky-blue circles indicate you've arrived at this impossibly hip concept shop, subtitled 'styledesignartfood' (yes, in English). Footwear,

Forum des Halles

fashion, homewares, books, art and cosmetics change according to the *Zeitgeist* (resulting in some astounding sales). In the basement, the wi-fi'd bar caters to Colette's model clientele with 100 varieties of water, plus salads and champagne.

☐ FORUM DES HALLES
Shopping Mall

☎ 01 44 76 96 56; rues Berger & Rambuteau, 1er; ⏰ 10am-7.30pm Mon-Sat; Ⓜ Les Halles
It seemed like a good idea at the time: move Paris' wholesale mar-

kets (and disease-breeding rats) outside the city, and replace them with an open park and underground mall. Today, the park attracts illicit 'vendors', while below, artificially lit, could-be-anywhere corridors of chain stores (including a vast Fnac) wrap around a sunken courtyard and the Julio Silva sculpture, *Pyegemalion*.

☐ GALERIE VÉRO DODAT
Arcade

19 rue Jean-Jacques Rousseau to 2 rue du Bouloi, 1er; ⏰ vary; Ⓜ Louvre Rivoli
Seek out bric-a-brac, antique dolls and curios in this covered passage.

QUARTERS

LOUVRE & LES HALLES

🏠 KENZO *Fashion & Perfume*
☎ 01 73 04 20 00; www.kenzo.com; 1 rue Pont Neuf, 1er; ⏰ 11am-7.30pm Mon-Sat; Ⓜ Pont Neuf

While landmark La Samaritaine next door undergoes renovations, Kenzo flies the flag for fashion on this high-profile strip. Kenzo himself has retired from designing, but Antonio Marras is keeping Kenzo at the cutting edge, bolstered by the addition of a Philippe Starck–designed bar, Kong, (p84) on the top two levels.

🏠 VACHE & COW *Homewares*
☎ 01 40 26 60 36; www.vacheandcow .com in French; 12 rue de la Ferronnerie, 1er; ⏰ 1-7pm Mon, 11am-7pm Tue-Sat; Ⓜ Châtelet

Staking its claim as '100% cow', this boutique is a testament to its owners' resourcefulness in sourcing cow-adorned items – from towels to soaps to kitchen utensils to toys. Look for the life-size black-and-white fibreglass cow out front.

🍴 EAT

There are a slew of inexpensive cafés of varying quality in the maze of pedestrian streets ensnaring Les Halles. One of the most atmospheric spots for dining is along lively rue Montorgueil – see the boxed text, below. At the *haute* end of the spectrum is one of the world's most magnificent dining rooms, Le Grand Véfour (p83).

🍴 AU PIED DE COCHON
French €€
☎ 01 40 13 77 00 6; rue Coquillère, 1er; ⏰ 24hr; Ⓜ Les Halles

The former *halles* (markets; described by novelist Emile Zola as the 'belly of Paris') may have shifted out of the centre nearly 50 years ago, but this enduring brasserie specialising in pig's trotters still opens around the clock, just as it did when marketeers started and ended their day here. Trotters aside, there are hearty breakfasts and onion soup.

RUE MONTORGUEIL
Running north from Les Halles (G4), this cobblestone strip was once a splinter of the historic *halles* (markets). Pedestrianised rue Montorgueil crosses rue Étienne-Marcel (which showcases up-and-coming fashion designers), before changing names a bit further north to become rue Petite Carreaux (G3; look out for horse-meat butcher J Davin at No 9). It continues north through the Sentier garment-making quarter, where bolts of fabric and bowed clothing-racks are wheeled through the streets.

By day (except Monday), the street's grocers and speciality shops set up trellis-table stalls on the cobblestones, while both day and night, drinkers and diners spill from the street's bars, cafés and restaurants.

Specialist grocer, rue Montorgueil (p81)

🍽 AU ROCHER DE CANCALE
Seafood €€
☎ 01 42 33 50 29; www.aurocherde
cancale.fr in French; 78 rue Montorgueil,
2e; ⏰ 8am-2am; Ⓜ Les Halles or
Étienne Marcel

Rue Montorgueil was once the oyster market of the old *halles,* and this timberlined restaurant opened in 1846 is its legacy. Virtually unchanged since the days of the markets, there's a choice of three *plats du jour* plus two chef's suggestions (crab ravioli, say), alongside oysters from Cancale, Brittany's foremost oyster port.

Everything here, including wine by the pitcher, is great value.

🍽 CAFÉ MARLY *French* €€
☎ 01 46 26 06 60 93; rue de Rivoli, 1er;
⏰ 8am-2am; Ⓜ Palais Royal–Musée du Louvre

The glittering views of IM Pei's glass pyramid, and of the French movers, shakers and stars who frequent this café, make drinking or dining or both here a classic Parisian experience. If you're gearing up for an afternoon at the Louvre, carb-load first on Marly's excellent pastas.

🍽 COMPTOIR DE LA GASTRONOMIE

Gastronomic €€

☎ 01 42 33 31 32; www.comptoir-gastronomie.com; 34 rue Montmartre, 1er; ⏱ épicerie 6am-11pm Mon-Sat, to 7pm Sun, restaurant 11am-11pm Mon-Sat, to 7pm Sun; Ⓜ Les Halles; ♿

Here since 1894, this gorgeous Art Nouveau establishment has an elegant dining room where dishes are constructed around delicacies such as foie gras, truffles and caviar. The adjoining *épicerie* (specialist grocer) stocks a scrumptious array of gourmet goods to take home.

🍽 GEORGES

International €€€

☎ 01 44 78 47 99; www.centrepompidou.fr; 6th fl, Centre Pompidou, place Georges Pompidou, 4e; ⏱ lunch & dinner Wed-Mon; Ⓜ Rambuteau

Encased in aluminium sheeting with modular arctic-white seats, the Pompidou Centre's hyper-industrial dining room has stunning views over Paris' rooftops, especially from its terrace. But a cautionary tale from a non-French-speaking friend: 'The menu's words don't necessarily mean anything – my main course translated to 'the Crying Tiger'. It was divine, but I still have absolutely no idea what it was.'

🍽 LE GRAND VÉFOUR

Gastronomic €€€€

☎ 01 42 96 56 27; vefour@relaischateaux.com; 17 rue de Beaujolais, 1er; ⏱ lunch Mon-Fri, dinner Mon-Thu, closed third week of Apr, Aug, & last week of Dec; Ⓜ Pyramides

Chef Guy Martin preserves the reputation of this 1784-opened splendour, replete with gilt-edged mirrors and chandeliers, whose past guests included Napoleon. Martin's signature foie gras ravioli in truffle cream sauce is incomparable; and a sommelier is on hand to pair Martin's opuses with the finest of French wines.

Street café, rue Montorgueil (p81)

NOSHING WITH NIPPERS

If you're travelling with littlies, be warned that most restaurants in Paris don't have high-chairs or children's menus. But you don't have to resort to junk food. Cafeterias, such as the Bazar de l'Hôtel de Ville (BHV)'s cafétéria (p123), are an alternative for healthy, kid-friendly fare. Another option is to pick up sandwiches and crêpes from a street stall or, better yet, pack a market-fresh picnic, and head to parks such as the Jardin du Luxembourg (see p149), where the kids can run around to their hearts' content.

We've mentioned in eating reviews where places are especially good for children.

⑪ L'ESCARGOT French €€€
☎ 01 42 36 33 51; 38 rue Montorgueil, 1er; ☽ dinner daily, closed August; Ⓜ Les Halles

A giant gold snail adorns the forest-green façade of this heritage-listed monument. Snails also feature on the menu, along with frogs' legs, Chateaubriand steak with Béarnaise sauce, veal sweetbreads and whisky-flambéed Breton lobster. Try for the intimate loggia, perched above the entrance like a private box at the theatre. Past guests range from Proust to Bogie and Bacall.

⑪ STOHRER
Patisserie & Tratieur €

☎ 01 42 33 38 20; www.stohrer.fr; 51 rue Montorgueil, 2e; ☽ 7.30am-8.30pm; Ⓜ Étienne-Marcel or Sentier

Opened during the reign of Louis XV in 1730, this beautiful patisserie's pastel murals were added in 1864 by Paul Baudry, who also decorated the Garnier Opèra's Grand Foyer. All of the cakes, pastries, ice cream and savoury delicacies are made on the premises, with specialities including baba rhum (rum-drenched brioche) and puit d'amour (cream-filled, caramel-topped puff pastry).

⑂ DRINK
⑂ ANGÉLINA Salon de Thé
☎ 01 42 60 82 00; 226 rue de Rivoli, 1er; ☽ 9am-7pm; Ⓜ Tuileries

Situated under the cloisters, this glorious 1903 belle époque tea-room is renowned for its wonderful African hot chocolate, served with a pot of whipped cream. If you're travelling with kids, accommodating staff make them welcome here. If you're travelling toute seule (on your own), pick up a book from Gagliani, France's first English-language bookstore, at neighbouring 224 rue de Rivoli.

⑂ KONG Bar
☎ 01 40 39 09 00; 1 rue du Pont-Neuf, 1er; ☽ noon-2am; Ⓜ Pont Neuf

With its Philippe Starck–designed postmodern décor, including iridescent champagne-coloured vinyl booths, Japanese cartoon cutouts and garden gnome stools, nights here see Paris' glam young set guzzling Dom Pérignon and shaking their Chloé-clad booty on the tables. But the best time to visit this bar/restaurant/club atop the Kenzo building is at sunset, when you have magical views of the river.

⅄ LE TAMBOUR Bar
☎ 01 42 33 06 90; 41 rue Montmartre, 2e; ⏱ noon-6am Tue-Sat, 6pm-6am Sun & Mon; Ⓜ Étienne Marcel or Sentier

Insomniacs head to this local landmark for its rowdy, good-natured atmosphere, décor salvaged from Parisian public transport and street furniture, and filling French fare for under €20 served until 3.30am.

★ PLAY
★ COMÉDIE FRANÇAISE
Theatre
☎ 08 25 10 16 80; www.comedie-fran caise.fr in French; place Colette, 1er; tickets €10-35; ⏱ box office 11am-6pm Tue-Sat, 1-6pm Sun & Mon; Ⓜ Palais Royal–Musée du Louvre
Founded in 1680, the oldest theatre in France stages works

Street theatre

André Camboulas
Proprietor, Le Tambour (p85)

Philosophy behind the bistro's décor? To honour Paris… It's a temple to the soul of Paris. **Where do you find the street signs and memorabilia?** Life brings them to us. People give us thousands of things, but everything must find the right place in the room – like a shrine. **Best thing about working here?** The organic social matter – you can study life. The interactive relations with the diners are alchemy, because the place has its own personality. It's lovely work. **Where do you shop for the menus' ingredients?** At MIN (Marché d'Interest Nationale), which replaced Les Halles, in the *banlieue* (suburb) of Rungis. **Favourite wine?** For red wines, the Val de Loire (Loire Valley) – very fruity and light. **Best dessert on the menu?** All of them! Ah, OK, the *tarte tatin* (traditional upside-down caramelised-apple tart).

by playwrights such as Molière, Racine and Beaumarchais. The 'French Comedy' encompasses the main **Comédie Française Salle Richelieu** (place Colette, 1er), just west of the Palais Royal, as well as the **Comédie Française Studio Théâtre** (99 rue de Rivoli, 1er), and the Théâtre du Vieux Colombier (see p168). Performances are mostly in French.

⭐ FORUM DES IMAGES
Cinema
☎ 01 44 76 62 00; www.forumdesim ages.net in French; 1 Grande Galerie, Porte St-Eustache, Forum des Halles, 1er; tickets €6.50/5.50; ⏱ 1-10pm Tue, to 9pm Wed-Sun; Ⓜ Les Halles
Located in the depths of Les Halles, this archive cinema screens rare and little-known films, many of them set in Paris.

JAZZ IN THE CITY
Several stellar jazz clubs swing on rue des Lombards.

Le Baiser Salé (The Salty Kiss; ☎ 01 42 33 37 71; 58 rue des Lombards, 1er; admission free-€22; ⏱ 7pm-6am; Ⓜ Châtelet) Unearths trad, Afro- and fusion-jazz talent, and hosts occasional pop rock and *chansons*.

Le Duc des Lombards (☎ 01 42 33 22 88; www.ducdeslombards.com; 42 rue des Lombards, 1er; admission €16-20; ⏱ 9pm-4am; Ⓜ Châtelet) This laidback club recalls jazz greats (including the eponymous Duke).

Sunset & Sunside (☎ 01 40 26 46 60, 01 40 26 21 25; 60 rue des Lombards, 1er; admission €10-22; ⏱ 9.30pm-4am Mon-Sat; Ⓜ Châtelet) Respected double-venue leaning towards world music.

>MONTMARTRE

In the 1960s' bittersweet hit *La Bohème,* French crooner Charles Aznavour laments a bohemian Montmartre whose days are numbered. Half a century later, it's true that much of modern-day Montmartre, abutting Paris' northern boundary, *is* overrun with tourists. Yet somehow it retains its intimate village air.

Crowned by the Roman-Byzantine basilica, Sacré-Cœur, Montmartre is the city's steepest quarter (*mont* means hill – the martyr was St Denis, who was beheaded here about AD 250). Its lofty views, gnarled wine-producing vines, and tangle of streets, ivy-trailed staircases and squares, lured painters from the 19th century on. Picasso, Pissarro, Toulouse-Lautrec and Van Gogh were among those who set up here; and, though the rents no longer support bohemian budgets, Montmartre is still frequented by artists and their easels today.

Hedonists revel in Montmartre's southern neighbours, Pigalle and Clichy, home to cabarets including the Moulin Rouge, bawdy bars, neonlit strip clubs, and, yes, an erotica museum.

Montmartre's steep streets make for an enchanting stroll – see p16.

MONTMARTRE

☉ SEE
Basilique
du Sacré Cœur **1** C4
Cimetière
de Montmartre.............**2** B4
Dalí Espace
Montmartre **3** C4
Musée de l'Érotisme.......**4** B4
Musée
de Montmartre.............**5** C3

🛍 SHOP
Marché aux Puces
de St-Ouen **6** C1
Rebecca Rils **7** B4

Tati.................................**8** D4
Zut! **9** C4

🍴 EAT
À la Cloche d'Or **10** B4
Aux Négociants **11** D3
Charlot, Roi
des Coquillages **12** B4
Chez Marie.....................**13** C4
Chez Toinette **14** C4
La Maison Rose **15** C3
Le Relais Gascon **16** C4
Marché
Batignolles-Clichy........**17** A4
Ripaille **18** A4

🍷 DRINK
Café Le Refuge **19** C3
Drôle d'Endroit
pour une Rencontre **20** B3
Les Deux Moulins **21** B4

⭐ PLAY
Académie de Billard **22** B4
Au Lapin Agile **23** C3
Chez Louisette.............(see **6**)
Folies-Bergère............... **24** D6
La Cigale **25** C4
L'Élysée-
Montmartre **26** D4
Moulin Rouge............... **27** B4

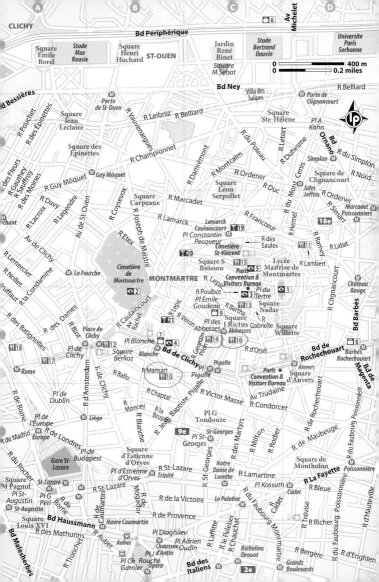

👁 SEE

👁 BASILIQUE DU SACRÉ-CŒUR

☎ 01 53 41 89 00; www.sacre-coeur
-montmartre.com; place du Parvis du
Sacré-Cœur, 18e; basilica free, dome €5;
🕐 basilica 6am-11pm, dome 9am-7pm
Apr-Sep, to 6pm Oct-Mar; Ⓜ Anvers, or
funicular

The chapel-lined 'Sacred Heart' basilica was built in 1873 to atone for
the Franco-Prussian War (1870–1),
but wasn't consecrated until 1919.
There are breathtaking views over
Paris from the front steps, which
just get better if you climb the 234
steps to the dome; you can see up
to 30km on a clear day.

👁 CIMETIÈRE DE MONTMARTRE

☎ 01 53 42 36 30, conservation office
01 53 42 36 30; conservation office
20 av Rachel, 18e; admission free;
🕐 8am-6pm Mon-Fri, 8.30am-6pm Sat,
9am-6pm Sun mid-Mar–early Nov, 8am-
5.30pm Mon-Fri, 8.30am-5.30pm Sat,
9am-5.30pm Sun early Nov–mid-Mar;
Ⓜ Place de Clichy

Steps of rue Foyatier, behind Basilique du Sacré-Cœur

The famous graves in this charming cobbled cemetery, established
in 1798, include writers Alexandre
Dumas and Stendhal (Marie-
Henri Beyle), composer Jacques
Offenbach, artist Edgar Degas,
film director François Truffaut and
dancer Vaslav Nijinsky. Pick up a
free map from the conservation
office.

PLACE DU TERTRE

The main square of the original village before it was incorporated into Paris proper, place du
Tertre (C4) has drawn countless artists and their palettes in its time. Now, particularly at weekends and in summer, it's almost a caricature of its former self; the prevalence of portraitists
touting to sketch tourists' likenesses makes it feel a bit like a theme park. Still, the buskers and
crowds do create a carnival atmosphere, and some of the portraitists are actually quite good.

◉ DALÍ ESPACE MONTMARTRE

☎ 01 42 64 40 10; www.daliparis.com; 11 rue Poulbot, 18e; admission €10/7; ☼ 10am-6pm; Ⓜ Abbesses

Catalan surrealist Dalí lived in Montmartre (at one point becoming its 'Emperor' at the invitation of self-titled Empress Lucie Valore, though their affair was shortlived). Dalí's illustrations, sculptures, engravings and furniture, such as his 'lips' sofa, are displayed against the dramatic black-painted walls of this museum.

◉ MUSÉE DE L'ÉROTISME

☎ 01 42 58 28 73; www.musee-ero tisme.com; 72 blvd de Clichy, 18e; admission €8/6; ☼ 10am-2am; Ⓜ Blanche

Exhibits at this museum are surprisingly artistic and represent the history of erotica from around the world, incorporating 5000-plus statues, paintings, black-and-white 1920s silent porn and mind-boggling toys. If you're inspired, the Rebecca Rils sex supermarket is next door (see p92).

◉ MUSÉE DE MONTMARTRE

☎ 01 49 25 89 39; www.museedemont martre.fr in French; 12-14 rue Cortot, 18e; admission €7/5.50; ☼ 10am-6pm Tue-Sun; Ⓜ Lamarck Caulaincourt

Housed in Montmartre's oldest building, a 17th-century garden-set manor, this is no dusty old local museum. The quarter's

Place du Tertre

TOP 10 MONTMARTRE ARTISTS

These are just some of the seminal artists who have lived in Montmartre over the years. Works by all these masters are on display in Paris' museums and galleries.

> Edouard Manet (born 1832, died 1883)
> Edgar Degas (1834–1917)
> Pierre-August Renoir (1841–1919)
> Vincent Van Gogh (1853–90)
> Henri de Toulouse-Lautrec (1864–1901)
> Raoul Dufy (1877–1953)
> Pablo Picasso (1881–1973)
> Maurice Utrillo (1883–1955)
> Amedeo Modigliani (1884–1920)
> Salvador Dalí (1904–89)

bohemian history comes to life through a series of paintings and documents, but it's also worth making a visit here for the bookshop alone, which sells wine from Montmartre's own little vineyard, Fête des Vendages de Montmartre.

🛍 SHOP

🏛 MARCHÉ AUX PUCES DE ST-OUEN *Market*
www.les-puces.com; rue des Rosiers, av Michelet, rue Voltaire, rue Paul Bert & rue Jean-Henri Fabre, 18e; ⏰ 10am-7pm Sat-Mon; Ⓜ Porte de Clignancourt
Europe's largest flea market has 2500 stalls spread across 10 spe-

ciality villages, including amazing antiques and vintage hats and jewellery. The market is at its best on Sunday; Mondays can be very quiet. While here, don't miss lunch at the legendary Chez Louisette (p99). See p184 for more on markets, as well as www.libertys.com and www.vernaison.com.

🏛 REBECCA RILS *Sex Shop*
76-78 blvd de Clichy; ⏰ 10am-1.30am; ⏰ 10am-2am; Ⓜ Blanche
Located next to the Musée de L'Érotisme (p91), this sex supermarket has aisles of toys, plus B&D gear, DVDs and outfits (and fitting rooms with red-velour chaise longues).

🏛 TATI *Department Store*
☎ 01 55 29 50 00; www.tati.fr; 4 blvd de Rochechouart, 18e; ⏰ 10am-7pm Mon-Fri, 9.15am-7pm Sat; Ⓜ Barbès Rochechouart
This no-frills department store is every fashionable Parisian's guilty secret – where customers fight for bargains (and there are some great ones stuffed in the clothes bins and piled on tables) – but never admit it.

🏛 ZUT! *Antiques*
☎ 01 42 59 69 68; www.antiquites-industrielles.com; 9 rue Ravignan, 18e; ⏰ 11am-1pm & 4-7pm Wed-Sat, 11am-1pm Sun, & by appointment; Ⓜ Abbesses

Tati

If you're looking for a conversation piece to dominate your lounge room, such as a turn-of-the-20th-century railway clock or other oversize industrial object, Zut's proprietor, Frédéric Daniel, can help you track it down. Even if you're not, it's worth sticking your head around the doorway to see some resplendent relics of Paris' past. Frédéric also does repairs.

EAT

Montmartre has more than its fair share of tourist traps. As a rule, places with English-language menus out front are more likely to have a bad price-to-quality ratio, but non-French speakers shouldn't be deterred as more authentic options (usually just off main drags) often have English menus inside.

QUARTERS

MONTMARTRE

À LA CLOCHE D'OR
French €€

☎ 01 48 74 48 88; 3 rue Mansart, 9e;
🕐 lunch & dinner to 4am; Ⓜ Blanche
or Pigalle

Once owned by the family of actress Jeanne Moreau, the 'Golden Bell' has vaudeville charm with its photos of stars, a roaring open fire in winter, and a wonderful house special of steak tartare.

AUX NÉGOCIANTS
French €

☎ 01 46 06 15 11; 27 rue Lambert,
18e; 🕐 lunch Mon-Fri, dinner daily;
Ⓜ Château Rouge

The Montmartre known and loved by Charles Aznavour is alive and well at this jovial, locally patronised wine bar serving rib-sticking classics such as bœuf bourguignon.

Basilique du Sacré-Cœur (p90) above Paris' rooftops

🍽 CHARLOT, ROI DES COQUILLAGES
Seafood €€€

☎ 01 53 20 48 00; 12 place de Clichy, 9e; 🕙 lunch & dinner to midnight Sun-Wed, to 1am Thu-Sat; Ⓜ Place de Clichy
These Art Deco premises enjoy a regal reputation among Parisians because of the trademark seafood platters on offer, but Charlot also does delicious grilled sardines, and bouillabaisse to make any Marseillais homesick. Lunch *menus,* starting at €19, are terrific value.

🍽 CHEZ MARIE
French €

☎ 01 42 62 06 26; 27 rue Gabrielle, 18e; 🕙 lunch & dinner; Ⓜ Abbesses
Decoupaged with old theatre and advertising posters, this little place away from the tourist crowds isn't the venue for a blow-out gourmet meal, but if you're after simple French standards, such as thigh of duck or well-cooked fish, served to you by kindly staff, then it's a treat.

🍽 CHEZ TOINETTE
French €€

☎ 01 42 54 44 36; 20 rue Germain Pilon, 18e; 🕙 dinner Tue-Sat; Ⓜ Abbesses
Game such as partridge, doe and roebuck are among the simply but superbly prepared dishes chalked on the blackboard of this vaunted bistro, along with the house speciality, duck fillet with sage and honey.

🍽 LA MAISON ROSE
French €€

☎ 01 42 57 66 75; 2 rue de l'Abreuvoir, 18e; 🕙 lunch & dinner daily Mar-Oct, lunch Thu-Mon, dinner Mon & Thu-Sat Nov-Feb; Ⓜ Lamarck Caulaincourt
Perched on the hillside just far enough north of place du Tertre to evade the coach-loads of tourists, this sweet little rose-pink cottage was rendered in lithographs by Utrillo. Reasonably priced bistro fare is dished up in the cosy rooms and on the tiny terrace in fine weather.

🍽 LE RELAIS GASCON
Brasserie €€

☎ 01 42 58 58 22; lerelaisgascon@yahoo.fr; 6 rue des Abbesses, 18e; 🕙 10.30am-2am; Ⓜ Abbesses
Climbing the wooden staircase to this narrow townhouse's 1st-floor dining room rewards with rooftop views of Montmartre. The solidly French menu includes seafood and meat dishes, but the reason that locals pack the communal tables here is to tuck into one of Gascon's gargantuan salads, served in giant bowls with thin-sliced fried potatoes sautéed in garlic.

QUARTERS

MONTMARTRE

La Maison Rose (p95)

🍴 MARCHÉ BATIGNOLLES-CLICHY *Market* €

blvd des Batignolles between rue des Batignolles & rue Puteaux, 8e & 17e; 🕙 **9am-2pm Sat;** Ⓜ **Place de Clichy or Rome**

Saturday mornings see this *marché biologique* (organic market) busy with shoppers stocking up for the week.

🍴 RIPAILLE *French* €€

☎ **01 45 22 03 03; 69 rue des Dames, 17e;** 🕙 **lunch Mon-Fri, dinner Mon-Sat;** Ⓜ **Rome**

Forget the fast-food joints around blvd de Clichy and head a few blocks south to owner/chef Philippe Fauré's year-old restaurant, which serves expertly prepared dishes such as St-Jacques scallops and salmon risotto, on funky, brightly coloured china in an arty, tangerine-toned dining room. The wines are well-chosen, the service warm and personal, and the three-course €15 lunch *menu* is an absolute steal.

🍸 DRINK

There's no shortage of great little cafés in this area, and again, the backstreets are your best bet for finding genuine local haunts. For more action, Pigalle and place de Clichy have a plethora of places to drink.

🍸 CAFÉ LE REFUGE *Café*

☎ **01 42 55 27 58; 72 rue Lamarck, 18e;** 🕙 **7.15am-midnight Mon-Sat, 9am-8pm Sun;** Ⓜ **Lamarck Caulaincourt**

This gem of a *café du quartier* (local café) has fantastic interior vintage tiling, a gleaming timber bar and *sympa* (cool) staff. Perfect for a sundowner and oysters on the terrace in season.

DRÔLE D'ENDROIT POUR UNE RENCONTRE *Café*

☎ 01 42 55 14 25; www.droledendroit .com in French; 46 rue Caulaincourt, 18e; ☽ 10am-1.30am Tue-Sat, noon-midnight Sun; Ⓜ Lamarck Caulaincourt

Overlooking a leafy stretch of rue Caulaincourt, this breezy café is onto it: great coffee (plus still-warm croissants from the neighbouring *boulangerie*), free wi-fi, a topnotch menu, and above all, a quirky name (it means 'a funny place to meet someone').

LES DEUX MOULINS *Café*

☎ 01 42 54 90 50; 15 rue Lepic, 18e; ☽ 7am-2am Mon-Sat, 8am-2am Sun; Ⓜ Blanche; ♿

The 'Two Windmills', where Amélie (p208) waitressed, remains, bless it, a down-to-earth local for lingering over the newspapers, chatting with regulars, or just sitting by the windows and watching Montmartre go by. Wi-fi's free, though annoyingly you need to log on again every half hour.

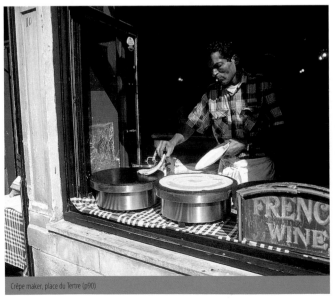

Crêpe maker, place du Tertre (p90)

⭐ PLAY

Paris' main red-light district (albeit a tame one) stretches from Clichy to Pigalle, keeping this quarter lively after dark. Around place de Clichy you'll find multiplex cinemas (often screening films in English), as well as late-night dining spots.

Red-light district, Pigalle

⭐ **ACADÉMIE DE BILLARD**
Pool Hall
☎ 01 48 78 32 85; 84 rue de Clichy, 18e;
pool per hr from €5; ⏰ 11am-6am;
Ⓜ Place de Clichy
Beneath stained-glass ceilings,
this old-fashioned pool hall lit by
antique lamps is staffed by bow
tie–wearing waiters, who deliver
your drinks while you snooker
your opponents. Players must be
over 18; bring photo ID.

⭐ **AU LAPIN AGILE** *Cabaret*
☎ 01 46 06 85 87; www.au-lapin-agile
.com; 22 rue des Saules, 18e; tickets
€24/17, no concession Sat; ⏰ 9pm-2am
Tue-Sun; Ⓜ Lamarck Caulaincourt
Four-hour shows incorporating
chansons and poetry kick off at
9.30pm at this rustic venue that's
scarcely changed since its early-
20th-century heyday. Its name
(the 'agile rabbit') comes from *Le
Lapin à Gill,* a mural of a rabbit
jumping out of a cooking pot
by caricaturist André Gill, which
can still be seen on the western
exterior wall.

⭐ **CHEZ LOUISETTE** *Chansons*
☎ 01 40 12 10 14; Marché aux Puces
de St-Ouen; ⏰ noon-6pm Sat-Mon;
Ⓜ Porte de Clignancourt
This trip of a place, bedecked with
gaudy Christmas decorations
year-round, is a priceless spot
to catch old-time *chanteurs* and

TIP OF THE HAT
For *chanson* venues that don't charge
an entry fee or cover charge, such as restaurants like Chez Louisette (left), performers typically pass around the hat at
the end of a set. You're not obliged to
tip, but it's the way that these artists –
many of them very talented – earn a
crust, and being generous helps keep
this classic Parisian tradition alive. Don't
spend all your money at once, though –
over the course of *chansons,* there are
often several different performers with
a short interval between them, each
with their own hat.

chanteuses (such as the incomparable Manuella, whose rendition
of Piaf's *Milord* tears the roof off),
accompanied by accordion players swaying with gusto. The food
(hearty French) is great and the
wine flows, invariably inspiring
you to dance between the tightly
packed tables.

⭐ **FOLIES-BERGÈRE** *Cabaret*
☎ 01 44 79 98 98; www.foliesbergere
.com in French; 32 rue Richer, 9e;
Ⓜ Cadet
If only the walls could talk. This is
the legendary club where Charlie
Chaplin, WC Fields and Stan Laurel
appeared on stage together one
night in 1911, and where Josephine Baker – accompanied by her
diamond-collared pet cheetah and
wearing only stilettos and a skirt

QUARTERS

MONTMARTRE

made from bananas – bewitched audience members including Hemingway. These days it mounts musicals such as *Cabaret*.

⭐ LA CIGALE *Live Music*
☎ 01 49 25 89 99; www.lacigale.fr; 120 blvd de Rochechouart, 18e; tickets from €25; 🕑 box office noon-7pm Mon-Fri; Ⓜ Anvers or Pigalle
A heritage-listed monument, this 1887 music hall was overhauled by

Philippe Starck a century later and now presents edgy rock and jazz.

⭐ L'ÉLYSÉE-MONTMARTRE *Live Music*
☎ 01 44 92 45 36; www.elyseemont martre.com; 72 blvd de Rochechouart, 18e; tickets from €10; Ⓜ Anvers
In the heart of party-hard Pigalle, this old-style music hall hosts indie artists such as the Hush Puppies, Sabotage, Killswitch and Sorel, as

Moulin Rouge

WORTH THE TRIP

Football reaches fever pitch at the **Stade de France** (☎ 08 92 70 09 00; www.stade france.com; rue Francis de Pressensé, ZAC du Cornillon Nord, 93216 St-Denis la Plaine; tours €10/8; ⏱ tours on the hour in French 10am-5pm year-round, in English 10.30am & 2.30pm Jun-Aug; M St-Denis-Porte de Paris; ♿), located just north of the ring road in St-Denis. Built for the 1998 World Cup, which France hosted and ultimately won in this stadium before 80,000 elated spectators, this immense, futuristic structure also hosts rugby (including 2007 rugby World Cup fixtures) and other sporting events, as well as major concerts.

Guided tours lasting one hour are the only way to see the stadium (bar attending a match or event), but are well worth it, taking you into the dressing rooms, the edges of the pitch, and into the presidential stand.

Upcoming events are posted on the stadium's website. You can also book tickets for events directly on the website, or via booking agency **Ticketnet** (www.ticketnet.fr).

well as putting on club nights and DJs. Doors open at 7.30pm.

⭐ **MOULIN ROUGE** *Cabaret*
☎ 01 53 09 82 82; www.moulinrouge.fr; 82 blvd de Clichy, 18e; M Blanche
The most famous cabaret of all, immortalised in the posters of Toulouse-Lautrec and later on screen by Baz Luhrmann, Moulin Rouge twinkles beneath a 1925 replica of its original red windmill. It's rife with bus tour crowds, but from the first bars of opening music to the last high kick, it's a whirl of fantastical costumes, sets and choreography; the experience is best soaked up with champagne.

>BELLEVILLE & SURROUNDS

In a few years' time, today's Belleville may well be remembered with the same sentimentality as is given to Montmartre's heyday. This is the long-impoverished district where songstress Édith Piaf was born in the gutter, so legend claims, in 1915. Later Belleville became home to thousands of immigrants, particularly from Northern Africa and China. Like Montmartre, Belleville sits on a hill (its name derives from *belle vue* – beautiful view), and an influx of artists established ateliers and collectives here and in neighbouring Ménilmontant. And like Montmartre before it, Belleville is edging towards becoming *branché* (trendy), with rising rents threatening to drive artists out. For now, its eclectic streets and diverse ethnic mix offer an authentic, off-the-tourist-track experience.

To the west of Belleville is Canal St-Martin, crisscrossed with iron footbridges and lined with *bobo*-chic cafés and boutiques. East, you'll find Cimetière du Père Lachaise, a maze of cobbled lanes where the residents include Belleville's Édith Piaf.

BELLEVILLE & SURROUNDS

◎ SEE
Cimetière du Père
Lachaise **1** F5
Cité des Sciences
et de l'Industrie **2** E1
Maison de l'Air **3** E4
Musée Édith Piaf **4** E5
Parc de Belleville **5** E4
Parc de la Villette **6** F1

◻ SHOP
Marché aux Puces de
Montreuil **7** H6
Tati **8** C4

⊞ EAT
Au Village **9** D5
Bistro Indien **10** B4
Le Chansonnier **11** C3
Le Krung Thep **12** E4
Le Villaret **13** D5
Marché
Belleville **14** E4
Marché
St-Quentin **15** C3

▼ DRINK
Café Charbon **16** E5
Café Chéri(e) **17** D4

Chez Prune **18** C4
L'Atmosphère **19** C3
L'Autre Café **20** D4

★ PLAY
La Java **21** D4
Le Nouveau Casino **22** E5
Le Vieux Belleville **23** E4
New Morning **24** C4

Please see over for map

👁 SEE

👁 ÇA SE VISITE! BELLEVILLE WALKING TOURS

☎ 01 48 06 27 41; www.ca-se-visite.fr; walks €12/9

This local initiative arranges two- to 2½-hour 'urban discovery tours' (some in English) through the fascinating Belleville quarter. Residents lead small groups (up to 15 people) through their streets, introducing you to artists and craftspeople and teaching you about the area's history. Tour schedules are posted on the website. Tours in other disadvantaged parts of Paris are in the works.

👁 CIMETIÈRE DU PÈRE LACHAISE

☎ 01 55 25 82 10; Blvd de Ménilmontant; admission free, maps (sold at nearby kiosks) €5; 🕑 8am-6pm Mon-Fri, 8.30am-6pm Sat, 9am-6pm Sun mid-Mar–early Nov, 8am-5.30pm Mon-Fri, 8.30am-5.30pm Sat, 9am-5.30pm Sun early Nov–mid-Mar; Ⓜ Philippe Auguste, Gambetta or Père Lachaise; ♿

In addition to the famous names buried here and their tombs' time-honoured traditions (see p20), one particularly haunting set of graves in the world's most visited cemetery is that of the last Communard insurgents. Cornered by government forces, survivors were lined up against the Mur des Fédérés (Federalists' Wall) and systematically shot, then buried where they fell.

CANAL ST-MARTIN

Bordered by shaded towpaths, this postcard-perfect canal (C4) is the centre of *bobo* (bohemian bourgeois) life in Paris, with quirky shops and cafés buzzing on its newly gentrified banks. Road-bridges straddling the canal pivot 90 degrees when barges pass through the canal's nine locks. The canal is especially pleasant for a Sunday stroll, when the surrounding streets are closed to traffic.

The canal is easily reached from metro stations République, Jaurès, Jacques Bonsergent and Gare de l'Est.

👁 CITÉ DES SCIENCES ET DE L'INDUSTRIE

☎ 01 40 05 80 00; www.cite-sciences .fr; 30 av Corentin Cariou; admission free-€12; 🕑 10am-6pm Tue-Sat, to 7pm Sun; Ⓜ Porte de la Villette; ♿

High-tech exhibits abound at the enormous City of Science and Industry, situated in the Parc de la Villette (p107). Some attractions are free, while others, such as the iconic silver sphere Géode, screening 180-degree films, and the Cité des Enfants ('Children's City'; lots of robots) incur fees. Orient yourself with a free *Keys to the Cité* map from the main entrance.

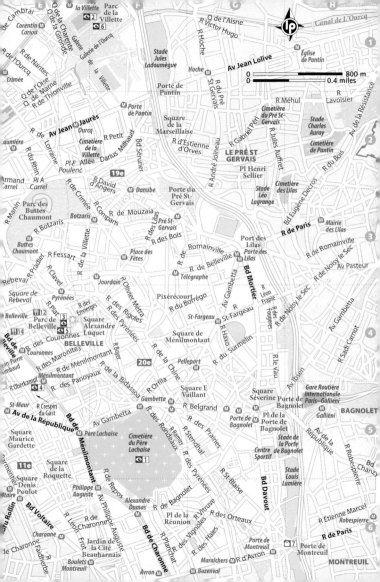

Oscar Wilde's grave, Cimetière du Père Lachaise (p103)

◉ MAISON DE L'AIR
☎ 01 43 28 47 63; admission €2;
🕑 1.30-5.30pm Mon-Fri, to 6.30pm Sun
Mar-Oct, 1.30-5pm Mon-Fri, to 5.30pm
Sun Nov-Feb; Ⓜ Pyrénées

The concrete-bound 'Museum of
Air', located in Parc de Belleville
(below), has environmental
exhibits.

◉ MUSÉE ÉDITH PIAF
☎ 01 43 55 52 72; 5 rue Crespin du Gast,
11e; 🕑 by appt btwn 1-6pm Mon-Wed,
10am-noon Thu; Ⓜ Ménilmontant

You need to reserve ahead but it's
worth it to visit this small museum
cluttered with memorabilia,
recordings and video footage
of legendary Parisian chanteuse
Édith 'Non, je ne regrette rien' Piaf.
Born Édith Gassion, the diminutive
(142cm) singer was nicknamed
la Môme Piaf (the Little Sparrow)
by nightclub-owner Louis Leplée,
who launched her immortal
career.

◉ PARC DE BELLEVILLE
admission free; 🕑 sunrise to sunset;
Ⓜ Couronnes

One of the best panoramas
of Paris unfolds alongside the
teensy vineyard at the top of this
little-known park. Terraced down
the slopes over 4.5 hectares,
early mornings see locals from the
nearby Chinese community practising t'ai chi on the upper lawns.

The Maison de l'Air (opposite) is located at the bottom of the park.

PARC DE LA VILLETTE

☎ 01 04 03 75 75; www.villette.com; admission free; ⏰ 6am-1am; Ⓜ Porte de la Villette or Porte de Pantin; ♿

At this 35-hectare pavilion-filled 'park of the future' you can wander between 10 themed gardens/ playgrounds including the Jardin des Îles (Garden of Islands), Jardin des Bambous (Bamboo Gardens), Jardin des Miroirs (Mirror Gardens) and Jardin du Dragon (Dragon

AROUND THE WORLD IN AN AFTERNOON
Take in a host of multicultural Parisian sights in an afternoon's stroll by plotting a course loosely in line with the metro stations of the city's northeast. Start at Château Rouge, meander south to Strasbourg St-Denis, east via République to Belleville, south to Couronnes and zigzag north to Pyrénées.

Garden). Situated at the northern end is the Cité des Sciences et de l'Industrie (p103).

Parc de la Villette

BELLEVILLE & SURROUNDS

THE ARTISTS OF BELLEVILLE

More than 240 of Belleville's artists open their studios each May during the **Portes Ouvertes des Ateliers d'artistes de Belleville** (open doors of the studios of the artists of Belleville).

Neighbouring Ménilmontant runs its own **Portes ouvertes des ateliers de Ménilmontant** each October with 130 artists taking part.

And the artists of the Père Lachaise quarter recently began opening their doors each December.

Dates for all three programs are at www.parisinfo.com.

It's often possible to visit the areas' ateliers outside these events: info about Belleville's artists is available at www.ateliers-artistes-belleville.org (in French), and Ménilmontant's at www.ateliersdemenilmontant.org or www.artotal.com/menil (both in French).

🗂 SHOP

Canal St-Martin (p103) is home to some offbeat designer boutiques.

Many artists in Belleville and its surrounds sell works direct from their ateliers – see above.

🗂 MARCHÉ AUX PUCES DE MONTREUIL *Market*

av du Professeur André Lemière, 20e; ⏰ **8am-6pm Sat-Mon;** Ⓜ **Porte de Montreuil**

This 19th-century flea market has great vintage clothes and designer castoffs, as well as stalls selling antique jewellery, linen and crockery.

🗂 TATI *Department Store*

174 rue du Temple, 3e; ⏰ **10am-7pm Mon-Fri, 9.15am-7pm Sat;** Ⓜ **République**

This is a small branch of the bargain-basement department store (p92).

🍴 EAT

Belleville and its surrounds offer a kaleidoscope of international restaurants, many of them inexpensive, and unlike many other parts of Paris, there's often no need to book ahead. Wander around and you'll find African, Thai, Korean, Japanese, Chinese, Indian and dozens of others, with plenty of traditional French bistros in between. See p198 for a rundown of Paris' mondial communities, many of them at home in this area.

🍴 AU VILLAGE

Senegalese   €€

☎ **01 43 57 18 95; 86 av Parmentier, 11e;** ⏰ **dinner to midnight Mon-Thu, to 2am Fri-Sun;** Ⓜ **Parmentier**

Fried plantain bananas with red sauce is among the delicious dishes at this funky, friendly African restaurant.

⚑ LE CHANSONNIER
French   €€

☎ 01 42 09 40 88; www.lechansonnier
.com in French; 14 rue Eugène-Varlin,
10e; ⏱ lunch Mon-Fri, dinner Mon-Sat;
Ⓜ Château Landon

Behind a claret-coloured façade, Le
Chansonnier's antique zinc bar and
moulded cornices are lined with
autographed photos of the singers
who've performed at *soirées* here.
Classic French bistro fare includes
confit of duck with garlic potatoes
or a traditional *mijoté* pot of rabbit
with green olives, and there's a
good children's menu, too.

Marché Belleville (p110)

PASSAGE BRADY

Unlike some of the ornate arcades, the dilapidated Passage Brady (C4) isn't aesthetically beautiful, but aromatically, it's just as tantalising. Located at 46 rue du Faubourg St-Denis and 33 blvd de Strasbourg, the arcade is crammed wall-to-wall with Indian, Pakistani and Bangladeshi cafés. You can get a fantastic lunch for well under €10, and dinner for only slightly more. Nearby, the slightly more upmarket **Bistro Indien** (☎ 01 53 34 63 08; 42 rue Faubourg St-Denis, 10e; Ⓜ Château d'Eau or Strasbourg St-Denis) has terrific tandoori-oven naan, veggie options galore, and set *menus* to defeat the heartiest *flâneur's* appetite.

For curry fiends, **Indeaparis** (www.indeaparis.com in French) lists every Indian restaurant in Paris.

🍴 LE KRUNG THEP *Thai*   €
☎ 01 43 66 83 74; 93 rue Julien Lacroix, 20e; 🕙 dinner; Ⓜ Pyrénées

This aromatic restaurant cluttered with kitsch décor serves green curries, chicken steamed in banana leaves and vegetarian dishes galore, which are all as good as any you'll find in the Thai dining paradise of Sydney, and very possibly in Le Krung Thep's namesake Bangkok.

🍴 LE VILLARET *French*   €€€
☎ 01 43 57 89 76; 13 rue Ternaux, 11e; 🕙 lunch Mon-Fri, dinner to 11.30pm Mon-Thu, to 1am Fri & Sat; Ⓜ Parmentier or Oberkampf

In-the-know Parisians come from all over the city to this simple but buzzing bistro for its *menus,* which change daily, featuring French classics, such as succulent leg of lamb and crispy roast chicken, accompanied by a strong wine list.

🍴 MARCHÉ BELLEVILLE
Market   €

blvd de Belleville btwn rue Jean-Pierre Timbaud & rue du Faubourg du Temple, 11e & 20e; 🕙 7am-1.30pm Tue & Fri; Ⓜ Belleville or Couronnes

Belleville's diverse community comes together at this vibrant market, which has African, Middle Eastern and Asian stalls piled high with fruit, vegetables, spices, condiments and delicacies. There's also local artists selling their works here.

🍴 MARCHÉ ST-QUENTIN
Market   €

85 blvd de Magenta, 10e; 🕙 8.30am-1pm & 4-7.30pm Tue-Sat, 8.30am-1pm Sun; Ⓜ Gare de l'Est

Since 1866, the corridors beneath the iron-and-glass roof of this covered market have sold a vast array of foodstuffs; these days the offerings are often very gourmet.

▾ DRINK

Rue Oberkampf (E5) is the area's main drag for edgy bars. Cafés line Canal St-Martin (C3), and there are more throughout Belleville proper, many unchanged in decades. Others have had a recent facelift in line with the area's new gritty-chic status, but this is still a world away from the touristy parts of Paris.

▾ CAFÉ CHARBON *Café*

☎ 01 43 57 55 13; 109 rue Oberkampf, 11e; ☽ 9am-2am Sun-Thu, to 4am Fri & Sat; Ⓜ Parmentier

The distressed *belle époque* Café Charbon was the first of rue Oberkampf's hip cafés. It also does a standout Sunday brunch. The performance venue, Le Nouveau Casino, is next door (p113).

▾ CAFÉ CHÉRI(E) *Bar*

☎ 01 42 02 02 05; 44 blvd de la Villette, 19e; ☽ 8am-2am; Ⓜ Belleville

Electro beats, a redlit bar and rum punches make this a happenin' spot to kick the night off, especially in summer out on the terrace.

▾ CHEZ PRUNE *Café*

☎ 01 42 41 30 47; 71 quai de Valmy, 10e; ☽ 8am-2am Mon-Sat, 10am-2am Sun; Ⓜ Jacques Bonsergent or République

The original Parisian *bobo* hang-out, this canalside café has mosaic-tiled wrought-iron tables, views over the bridges, an outdoor terrace and a lively, yet earthy vibe.

▾ L'ATMOSPHERE *Café*

☎ 01 40 38 09 21; 49 rue Lucien-Sampaix, 10e; ☽ 10am-midnight; Ⓜ Château Landon or Jacques Bonsergent

This clattering timber-and-tile café; sitting on the kink of Canal St-Martin's western bank, has an artsy, spirited ambience and stellar wines. Soak both up with *plats du jour* (dishes of the day) for under €15.

▾ L'AUTRE CAFÉ *Café*

☎ 01 40 21 03 07; 62 rue Jean-Pierre Timbaud, 11e; ☽ 8am-1.30am Mon-Fri, 11.30am-1.30am Sat & Sun; Ⓜ Parmentier

Exhibitions by up-and-coming local artists and film screenings are among the events at this art-oriented café, which also serves decent food at artist-budget prices.

COFFEE TALK

un café A single shot of espresso.
un café allonge An espresso lengthened with hot water (usually, but not always, served separately).
un café au lait A coffee with milk (closest thing to a flat white).
un café crème A shot of espresso lengthened with steamed milk (closest thing to a *caffè latte*).
un double A double shot of espresso.
une noisette A shot of espresso with a spot of milk.

Alex Freiman
Jazz Guitarist

Style of jazz? All instrumental; a mixture of standards and original modern jazz compositions. **Favourite composer?** Miles, Duke, Charlie, Branford Marsalis, John Coltrane (and too many others to list here). When you play jazz you're responsible for knowing the history. It's all the same music – there's no break. **Best thing about living in Paris?** It's a very inspiring city, and very beautiful. I like the paradox of the roughness of the city and the delicacy of the architecture. **How did you get your musical break?** I busked a lot and got gigs from that, and got invited to play some festivals, which led to more gigs. (Alex's gigs are listed in free street mag *Lilo*, available at bars and venues.) **Philosophy on jazz?** People try to intellectualise it but there's nothing snobbish about jazz. Jazz is intuitive – that's what makes jazz jazz.

⭐ PLAY

⭐ LA JAVA *Live Music*

☎ 01 42 02 20 52; 105 rue du Faubourg du Temple, 10e; tickets €10-20; ⏱ 11pm-5am Thu-Sat, 2-7pm Sun; Ⓜ Goncourt

Belleville's Édith Piaf got her first break in this dance hall. These days it features world music concerts, and DJs spinning salsa beats.

⭐ LE NOUVEAU CASINO *Live Music*

☎ 01 43 57 57 40; www.nouveau casino.net in French; 109 rue Oberkampf, 11e; admission free-€20; ⏱ vary; Ⓜ Parmentier

Intimate concerts, top DJs. Electro, pop, deep house, and rock all feature at this performance venue annexed to Café Charbon (p111).

⭐ LE VIEUX BELLEVILLE *Chansons*

☎ 01 44 62 92 66; 12 rue des Envierges, 20e; ⏱ performances from 8.30pm Tue & Sat; Ⓜ Pyrénées

Perched at the top of the Parc de Belleville, this old-fashioned bistro is an atmospheric and not even slightly touristy venue for twice-weekly *chansons* performances featuring accordions and an organ grinder. It's a lively favourite with locals, though, so booking ahead is advised. 'The old Belleville' also serves classic French *menus* (it is open for lunch Monday to Saturday and dinner Tuesday to Saturday).

⭐ NEW MORNING *Jazz*

☎ 01 45 23 51 41; www.newmorning .com; 7-9 rue des Petites Écuries, 10e; tickets €15-25; ⏱ 8pm-2am most days, box office 4.30-7.30pm Mon-Fri; Ⓜ Château d'Eau

The excellent acoustics at this former printing press makes New Morning a superb place to catch the headlining jazz acts, as well as a diverse range of music including blues, rock, funk, salsa, Brazilian and Afro-Cuban styles.

>MARAIS & BASTILLE

Funky bars, sophisticated clothing and homewares boutiques, glam restaurants, and the city's thriving gay and Jewish communities all squeeze cheek-by-jowl into this vibrant patch.

Paris' *marais* (marsh) was cleared in the 12th century, and from the 16th century onwards grand mansions were built here for the aristocracy. Haussmann's reformations largely bypassed the area, leaving an atmospheric jumble of laneways intact to this day. After falling from grace, the Marais underwent a renaissance in the 1960s that hasn't stopped since, and is now a see-and-be-seen spot for a *soirée* (evening out) on the town.

MARAIS & BASTILLE

🜨 SEE
Guimard Synagogue	**1**	D3
Hôtel de Sully	**2**	D4
Hôtel de Ville	**3**	B3
Jeu de Paume – Site Sully	(see **2**)	
Maison de Victor Hugo	**4**	E4
Maison Européenne de la Photographie	**5**	C3
Musée Carnavalet	**6**	D3
Musée Cognacq-Jay	**7**	D3
Musée d'Art et d'Histoire du Judaïsme	**8**	C2
Musée des Arts et Métiers	**9**	C1
Musée Picasso	**10**	D2
Place de la Bastille	**11**	E4
Promenade Plantée	**12**	F5

🛍 SHOP
Antoine et Lili	**13**	C3
Azzedine Alaïa	**14**	C3
Bazar de l'Hôtel de Ville (BHV)	**15**	C3
Boutique Paris-Musées	**16**	D3
Le Mots à la Bouche	**17**	C3
Les Belles Images	**18**	D1
Marché aux Puces d'Aligre	**19**	F5
Red Wheelbarrow Bookstore	**20**	D4
Shine	**21**	D2
Un Chien dans le Marais	**22**	C3
Viaduc des Arts	**23**	F5

🍴 EAT
Bazar de l'Hôtel de Ville (BHV) Cafétéria	(see **15**)	
Brasserie Bofinger	**24**	E4
Chez Marianne	**25**	C3
Crêperie Bretonne	**26**	G4
Grand Apétit	**27**	E4
La Boutique Jeune	**28**	C3
L'As de Felafel	**29**	C3
Le Clown Bar	**30**	E1
Le Coude Fou	**31**	C3
Le Loir dans la Theiere	**32**	D3
Le Petit Bofinger	**33**	E4
Le Train Bleu	**34**	F6
Marché aux Enfants Rouges	**35**	D1
Marché Bastille	**36**	E4
Marché Beauvau	(see **19**)	
Pozzetto	**37**	C3

🍸 DRINK
3W Kafé	**38**	C3
Andy Wahloo	**39**	C1
Café Baroc	**40**	C3
Café des Phares	**41**	E4
Curieux Spaghetti Bar	**42**	B2
Le Progrès	**43**	D2
Le Pure Café	**44**	G4
Le Quetzal	**45**	C3
Le Viaduc Café	(see **23**)	
Mariage Frères	**46**	C3
Open Café	**47**	C3

⭐ PLAY
Barrio Latino	**48**	F4
Bistrot Latin	**49**	C3
China Club	**50**	F5
Le Balajo	**51**	E4
Le Bastille	**52**	E4
Opéra Bastille	**53**	E4

Please see over for map

Nearby is the Bastille, which was a flashpoint for the French Revolution and is still the focal point of Paris' not-infrequent political protests. A long-time grassroots district, recently the Bastille has boomed alongside the neighbouring Marais as a pumping party hub.

Above the Bastille, the raised Promenade Plantée walkway provides a peaceful retreat from the urban action.

◉ SEE

◉ HÔTEL DE SULLY

☎ 01 47 03 12 52; www.jeudepaume
.org; 62 rue St-Antoine, 4e; admission
incl Jeu de Paume – Site Concorde €8/4;
☾ noon-7pm Tue-Fri, 10am-7pm Sat &
Sun; Ⓜ St-Paul; ♿

Housed in a 17th-century mansion, the Jeu de Palme – Site

Sully is an annexe of the national photography centre (p76), and focuses on monograph and thematic photography exhibitions. In the same building, framed by two Renaissance courtyards, is the headquarters of the Monuments Nationaux (www.monum
.fr), which has reams of info about France's national monuments.

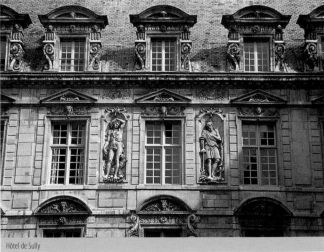

Hôtel de Sully

 HÔTEL DE VILLE

☎ 01 42 76 50 49; www.paris.fr; place de l'Hôtel de Ville, 4e; exhibitions free; ⏱ 10am-7pm Mon-Sat; Ⓜ Hôtel de Ville; ♿

Paris' beautiful neo-Renaissance town hall, completed in 1882, is adorned with 108 statues of illustrious Parisians. Regular temporary exhibitions are held here, usually with a Paris theme, such as the photography of Robert Doisneau (who snapped his world-famous black-and-white *Kiss at the Hôtel de Ville* here in 1950). A winter ice-skating rink sets up outside – see p28.

MAISON DE VICTOR HUGO

☎ 01 42 72 10 16; 6 place des Vosges; permanent collection free, temporary exhibitions €7.50/5; ⏱ 10am-6pm Tue-Sun; Ⓜ St-Paul or Bastille

Hôtel de Ville

One of the symmetrical houses on the place des Vosges (p125), the former home of Victor Hugo is where he wrote much of *Les Misérables*. The museum offers an evocative insight to the writer's life, featuring drawings, portraits, and furnishings preserved just as they were when he resided here.

MAISON EUROPÉENNE DE LA PHOTOGRAPHIE

☎ 01 44 78 75 00; www.mep-fr.org; 5-7 rue de Fourcy, 4e; admission €6/3, free 5-8pm Wed; 11am-8pm Wed-Sun; M St-Paul or Pont Marie;

Exhibition prints, the printed page and films from the 1950s on feature in this light-filled photography museum housed in an early-18th-century Marais mansion. Documentaries and short films screen most weekend afternoons, while regular temporary exhibitions spotlight major French and international photographers.

MUSÉE CARNAVALET

☎ 01 44 59 58 58; www.v1.paris.fr/musees/musee_carnavalet in French; 23 rue de Sévigné, 3e; admission €7/3.50; 10am-6pm Tue-Sun; M St-Paul or Chemin Vert

Housed in two sumptuous private mansions dating from the 16th and 17th centuries, Paris' history museum weaves together the story of the city from the Gallo-Roman period through the heady days of the French Revolution to its Art Nouveau epoch. Among the 140 rooms, don't miss Marcel Proust's corklined bedroom, which was transplanted from his former home on blvd Haussmann.

PLETZL

The area around the Marais' rue des Rosiers and rue des Écouffes was traditionally known as the Pletzl (C3), and was home to a poor but vibrant Jewish community. The 1960s ushered in stylish boutiques, which now sit side-by-side with Jewish bookshops, *cacher* (kosher) pizza joints, butchers, delis, and takeaway-felafel windows.

The Art Nouveau **Guimard synagogue** (10 rue Pavée, 4e) was designed in 1913 by Hector Guimard, who also originated the city's famous metro entrances. The interior is closed to the public.

MUSÉE COGNACQ-JAY

☎ 01 40 27 07 21; www.paris.fr/musees/cognacq_jay in French; 8 rue Elzévir, 3e; admission free; 10am-6pm Tue-Sun; M St-Paul or Chemin Vert

The oil paintings, pastels, sculpture, *objets d'art*, jewellery, porcelain and 18th-century furniture amassed by the founder of La Samaritaine department store are a great excuse to peek inside this museum, housed in the beautiful Hôtel de Donon.

V

QUARTERS

MARAIS & BASTILLE

Place de la Bastille

◉ MUSÉE D'ART ET D'HISTOIRE DU JUDAÏSME

☎ 01 53 01 86 60; www.mahj.org; 71 rue du Temple, 3e; admission €6.80/4.50; ⏱ 11am-6pm Mon-Fri, 10am-6pm Sun; Ⓜ Rambuteau; ♿

Documents from the Dreyfus Affair, famously championed by Parisian novelist Emile Zola in his open letter to the government, *J'accuse…!* (*I Accuse…!;* 1898), are the highlights of this comprehensive Jewish Art and History museum tracing Jewish communities throughout Europe from the Middle Ages to today. The 17th-century mansion is also an impressive showcase for works by Chagall and Modigliani.

◉ MUSÉE DES ARTS ET MÉTIERS

☎ 01 53 01 82 00; www.arts-et-metiers .net in French; 60 rue Réaumur, 3e; admission €6.50/4.50; ⏱ 10am-6pm Tue, Wed & Fri-Sun, to 9.30pm Thu; Ⓜ Arts et Métiers; ♿

Foucault's original pendulum, which he used in 1855 to prove the world turns on its axis, is among the 80,000 instruments, machines and working models displayed at Europe's oldest science and technology museum. The metro station of the same name is one of Paris' most artistic, with gleaming copper panelling and crafts.

◉ MUSÉE PICASSO
☎ 01 42 71 25 21; www.musee-picasso .fr; 5 rue de Thorigny, 3e; admission €6.50/5.20; ⏲ 9.30am-6pm Wed-Mon Apr-Sep, to 5.30pm Wed-Mon Oct-Mar; Ⓜ St-Paul or Chemin Vert; ♿
Small enough to feel intimate yet large enough to trace the artist's life through his evolving body of work (some 3500 pieces), this 17th-century mansion is a must during any visit to Paris. Also on display is Picasso's prized personal art collection, including works by Braque, Cézanne, Matisse and Degas.

◉ PLACE DE LA BASTILLE
Ⓜ Bastille
Nothing remains of the former prison that was mobbed on 14

July 1789, igniting the French Revolution, but you can't miss the 52m green-bronze column topped by a gilded, winged Liberty. Revolutionaries from the uprising of 1830 are buried beneath. Now a skirmishly busy roundabout, the *place* is still Paris' most symbolic destination for traffic-stopping political protest marches.

◉ PROMENADE PLANTÉE
www.promenade-plantee.org in French; 12e; admission free; ⏲ 8am-5.30pm to 9.30pm Mon-Fri, 9am-5.30pm to 9.30pm Sat & Sun; ♿
This pioneering park, with its walking path, flowers and park benches extending above the rooflines, has led to the construction of similar projects in the US and UK. It was a romantic backdrop for one of the central scenes in the film *Before Sunset* (see the boxed text, p132), and a highlight of any visit to Paris – see p15. And it's free.

UNE NUIT EN MÉTRO (A NIGHT IN THE METRO)
The ghosts of Paris' metro come out during this all-night tour by vintage train. Embarking from a ramshackle railyard (you're given directions when you secure tickets), these underground tours travel to phantom stations including those that closed during WWII and never reopened, and others that were built but never actually opened at all. An organist plays during atmosphere-charged stops where passengers can waltz on the deserted platforms or investigate the empty passages. There's an onboard bar, and croissants and champagne are served at dawn. Tickets (around €50) are like hens' teeth – contact **ADEMAS** (☎ 01 48 25 13 32; http://ademas.assoc.free.fr in French; ademas@orange.fr).

WORTH THE TRIP

Blanketing 995 hectares of Paris' southeast, the **Bois de Vincennes** (pull-out map, S12; blvd Poniatowski, 12e; Ⓜ Porte de Charenton or Porte Dorée; ♿) is best known and loved for its giant annual funfair, the Foire du Trône (p25).

During the rest of the year, these sprawling woods merit a visit for the romantic royal palace, the **Château de Vincennes** (☎ 01 48 08 31 20; www.monum.fr; av de Paris, 12e; grounds free, palace by guided tour only from €5/3.50; ☉ gardens 10am-noon & 1.15-6pm May-Aug, 10am-noon & 1.15-5pm Sep-Apr, call for guided tour departure times; Ⓜ Château de Vincennes), complete with dungeons (closed to visitors at the time of writing, but expected to reopen). Adjacent to the chateau is the flower-filled **Parc Floral de Paris** (☎ 08 20 00 75 75; www.parcfloraldeparis.com in French; esplanade du Château de Vincennes, 12e; admission €3/1.50; ☉ 9.30am-5pm to 8pm; Ⓜ Château de Vincennes), with its delightful Jardin des Papillons (Butterfly Garden).

If you go down to the woods, you'll also be in for a surprise in the form of the very non-European **Aquarium Tropical** (☎ 01 44 74 84 80; www.musee-afriqueoceanie.fr in French; Palais de la Porte Dorée, 293 av Daumesnil, 12e; €5.50/4; ☉ 10am-5.15pm Wed-Mon; Ⓜ Porte Dorée). A legacy of France's colonial past, the aquarium is housed in a 1931 pavilion from the Exposition Coloniale. Today it's a teaching facility as well as a place where visitors can see multicoloured fish and marine life.

Along with sea creatures, around 600 animals call the woods home over at **Paris Zoo** (Parc Zoologique de Paris; ☎ 01 44 75 20 10; www.mnhn.fr; 53 av de St-Maurice, 12e; admission €5; ☉ 9am-6pm Mon-Sat, to 6.30pm Sun Apr-Sep, to 5pm Mon-Sat, to 5.30pm Sun Oct-Mar; Ⓜ Porte Dorée).

🛍 SHOP

The Marais' miniature streets are like a jewellery box, spilling over with brightly coloured shops filled with lots of quirky, one-off items. And unlike St-Germain des Prés and the Champs-Élysées area, with their concentration of luxury labels, shopping in the Marais is (generally) not only an enjoyable experience but an affordable one as well.

🛍 **ANTOINE ET LILI**
Fashion & Homewares
☎ **01 42 72 26 60; www.antoineetlili .com; 51 rue des Francs Bourgeois, 3e;** ☉ **10.30am-7.15pm Tue-Sat, 2-7pm Sun & Mon;** Ⓜ **St-Paul**
Flower-children of the new millennium flock to this urban-grunge-meets-tribal boutique. Along with offbeat clothing by Antoine and Lili's designers, you can pick up earthy homewares such as votive candles from Nepal. There's a

handful of smaller branches in Paris and throughout France.

🏠 AZZEDINE ALAÏA *Fashion*
☎ 01 42 72 19 19; 7 rue Moussy, 4e; ⏰ 10am-7pm Mon-Sat; Ⓜ St-Paul

If you can't get enough of the slimline designs at Tunisian-born Azzedine Alaïa's clothing store, you can bed down next door at his very select three-room hotel, called, simply, **3 Rooms** (☎ 01 44 78 92 00). Actually, there are more than three rooms per se: two apartments have

separate double bedrooms, and the third has two double bedrooms.

🏠 BAZAR DE L'HÔTEL DE VILLE (BHV) *Department Store*
☎ 01 42 74 90 00; www.bhv.fr in French; 14 rue du Temple, 4e; ⏰ 9.30am-7.30pm Mon, Tue, Thu & Fri, to 9pm Wed, to 8pm Sat; Ⓜ Hôtel de Ville

The basement hardware section of this otherwise-straightforward department store is where Parisians come when renovating their ancient apartments; which has every

Place des Vosges (p125)

hammer, nail and drill bit imaginable cramming the chaotic shelves. There's also a *caféteria* (p126).

 BOUTIQUE PARIS-MUSÉES
Arts & Crafts

☎ 01 42 74 13 92; 29bis rue des Francs Bourgeois, 4e; ⊙ 2-7pm Mon, 11am-1pm & 2-7pm Tue-Sun; Ⓜ Chemin Vert or St-Paul

Innovative works by young, up-and-coming Parisian artists share shelf space with quality reproductions of paintings and sculptures on display at Paris' museums.

LE MOTS À LA BOUCHE
Books

☎ 01 42 78 88 30; www.motsbouche .com in French; 6 rue Ste-Croix de la Bretonnerie, 4e; ⊙ 11am-11pm Mon-Sat, 2-8pm Sun; Ⓜ Hôtel de Ville

'On the Tip of the Tongue' is Paris' premier gay and lesbian bookshop, with stacks of info about gay Parisian life. On the ground floor you'll find English-language books, including travel guides; things steam up when you go down (stairs).

LES BELLES IMAGES
Fashion

☎ 01 42 76 93 61; www.lesbellesim ages.com; 74 rue Charlot, 3e; ⊙ 11am-7.30pm Tue-Sat; Ⓜ Filles du Calvaire

The kind of place that would be at home on London's Carnaby St c 1970, this retro boutique stocks Vivienne Westwood originals among other wild-child designers as well as a range of ab-fab homewares.

MARCHÉ AUX PUCES D'ALIGRE *Market*

place d'Aligre, 12e; ⊙ 7am-1.30pm Tue-Sun; Ⓜ Ledru Rollin

Rummage through boxes and racks jammed with vintage fashions at Paris' most central

Viaduc des Arts

PLACE DES VOSGES

The stone cloisters of this 1612-built ensemble of mansions (D3) resonate with busking violinists and cellists, who provide an atmospheric soundtrack for sipping tea in one of several elegant cafés or browsing the arcaded galleries and antique shops. Victor Hugo's former residence-turned-museum (p118) is at No 6, while today's most famous resident is Japanese designer Issey Miyake, whose Paris' headquarters are at No 3.

In the centre you'll see *au pairs* playing with their charges in the little gated park.

flea market. Food market Marché Beauvau (p129) is next door.

🖽 RED WHEELBARROW BOOKSTORE *Books*

☎ 01 48 04 75 08; www.theredwheel barrow.com; 22 rue St-Paul, 4e; ☽ 10am-7pm Mon-Sat, 2-6pm Sun; Ⓜ St-Paul
Brimming with quality English-language literature, this terrific little Canadian-run bookshop has a dedicated clientele and lots of info on literary events in Paris.

🖽 SHINE *Fashion*

☎ 01 48 05 80 10; 5 rue de Poitou, 3e; ☽ 11am-7.30pm Mon-Sat; Ⓜ Filles du Calvaire
Get glammed up at this trendsetting boutique stocking hand-picked pieces from the current crop of designer darlings such as Stella McCartney's creations for Chloé.

🖽 UN CHIEN DANS LE MARAIS *Fashion*

☎ 01 42 74 30 06; www.unchiendansle marais.com; 35bis rue du Roi de Sicile, 4e; ☽ 11am-7pm; Ⓜ St-Paul

For the dog that has everything. This little boutique stocks nothing but dog outfits in all sizes. Pick out a design perfectly suited to your pooch from the latest winter and summer 'collections' while owner Franck Woerther's pet rabbits, Thelma and Louise, lope underfoot (Thelma was actually belatedly discovered to be a boy, but hey, this is the Marais, baby).

🖽 VIADUC DES ARTS *Arts & Crafts*

www.viaduc-des-arts.com; av Daumesnil, 12e; ☽ vary; Ⓜ Bastille or Gare de Lyon
Beneath the Promenade Plantée, in the brick arches of its 19th-century viaduct, traditional craftsmen and women carry out renovations and repairs of all manner of antiques, and create new items using traditional methods. The 50 artisans include furniture and tapestry restorers, interior designers, cabinet makers, violin- and flute-makers, embroiderers and jewellers.

> **MARAIS ONLINE**
> A handy resource for discovering the Marais is the website **Marais Evous** (http://marais.evous.fr), which details the most interesting streets and includes aerial photographs.

🍴 EAT

🍴 BAZAR DE L'HÔTEL DE VILLE (BHV) CAFÉTERIA
Caféteria €

14 rue du Temple, 4e; 🕒 **11.15am-6.30pm Mon, Tue & Thu-Sat; 11.15am-8.30pm Wed;** Ⓜ **Hôtel de Ville**

This *caféteria*, on the 5th floor of the department store (p123), is a kid-friendly (and wallet-friendly) choice, offering a carvery and desserts such as parfaits. There's eye-level views of the statues adorning the Hôtel de Ville's roofline.

🍴 BRASSERIE BOFINGER
Brasserie €€€

☎ **01 42 72 87 82; www.bofingerparis .com; 5-7 rue de la Bastille, 4e;** 🕒 **lunch & dinner;** Ⓜ **Bastille**

To experience brasserie dining in all its Art Nouveau splendour, there's no better place in town than here. The historic Bofinger's food is first-rate, its service genuine, and a seat under its glass cupola sublime. Past diners span from Mikhail Gorbachev to Madonna, but it's the little snippets

of Parisian life you see around you as you dine that make the experience unforgettable.

🍴 CHEZ MARIANNE *Kosher* €

☎ **01 42 72 18 86; 2 rue des Hospitalières St-Gervais, 4e;** 🕒 **noon-midnight;** Ⓜ **St-Paul**

There's often a wait for a table at Chez Marianne's black-and-white-tiled restaurant space, but the phenomenal mix-and-match platters, with choices including olives, hummus, eggplant and much more, are worth every minute. Otherwise you can pack a picnic from the deli to take to the place des Vosges, or pick up felafel sandwiches from the takeaway window.

🍴 CRÊPERIE BRETONNE
Breton & Crêperie €

☎ **01 43 55 62 29; 67 rue de Charonne, 12e;** 🕒 **lunch Mon-Fri, dinner Mon-Sat;** Ⓜ **Charonne**

Authentic down to its buckwheat *galettes* and perfectly buttered sweet crêpes (with salted butter, of course), this place is filled with emotive photos of Brittany, and, joy of joys, serves brut Val de Rance cider. *Yec'hed mat* (cheers)!

🍴 GRAND APÉTIT
Vegetarian €

☎ **01 40 27 04 95; 9 rue de la Cerisaie, 4e;** 🕒 **lunch Mon-Fri, dinner Mon-Wed;** Ⓜ **Bastille or Sully Morland;** Ⓥ

Just when you were thinking there were no vegan eateries in Paris, along comes this excellent place, which has a blackboard crammed with filling dishes made with organic cereals, raw and cooked vegetables and seaweed. There's a macrobiotic shop next door (open 9.30am to 7.30pm Monday to Thursday, to 4pm Friday).

🍴 LA BOUTIQUE JEUNE
Kosher €

☎ 01 42 72 78 91; www.laboutique jaune.com in French; 27 rue des Rosiers, 4e; 🕐 11am-7pm Mon, 10am-7pm Wed & Thu, to 7.30pm Fri-Sun; Ⓜ St-Paul

Since 1946 this bright yellow–fronted Yiddish *traiteur* has been purveying fantastic cakes, breads, *charcuterie,* and its famous 'Yiddish sandwich', filled with the flavours of Eastern Europe and served hot. There's a tiny sit-down area.

🍴 L'AS DE FELAFEL *Kosher* €
☎ 01 48 87 63 60; 34 rue des Rosiers, 4e; 🕐 noon-midnight Sun-Thu, to 5pm Fri; Ⓜ St-Paul

The famous fried chickpea balls here are flawlessly textured, but the platters are too heavy on the lettuce and too light on everything

Jewish food shops, the Pletzl (p119)

else, and beer, plonked down unopened in the can, is outrageously overpriced. Go for the felafel sandwiches and you can't go wrong, but to savour a sit-down meal, go down the road to Chez Marianne (p126).

⑪ LE CLOWN BAR
French €€

☎ 01 43 55 87 35; 114 rue Amelot, 11e; 🕐 lunch & dinner to midnight Mon-Sat; Ⓜ Filles du Calvaire

If you've ever harboured fantasies of running away with the circus, this wine bar and bistro's frescoes and mosaics of clowns and circus

Potato au gratin, Marché Bastille

memorabilia will make you feel like you already have. (The evil-themed clowns will scare the pants off kids and coulrophobes, though.) Traditional *menus* are good value, but desserts err on the pricey side.

⑪ LE COUDE FOU *French* €€

☎ 01 42 77 15 16; www.lecoudefou .com; 12 rue du Bourg-Tibourg, 4e; 🕐 lunch & dinner, bar until 2am; Ⓜ Hôtel de Ville

The bar of this cosy tiled and muraled bistro is always buzzing with local customers, who come for the specialist wines as well as hearty classic fare. It's at its most animated during its convivial Sunday brunch, which is more like a traditional French lunch.

⑪ LE PETIT BOFINGER
French €€

☎ 01 42 72 05 23; 6 rue de la Bastille, 4e; 🕐 lunch & dinner; Ⓜ Bastille

Considering its grandeur, the prices at Brasserie Bofinger (p126) are extremely reasonable. If you're on a budget, though, its splendidly tiled little brother across the street, Le Petit Bofinger, is an affordable but still atmospheric alternative, serving fresh market fare.

⑪ LE TRAIN BLEU *French* €€€

☎ 01 53 80 24 00; www.le-train-bleu .com; 26 pl Louis Armand, Gare de Lyon, 12e; 🕐 lunch & dinner; Ⓜ Gare de Lyon

BRUNCHING IN PARIS
Sunday lunch is traditionally France's main meal of the week, but numerous bars and cafés now offer brunch, often starting at noon and usually stretching out to around 4pm, and costing roughly €15 to €25.

Our favourite spot to spend a languorous Sunday is at **Le Loir dans la Theiere** (The Dormouse in the Teapot; ☎ 01 42 72 90 61; 3 rue des Rosiers, 4e; ⏰ 11.30am-7pm Mon-Fri, 10am-7pm Sat & Sun), a wonderful old space filled with retro toys, comfy couches and free wi-fi. Its farm-style wooden tables are laden at brunch, which is served here on both Saturday and Sunday.

This railway station's heritage-listed *belle époque* showpiece gives new meaning to travelling in style. Dine on vanilla-flavoured velvet crab, grilled lobster flambéed in Cognac, caramelised pear sorbet, and a pot of Blue Moon Ceylon tea. There's an excellent children's menu, and a sumptuous bar for a *digestif* before boarding your train to the Côte d'Azur.

🍴 MARCHÉ AUX ENFANTS ROUGES *Market* €
39 rue de Bretagne, 3e; ⏰ 9am-2pm & 4-8pm Tue-Fri, 9am-8pm Sat, to 2pm Sun; Ⓜ Filles du Calvaire
Just south of place de la République, this aromatic covered market brings together foodstuffs from Europe and North Africa.

🍴 MARCHÉ BASTILLE *Market* €
blvd Richard Lenoir, 11e; ⏰ 7am-2pm Tue, to 2.30pm Sun; Ⓜ Bastille or Richard Lenoir

If you only get to one open-air market in Paris, this one – with its traditional French and ethnic food stalls of every description stretching between the Bastille and Richard Lenoir metro stations – is among the very best.

🍴 MARCHÉ BEAUVAU *Market* €
place d'Aligre, 12e; ⏰ 8.30am-1pm & 4-7.30pm Tue-Sat, 8.30am-1.30pm Sun; Ⓜ Ledru Rollin
Adjacent to the place d'Aligre flea market (p124), this covered market sells Arab and North African food specialities such as couscous and sweet pastries.

🍴 POZZETTO *Ice Cream* €
☎ 01 42 77 08 64; 39 rue du Roi de Sicile, 4e; ⏰ noon-11pm Mon-Thu, to 2am Fri-Sun; Ⓜ St-Paul
Paris' best new gelato maker was born in the Marais when a group of friends from Italy's north couldn't find their favourite ice cream in >

Paris, and so imported the ingredients to create it here from scratch. Flavours (spatula'd, not scooped) include *fianduia* (chocolate-to-die-for) and *fiordilatte* (milk). The shop also sells Piedmontese hazelnut biscuits, and the staff pour a mean espresso as well.

DRINK

3W KAFÉ *Gay & Lesbian*
☎ 01 48 87 39 26; www.3w-kafe.com in French; 8 rue des Écouffes, 4e; ☷ 6pm-2am; Ⓜ Hôtel de Ville
Men are welcome but rare at this sleek lesbian lounge in the Marais.

ANDY WAHLOO *Bar*
☎ 01 42 71 20 38; 69 rue des Gravilliers, 3e; ☷ noon-2am; Ⓜ Arts et Métiers
This postmodern place peaks during happy hour (5pm to 8pm), when its candy-flavoured cocktails are half-price. Its name means 'I have nothing' in Arabic, but its eye-popping, tutti-frutti décor and ear-splitting house music owe a greater debt to the bar's almost-namesake, Andy Warhol.

CAFÉ BAROC *Bar*
☎ 01 48 87 61 30; 37 rue du Roi de Sicile, 4e; ☷ 5pm-2am Tue-Sun; Ⓜ St-Paul
Lined with old cinema seats and serving beers with a twist of syrup in flavours such as lemon or peach, Baroc is a chilled little place most of the week. Things

gets hyper on Wednesday and Thursday nights, though, when bar staff crank up fabulously camp '80s tunes. Downstairs there's a shoebox-size basement with vintage sofas.

CAFÉ DES PHARES *Café*
☎ 01 42 72 04 70; 7 place de la Bastille, 4e; ☷ 7am-3am Sun-Thu, to 4am Fri & Sat, philosophy debates 11am-1pm Sun; Ⓜ Bastille
Grappling with concepts such as existentialism is required for Parisians to pass the *baccalauréat* (school certificate) – hence the popularity of *philocafés,* where wide-ranging philosophical discussions take place. This is the original (and arguably best); and even if your French isn't up to following the convoluted conversations, it still offers a fascinating cultural insight.

CURIEUX SPAGHETTI BAR *Bar*
☎ 01 42 72 75 97; 14 rue St-Mérri, 4e; ☷ noon-4am Thu-Sat, to 2am Sun-Wed; Ⓜ Rambuteau
This loungey bar spins decent beats, and also serves spaghetti as part of a hip international menu, as well as test-tube shots of vodka in flavours such as pina colada and bubble gum. Post-clubbers descend for Sunday brunch from noon; it's best to book for this.

Café des Phares

▼ LE PROGRÈS *Café*

☎ 01 42 72 01 44; 1 rue de Bretagne, 3e; ⏱ 8am-10pm Mon-Sat; Ⓜ St-Sébastien Froissart

This sunlit, Art Deco–tiled café is a favourite with Paris' current 'Lost Generation' of expat writers, who come for the cheap bistro fare, strong coffee, and pitchers of wine.

▼ LE PURE CAFÉ *Café*

☎ 01 43 71 47 22; 14 rue Jean Macé, 11e; ⏱ 7am-2am Mon-Fri, 8am-2am Sat, noon-midnight Sun; Ⓜ Charonne or Faidherbe Chaligny

This rustic, cherry-red corner café is a classic Parisian haunt, which found its way onto the big screen

in *Before Sunset* (see the boxed text, p132). The kitchen turns out well-crafted fare (sometimes with a fusion twist), but above all it's an unpretentious place to kick back with a glass of wine.

▼ LE QUETZAL *Gay & Lesbian*

☎ 01 48 87 99 07; 10 rue de la Verrerie, 4e; ⏱ 5pm-3am Mon-Thu, to 5am Fri-Sun; Ⓜ Hôtel de Ville

A 30-something gay male crowd congregates at this house- and dance-spinning bar, which aptly sits opposite rue des Mauvais Garçons ('Bad Boys' Street'; named after the brigands who congregated here in 1540). Happy hour stretches from 5pm to midnight.

V

QUARTERS

MARAIS & BASTILLE

☐ LE VIADUC CAFÉ *Café*
☎ 01 44 74 70 70; 43 av Daumesnil, 12e;
🕐 9am-2am; Ⓜ Gare de Lyon
Live jazz plays from noon to
4pm during Sunday brunch, but
this snazzy place wedged into a
glassed-in arch of the Viaduc des
Arts (p125) is a sophisticated spot
for a drink any time of the day or
night.

☐ MARIAGE FRÈRES
Salon de Thé
☎ 01 42 72 28 11; www.mariagefreres
.com in French; 30 rue du Bourg Tibourg,
4e; 🕐 shop 10.30am-7.30pm, tearooms
noon-7pm; Ⓜ Hôtel de Ville
There are more than 500 varieties
of tea available at this 1854-
founded tea shop (the first established in Paris); the tea is best
enjoyed by sipping a cup in the
genteel tearoom. The company
also operates a couple of other
outlets in Paris.

☐ OPEN CAFÉ *Gay & Lesbian*
☎ 01 42 72 26 18; 17 rue des Archives,
4e; 🕐 11am-2am Sun-Thu, to 4am Fri-
Sat; Ⓜ Hôtel de Ville
This see-and-be-seen Marais institution is raining men, and is a primer
for a night out in gay Paree, but the
vibe is social rather than cruisey.

⭐ PLAY

BARRIO LATINO *Salsa Bar*
☎ 01 55 78 84 75; 46-48 rue du Faubourg
St-Antoine, 11e; 🕐 11am-2am Sun-Thur,
to 3am Fri-Sat; Ⓜ Bastille
You can salsa your socks off in this
vast venue. The crowd is as mixed
as a well-shaken cocktail: gay,
straight, locals and visitors.

☐ BISTROT LATIN *Club*
☎ 01 42 77 21 11; 20 rue du Temple, 4e;
admission from €6; 🕐 7pm-1am Mon,
Wed & Thu, to 2am Fri-Sun; Ⓜ Hotel
de Ville

SUNSET ON SCREEN
Richard Linklater's *Before Sunset* is a contemporary love letter to Paris. Shot in real time using
long takes, this arthouse film reunites New York author Jesse (Ethan Hawke) and Parisian
environmental activist Céline (Julie Delpy) almost a decade after their fateful first meeting.

Before Sunset opens in Shakespeare & Co (p12 and p158), where Jesse launches his novel
about his lost love, and spies her by the shelves.

With a handful of hours before Jesse is due to leave Paris, they stroll first to Le Pure Café
(p131), then along the Promenade Plantée (p15 and p121). Afterwards, Céline scoffs at
a boat ride on the Seine (p17), protesting 'it's for tourists', but as they glide beneath the
bridges she admits 'I forget how beautiful Paris is'. At twilight, en route to the airport, Jesse
escorts Céline to her apartment (near Bastille), as the minutes to his flight tick by...

If you want to perfect your salsa moves or dance your last tango in Paris, dance classes are held here most evenings from 7pm; upstairs is the Latino cinema, Le Latina.

☆ CHINA CLUB *Jazz*
☎ 01 43 43 82 02; http://chinaclub.cc; 50 rue de Charenton; jazz club €12-14 Thu, free Fri & Sat; ⏰ bar 7pm-2am, jazz club 8pm-2am Thu & 10pm-2am Fri & Sat; Ⓜ Ledru Rollin or Bastille
Opulent red-lacquered walls, chesterfield sofas, and a basement jazz club, Sing Song, styled like 1930s Shanghai, have made Paris' China Club a fixture on the international party circuit. From 7pm to 9pm you can swill a Long Island iced tea or stellar martini for €6 at the main bar; and you can tuck into Peking duck and spring rolls until midnight.

☆ LE BALAJO *Club*
☎ 01 47 00 07 87; www.balajo.fr; 9 rue de Lappe, 11e; admission from €10; ⏰ 9pm-2am Tue-Thu, 11pm-5am Fri & Sat, 3-7.30pm Sun; Ⓜ Bastille
A classic Parisian venue since 1936, this place still pulls in the crowds for a diverse range of offerings – from the ubiquitous salsa to rock, DJs and R & B. It

evokes its past during its Sunday *musette* (accordion gig) from 3pm to 7pm, which includes old-time tea dancing.

☆ LE BASTILLE
Club
☎ 01 43 07 79 95; 8 place de la Bastille, 11e; ⏰ 7am-6am; Ⓜ Bastille
With a lively terrace overlooking place de la Bastille and a sleek interior of dark timber, chocolate banquettes and amber lamps, Le Bastille serves lunch and dinner and at night turns into a happening club. It closes for just one hour each morning from 6am to 7am, before reopening to serve gratifyingly strong coffee.

☆ OPÉRA BASTILLE
Opera House
☎ 08 92 89 90 90; www.opera-de-paris .fr in French; 2-6 place de la Bastille, 12e; guided tours €11/9; ⏰ box office 10.30am-6.30pm Mon-Sat, tours 1.15pm Mon-Sat, tickets sold 15mins prior; Ⓜ Bastille
If you don't score tickets to a performance at Paris' 1989-built monolith, which was instigated by Mitterrand as the city's second opera house, you can go behind the scenes on a guided tour.

>THE ISLANDS

Paris' geographic and spiritual heart is situated in the Seine.

The city's watery beginnings took place on the Île de la Cité, the larger of the two inner-city islands. Today, all distances in France are measured from Kilometre Zéro, marked by a bronze star outside Notre Dame. The island is also home to the beautiful Ste-Chapelle; the Conciergerie, where Marie Antoinette was imprisoned; a colourful flower market; and picturesque parks such as place Dauphine and square du Vert Galant.

To the east, tranquil Île St-Louis is graced with elegant mansions that are among the city's most exclusive residential addresses, along with a handful of intimate hotels and exquisite boutiques.

Connecting the two islands, the Pont St-Louis is an impossibly romantic spot to watch the sun set.

THE ISLANDS

◎ SEE
Cathédrale de Notre
Dame **1** E4
Conciergerie **2** C2
Pont Neuf **3** B1
Ste-Chapelle **4** C2

🛍 SHOP
Clair de Rêve **5** G4
La Petite Scierie **6** G4

Librairie Ulysse **7** G4
Marché aux Fleurs **8** D2
O&Co **9** F4

🍴 EAT
Brasserie de l'Île
St-Louis **10** F4
Café le Flore en l'Île **11** F4
Esterina **12** F4
Maison Berthillon **13** G4

🍸 DRINK
La Charlotte en L'île **14** G4
Taverne Henri IV **15** A1

Please see over for map

SEE

CATHÉDRALE DE NOTRE DAME DE PARIS

☎ 01 42 34 56 10; www.cathedralede paris.com; place du Parvic Notre Dame, 4e; cathedral admission free, towers €7.50/4.80, museum €3/2; ⏲ cathedral 8am-6.45pm Mon-Fri, to 7.45pm Sat & Sun, towers 9.30am-7.30pm daily Apr-Jun & Sep, 9am-7.30pm Mon-Fri, to 11pm Sat & Sun Jul & Aug, 10am-5.30pm daily Oct-Mar, museum 2.30-6pm Wed, Sat & Sun; Ⓜ Cité; ♿

On the must-see list of 10 million visitors annually, this 14th-century Gothic wonder took 200 years to build. It was saved from demolition by a petition following the popularity of Victor Hugo's 1831 novel, *The Hunchback of Notre Dame*. Light streams through three rose windows into the cathedral's vast interior; climbing the 387 spiralling steps rewards with views from the towers. There's no wheelchair access to the towers.

Cathédrale de Notre Dame de Paris

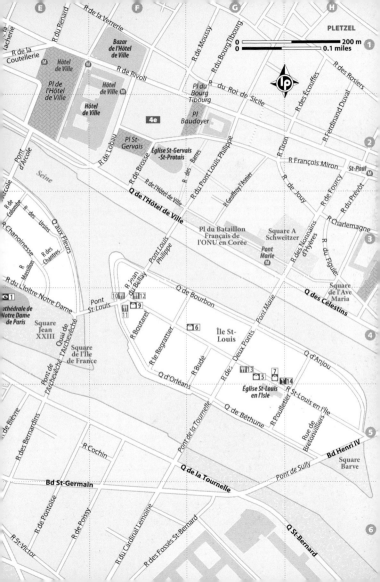

☉ CONCIERGERIE

☎ 01 53 40 60 97; www.monum.fr;
2 blvd du Palais, 1er; admission
€6.50/4.50, combined ticket with
Ste-Chapelle €9.50/7; ⏰ 9.30am-6pm
Mar-Oct, 9am-5pm Nov-Feb; Ⓜ Cité
This cross-vaulted 14th-century
palace was turned into a prison
and torture chamber where 2780
condamnés (condemned) that had
been brought before the Revolutionary Tribunal in the adjoining
Palais de Justice – notably Marie
Antoinette – were incarcerated
before being sent to the guillotine.
It's of most interest to history buffs
and French speakers, as there are
few English interpretations.

☉ PONT NEUF
Ⓜ **Pont Neuf**
Paris' oldest and most famous
bridge (ironically called 'new
bridge') was inaugurated in 1607,
linking the Île de la Cité with the
Seine's left and right banks. The
semicircular benches, recessed into
the bridge's sparkling white stone,

Pont Neuf

are a picturesque spot to stop and watch Paris' riverboats pass by.

☺ STE-CHAPELLE

☎ 01 53 40 60 97; www.monum.fr; 4 blvd du Palais, 1er; admission €6.50/4.50, combined ticket with Conciergerie €9.50/7; ☽ 9.30am-6pm Mar-Oct, 9am-5pm Nov-Feb; Ⓜ Cité; ♿

The stained-glass windows of this beautiful 'Holy Chapel', consecrated in 1248, give it an ethereal feel. Classical concerts by composers such as Vivaldi and Bach often take place here; costing between €16 and €25, these tickets offset much of the entry price – check outside for posters.

🛍 SHOP

The Île de Cité has a fabulous flower market. Little gift shops dot the tiny streets of Île St-Louis.

🛍 CLAIR DE RÊVE Toys

☎ 01 43 29 81 06; www.clairdereve .com; 35 rue St-Louis en l'Île, 4e; ☽ 11am-1pm & 1.45-7.45pm Mon-Sat; Ⓜ Pont Marie

Stringed marionettes bob from the ceiling of this endearing little shop. Papier-mâché and leather marionettes start at €100 for a petite puppet, going up to €630 for one made of porcelain. The shop also sells wind-up toys. See the boxed text, p153, for info on marionette shows in Paris.

BOUQUINISTES

Lining both banks of the Seine through the centre of Paris, the open-air *bouquiniste* stalls selling secondhand, and often out-of-print, books, rare magazines, postcards and old advertising posters are a definitive Parisian sight. The name comes from *bouquiner,* meaning 'to read with appreciation', which sums up the French love of literature. The *bouquinistes'* green metal stalls are folded down like suitcases and locked at night. Many open only from spring to autumn, but even in the depths of winter, you'll still find somewhere to barter for antiquarian treasures.

🍴 LA PETITE SCIERIE
Food & Drink

☎ 01 55 42 14 88; la.petite.scierie@ wanadoo.fr; 60 rue St-Louis en l'Île, 4e; ☽ 11am-8pm; Ⓜ Pont Marie

Strewn with feathery real-life (or rather formerly real-life) stuffed ducks, this tiny shop specialises in foie gras. Purchases (from €32.30 for 180g) include a gratis bottle of Coteaux du Layon wine, which you can also taste in-store along with foie gras on chunks of baguette.

🛍 LIBRAIRIE ULYSSE *Books*

☎ 01 43 25 17 35; www.ulysse.fr in French; 26 rue St-Louis en l'Île, 4e; ☽ 2-8pm Tue-Fri; Ⓜ Pont Marie

You can barely move in this jam-packed shop piled high with

AN ISLAND & ITS ICE CREAM

Just as champagne is synonymous with the Champagne region where it's produced, Berthillon ice cream is synonymous with the Île St-Louis.

The esteemed Berthillon *glacier* (ice-cream maker) was founded here in 1954, and is still run by the same family today. Among the 70 flavours, made with natural ingredients and no chemicals, are fruit sorbets such as pink grapefruit, rhubarb and fig, and much richer ice creams, made from fresh milk and eggs, such as honey nougat, Earl Grey tea, white chocolate and Grand-Marnier.

Maison Berthillon (☎ 01 43 54 31 61; www.berthillon-glacier.fr; 31 rue St-Louis en l'Île, 4e; ☼ 10am-8pm Wed-Sun; Ⓜ Pont Marie) sells its ice creams direct from its premises, as well as through a number of other outlets sprinkled around the island (and elsewhere in Paris).

Most tourists queue at the **Café le Flore en l'Île** (☎ 01 43 29 88 27; 42 quai d'Orléans; (1/2/3/4 small scoops €2.80/4/6/8; ☼ 8am-2am; Ⓜ Pont Marie), a beautiful gilded, timber-panelled tearoom with green-and-gold awnings and spectacular views of the Pont St-Louis, and a takeaway window doing a roaring trade on a hot day. And because of the queues, this is usually the first outlet you see as you cross onto the island. But the same celebrated ices are actually cheaper and the queues often shorter just around the corner at **Esterina** (88 rue St-Louis en l'Île; 1/2/3/4 small scoops €2/3.50/4.50/5.50; ☼ 11am-midnight May-Sep, 1-7pm Oct-Apr; Ⓜ Pont Marie) and at the takeaway counter of Maison Berthillon's own premises, which charges similar prices and has its own charming tearoom in the adjoining building.

Buying a cone and wandering through the island's tiny streets is a favourite pastime for Parisians as well as for tourists, and regardless of where you buy it from, a Berthillon ice cream is still a Berthillon ice cream (ie sublime).

Ice-cream connoisseurs should also check out the offerings at Parisian-Italian newcomer, Pozzetto (see p129).

antiquarian and new travel guides, *National Geographic* back-editions and maps. Opened in 1971 by intrepid travel writer Catherine Domaine, this was the world's first bookshop dedicated solely to travel. Ulysse's hours can be erratic, but knock on the door or telephone and Catherine will open up if she's around.

🏠 MARCHÉ AUX FLEURS
Market

place Louis Lépin, 4e; ☼ **8am-7.30pm Mon-Sat;** Ⓜ **Cité**

Blooms have been sold at this flower market since 1808, making it the oldest market of any kind in Paris. On Sunday, between 9am and 7pm, it transforms into a twittering **bird market**.

📷 **O&CO** *Food & Drink*
☎ 01 40 46 89 37; www.oliviersandco
.com; 81 rue St-Louis en l'Île, 4e;
🕐 11am-2pm & 3-7.30pm Mon-Fri,
11am-7.30pm Sat & Sun; Ⓜ Pont Marie
This olive oil shop (formerly Oliviers
& Co) was the first of what is now a
worldwide chain; created by Olivier
Baussan, who also founded natural
cosmetic company L'Occitane
(there's a L'Occitane boutique on
this street at No 55). In addition to
Baussan's native Provence, O&Co
also stocks oils from Italy, Greece,
Israel, Turkey and Portugal.

🍴 EAT

Restaurants on these two small
islands are few, but there are
some lovely tearooms which also
serve food. The islands' most
famous foodstuff is the legendary
Berthillon ice cream; see the
boxed text, opposite.

🍽 BRASSERIE DE L'ÎLE
ST-LOUIS *Brasserie* €€
☎ 01 43 54 02 59; 55 quai de Bourbon,
4e; 🕐 6pm-1am Thu, noon-midnight
Fri-Tue; Ⓜ Pont Marie
Renowned for Alsatian cuisine,
with various dishes doused in Ries-
ling, you might just as easily be in
a *winstub* on Strasbourg's Grand Île
a few kilometres from the German
border – were it not for the views
of Notre Dame from the terrace.

Even if you're not dining, it's a spectacular setting for a drink.

🍸 DRINK

🍸 LA CHARLOTTE EN L'ÎLE
Salon de Thé
☎ 01 43 54 25 83; 24 rue St-Louis en
l'Île; 🕐 2-8pm Thu-Sun; Ⓜ Pont Marie
The Île St-Louis has some wonderful tearooms, but this fairytale
place next door to the Librairie
Ulysse is the island's most enchanting. It serves Turkish coffee,
hot chocolate and pastries, along
with dozens of varieties of tea,
and cosying up at the tiny tables
here is especially atmospheric on
a winter's evening. If this doesn't
inspire romance, nothing will.

🍸 TAVERNE HENRI IV *Bar*
☎ 01 43 54 27 90; 13 place du Pont Neuf,
1er; 🕐 vary; Ⓜ Pont Neuf
Popular with Paris' legal eagles
thanks to the Palais de Justice
nearby, this wine bar is one of the
few options for a drink on the Île de
Cité. It regularly hosts functions, so
hours can fluctuate; call ahead or
drop by and try your luck.

⭐ PLAY

Aside from Ste-Chapelle's classical
music concerts, there's not a lot
doing on these little islands, but
the Left Bank's nightlife is just a
hop, skip and a jump away.

>LATIN QUARTER, ST-GERMAIN DES PRÉS & MONTPARNASSE

Literary lovers, shopaholics and scholars all flock to this fabled part of Paris, where Sartre, de Beauvoir and Camus, and later Hemingway, Fitzgerald and Joyce, hung out in cafés drinking and engaging in earnest debate.

The Latin Quarter (so named because university students here communicated in Latin until the French Revolution) is home to the Sorbonne's main campus, which is graced by fountains and lime trees. Nearby, intriguing museums, late-opening bookshops, pigeon-filled squares, iron-gated gardens, and markets such as medieval rue Mouffetard, make it one of the liveliest parts of the city.

St-Germain des Prés was once Paris' bohemian and beatnik nucleus. These days it accommodates chichi boutiques, though the legendary literary cafés still exist. Gentrification saw Paris' bohemians move south to Montparnasse. This is where Sartre and de Beauvoir among others are buried; and where you can descend to the skull-and-bone-lined catacombs, or ascend the smoked-glass '70s shrine Tour Montparnasse for a bird's-eye view of the city.

LATIN QUARTER, ST-GERMAIN DES PRÉS & MONTPARNASSE

⊙ SEE

Catacombes.................... 1 C6
Cimetière
du Montparnasse 2 B5
Église St-Germain
des Prés 3 D2
Église St-Sulpice 4 D3
Fondation Cartier Pour
l'Art Contemporain 5 C5
Galerie d'Anatomie
Comparée et de
Paléontologie................. 6 H4
Galerie de Minéralogie
et de Géologie 7 G5
Grande Galerie
de l'Évolution 8 G4
Institut du Monde Arabe.. 9 G3
Jardin des Plantes 10 G4
Jardin du Luxembourg.. 11 D4
Ménagerie du Jardin
des Plantes 12 G4
Mosquée de Paris 13 G5
Musée de la Poste 14 A5
Musée du Luxembourg... 15 D3
Musée National
du Moyen Age 16 E3
Musée National
Eugène Delacroix 17 D2
Panthéon...................... 18 E4
Sorbonne...................... 19 E3
Tour Montparnasse 20 B4

🛍 SHOP

Abbey Bookshop 21 E2
Alexandra Sojfer 22 C2
Cacharel....................... 23 C2
Carré Rive Gauche 24 C1
La Grande Épicerie
de Paris........................ 25 B3
Le Bon Marché.............. 26 B2
Librairie Gourmande.... 27 C2
Shakespeare
& Company 28 E2
Sonia Rykiel 29 C2
Village Voice................. 30 D2

🍴 EAT

Chez Nicos 31 F4
Godjo 32 F3
La Petit Légume 33 F4
La Tour d'Argent........... 34 G3
L'Atelier de Joël
Robouchon................... 35 C1
Le Dôme 36 C4
Le Salon d'Hélène ..... (see 43)
Le Ziryab.................. (see 9)
Les Dix Vins 37 A5
Marché Brancusi.......... 38 B6
Marché Maubert 39 F3
Marché Monge 40 F4
Marché Raspail............ 41 C3

Pho 67 Restaurant
Vietnam.................... 42 E2
Restaurant Hélène
Darroze 43 C3

🍸 DRINK

Bar Signature .... (see 35)
Bistro des Augustins 44 E2
Brasserie Lipp.............. 45 C2
Café de Flore 46 C2
Café Panis.................... 47 F2
La Closerie des Lilas 48 D5
La Palette..................... 49 D2
Le Select...................... 50 C4
Le Vieux Chêne 51 F4
Les Deux Magots 52 C2
Les Éditeurs................. 53 D2
Student Bar & Cie 54 F4

⭐ PLAY

La Coupole................... 55 C4
Le Caveau
de la Huchette............. 56 E2
Le Champo.................... 57 E3
Théâtre
du Luxembourg........... 58 D4
Théâtre du Vieux
Colombier.................... 59 C2

Please see over for map

QUARTERS

LATIN QUARTER, ST-GERMAIN DES PRÉS & MONTPARNASSE

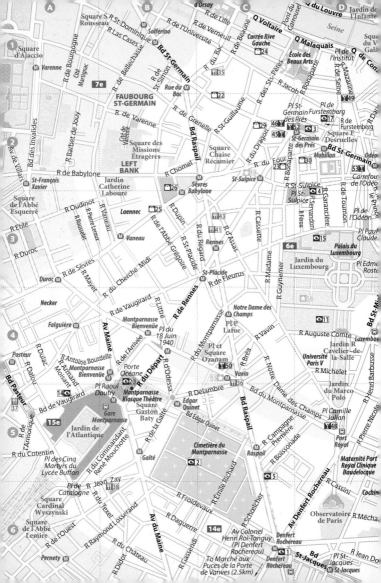

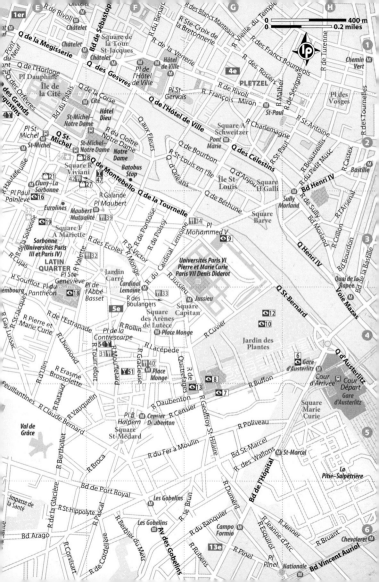

QUARTERS

LATIN QUARTER, ST-GERMAIN DES PRÉS & MONTPARNASSE

Catacombes

👁 SEE

🅲 CATACOMBES

☎ 01 43 22 47 63; www.catacombes
.paris.fr in French; 1 av Colonel Henri
Roi-Tanguy, 14e; admission €5/3.30;
🕑 10am-5pm Tue-Sun; Ⓜ Denfert
Rochereau

Paris' creepiest sight is its series of
macabre underground passages
lined with skulls and bones ex-
humed from the city's overflowing cemeteries and moved here
in 1785. From the *belle époque*
building on av Colonel Henri Roi-
Tanguy (formerly place Denfert
Rochereau), descend 130 steps to
prowl 1.7km of chilling tunnels.
Not for claustrophobes.

🅲 CIMETIÈRE DU MONTPARNASSE

☎ conservation office 01 44 10 86 50;
blvd Edgar Quinet & rue Froidevaux, 14e;
admission free; 🕑 8am-6pm Mon-Fri,
8.30am-6pm Sat, 9am-6pm Sun mid-
Mar–early Nov, 8am-5.30pm Mon-Fri,
8.30am-5.30pm Sat, 9am-5.30pm Sun
early Nov–mid-Mar; Ⓜ Edgar Quinet
or Raspail

Celebs laid to rest here include
writers Charles Baudelaire,
Guy de Maupassant, Jean-Paul
Sartre and Simone de Beauvoir;
playwright Samuel Beckett; and
photographer Man Ray. Montparnasse's tomb traditions include
fans leaving metro tickets on the
grave of singer Serge Gainsbourg
in reference to his song, 'Le
Poinçonneur des Lilas' (see the
boxed text, opposite). Free maps
are available from the conservation office.

🅲 ÉGLISE ST-GERMAIN DES PRÉS

☎ 01 55 42 81 33; 3 place St-Germain
des Prés; 🕑 8am-7pm Mon-Sat, 9am-
8pm Sun; ♿

Its spire rising above St-Germain
des Prés, this charming Roman-
esque church is Paris' oldest. Built
in the 11th century on the site of
an abbey, it was the city's main
centre of Catholic worship until it
was eclipsed by Notre Dame. It's
the (rumoured) resting place of its

namesake, Saint Germain (AD 496–576), the first bishop of Paris.

ÉGLISE ST-SULPICE

☎ 01 46 33 21 78; place St-Sulpice, 6e; 🕒 8.30am-7.15pm Mon-Sat, to 7.45pm Sun; Ⓜ St-Sulpice

Until recently, Église St-Sulpice's few visitors were fans of artist Eugène Delacroix, who painted the frescoes in the Chapelle des Stes-Agnes. Then Dan Brown set a murderous scene of *The Da Vinci Code* here, pivoting around the Rose Line (to the right of the middle of the nave). And yep, it's been mobbed by tourists ever since.

FONDATION CARTIER POUR L'ART CONTEMPORAIN

☎ 01 42 18 56 50; www.fondation .cartier.fr; 261 blvd Raspail; admission €6.50/4.50; 🕒 noon-8pm Tue-Sun; Ⓜ Raspail; ♿

Designed by architect *de jour* Jean Nouvel (see the boxed text, p149), this stunning space is worth checking out for the building alone, but it also hosts temporary exhibits spanning all facets of contemporary art from the 1980s on, including paintings, photography, video and fashion.

INSTITUT DU MONDE ARABE

☎ 01 40 51 38 38; www.imarabe.org; place Mohammed V, 5e; museum €5/4, temporary exhibitions extra; 🕒 museum 10am-6pm Tue-Sun, caféteria noon-2.30pm Tue-Sun; Ⓜ Cardinal Lemoine or Jussieu; ♿

The building that established the reputation of architect Jean Nouvel (see the boxed text, p149) blends modern and traditional Arab elements with western influences, such as photo-sensitive apertures built into the glass walls, inspired by latticed wooden windows. Museum exhibits

SERGE GAINSBOURG

Born Lucien Ginsburg in Paris in 1928 to a musician father fleeing turmoil in Russia, Serge Gainsbourg started out painting advertising signs before landing a cabaret pianist slot. His 1958 track 'Le Poinçonneur des Lilas' depicts work-a-day monotony through the eyes of a metro ticket-puncher. Gainsbourg enacted the soul-destroying job (since eclipsed by machines) on film when recording the song in the Porte des Lilas station.

Gainsbourg expanded his bohemian left bank following into widespread fame fuelled by scandal, excess and high-profile liaisons, most famously with Bridget Bardot, with whom he recorded his biggest international hits. He died in 1991.

Institut du Monde Arabe (p147)

encompass 9th- to 19th-century Arab arts, and there's a library, and a *caféteria*, Le Moucharabieh, as well as a panoramic restaurant/ tearoom, Le Ziryab (p162).

 JARDIN DES PLANTES
☎ 01 40 79 56 01; www.mnhn.fr; 57 rue Cuvier, 5e; admission €1.50 some sections free; ⏰ 7.30am-5.30pm to 7.30pm; Ⓜ Gare d'Austerlitz, Censier Daubenton or Jussieu; ♿

Founded in 1626 as Louis XIII's herb garden, Paris' botanical gardens are a serious institute rather than a leisure destination, but fascinating all the same. They're split into sections including a winter garden, tropical greenhouses and an alpine garden, as well as the school of botany. (There's also a menagerie; opposite.) The most scenic transport to get here is Batobus (p219).

◉ JARDIN DU LUXEMBOURG

🕑 7.30 to 8.15am-5pm to 10pm;
Ⓜ **Luxembourg**

This enchanting park is one of the loveliest places in Paris for a picnic (see p13) or just for relaxing and watching Parisians at play. The northern end is dominated by the Palais du Luxembourg. Built in the 1620s, it is occasionally possible to visit by guided tour – call ☎ 01 44 54 19 30. The *orangerie* houses the Musée du Luxembourg (p150).

◉ MÉNAGERIE DU JARDIN DES PLANTES

☎ 01 40 79 37 94; www.mnhn.fr; 57 rue Cuvier & 3 quai St-Bernard, 5e; admission €7/5 🕑 9am-6pm Mon-Sat, to 6.30pm Sun Apr-Sep, to 5pm Mon-Sat, to 5.30pm Sun Oct-Mar; Ⓜ **Gare d'Austerlitz, Censier Daubenton or Jussieu;** ♿

Like the Jardin des Plantes (opposite), in which it's located, this 1000-animal zoo is more than a

tourist attraction, also doubling as a research centre for the reproduction of rare and endangered species. The animals here were themselves endangered during the Prussian siege of 1870, when almost all were eaten by the starving Parisians.

◉ MOSQUÉE DE PARIS

☎ 01 45 35 97 33; www.mosquee-de -paris.org; 2bis place du Puits de l'Ermite, 5e; admission €3/2; 🕑 mosque 9am-noon & 2-6pm Sat-Thu, tearoom 9am-midnight daily, restaurant lunch & dinner daily, hamam 10am-9pm Mon, Wed, Thu, Sat & Sun, 2-9pm Tue & Fri; Ⓜ **Censier Daubenton or Place Monge;** ♿

Art Deco meets ornate Moorish style at this exquisitely tiled 1920s mosque. Provided you're modestly dressed, you can wander through the colonnaded courtyards (with incredible acoustics during the Call to Prayer) and see ancient Arabic texts in the library, but visitors aren't admitted to the prayer hall.

NOUVEL REVOLUTION

No architect has made as much of a splash on Paris' contemporary landscape as has Jean Nouvel (www.jeannouvel.fr). Born in 1945, Nouvel trained at the Paris' École des Beaux-Art, going on to design icons such as the Institut du Monde Arabe (p147), the Fondation Cartier Pour l'Art Contemporain (p147), the Musée de la Publicité (p79), and the Musée du Quai Branly (p44). His most famous edifice never to be built was his competition-winning Tour Sans Fin (ironically meaning 'tower without end') at La Défense (see the boxed text, p53). The 'Picasso of architecture's' latest creation is clothing retailer H&M's Champs-Élysées premises; slated to open late 2007.

BODY & SOUL

If too much relaxation is barely enough, for €58 at the Mosquée de Paris (p149) you can take a *hamam* (Turkish steam bath), followed by a *gommage* (black-soap scrubdown) and a massage, then nourish your body and soul on a *tajine* (slow-cooked meat) or couscous (including a drink) in the restaurant; it's all topped off with a pastry and sweet peppermint tea in the courtyard (which, on a cloudless day, transports you to Morocco). Alternatively, any of the above can be taken separately.

Note the *hamam* is open to women only on Monday, Wednesday, Thursday and Saturday, and men only on Tuesday and Sunday.

There's also a wonderful tearoom, mosaic-tiled restaurant and *hamam* (Turkish steam bath)– see the boxed text, above.

◐ MUSÉE DE LA POSTE
☎ 01 42 79 24 24; www.museedela poste.fr in French; 34 blvd de Vaugirard, 15e; admission €5/3.50, temporary exhibitions extra; ⊕ 10am-6pm Mon-Sat; Ⓜ Montparnasse Bienvenüe or Pasteur
You don't have to be a postie or a philatelist to appreciate this postal museum. Anyone inspired by travel and communications will enjoy its exhibits such as antique postal equipment, telecommunication and ancient French stamps. Imaginative temporary

exhibitions are based on quirky themes such as letter boxes that constitute works of art.

◐ MUSÉE DU LUXEMBOURG
☎ 01 42 34 25 95; www.museedu luxembourg.fr in French; 19 rue de Vaugirard, 6e; ⊕ 11am-10pm Mon, Fri & Sat, to 7pm Tue-Thu, 9am-7pm Sun, Ⓜ Luxembourg
Prestigious temporary art exhibitions take place in this beautiful former *orangerie* in the Jardin du Luxembourg (p149). Admission prices vary according to the specific exhibition (roughly around €10).

◐ MUSÉE NATIONAL D'HISTOIRE NATURELLE
☎ 01 40 79 30 00; www.mnhn.fr; 57 rue Cuvier, 5e; Grande Galerie de l'Évolution €8/6, others each €6/4; ⊕ 10am-5pm Wed-Mon, some sections close 6pm; Ⓜ Censier Daubenton or Gare d'Austerlitz; ♿
France's national museum of natural history incorporates three separate centres adjoining the Jardin des Plantes (p148): the Galerie de Minéralogie et de Géologie, dealing with minerals and geology; the Galerie d'Anatomie Comparée et de Paléontologie, focussing on anatomy and fossils; and the most interesting, the Grande Galerie de l'Évolution, with topical exhibits about humanity's effect on the ecosystem and global warming.

◎ MUSÉE NATIONAL DU MOYEN AGE

☎ 01 53 73 78 16; www.musee-moyen age.fr; 6 place Paul Painlevé, 5e; admission €6.50/4.50; ⏱ 9.15am-5.45pm Wed-Mon; Ⓜ Cluny–La Sorbonne or St-Michel; ♿

The National Museum of the Middle Ages (sometimes called the Musée de Cluny, or just Cluny), is fittingly housed in both the remains of Gallo-Roman baths (c AD 200), and the 15th-century Hôtel de Cluny, Paris' finest civil medieval building. The highlight is the series of 15th-century tapestries, *The Lady with the Unicorn*. Its foliage inspired the forest planted outside.

◎ MUSÉE NATIONAL EUGÈNE DELACROIX

☎ 01 44 41 86 50; www.musee-delac roix.fr in French; 6 rue de Furstemberg, 6e; admission €5; ⏱ 9.30am-5pm Wed-Mon; Ⓜ Mabillon or St-Germain des Prés; ♿

The father of French Romanticism lived at this intimate courtyard studio until his death in 1863.

Musée National du Moyen Age

Although his most famous works are at the Louvre (p77) and the Musée d'Orsay (p43), as well as St-Sulpice (p147), the museum's collection of oils, watercolours, pastels and drawings, and, especially, its location off a magnolia-shaded square, make it a delight.

Eiffel Tower from Tour Montparnasse

PARISIAN PUPPETS

You don't have to be a kid and you don't have to speak French to be delighted by marionette shows, which have entertained audiences in France since the Middle Ages.

The stringed puppets perform in the Jardin du Luxembourg's little **Théâtre du Luxembourg** (☎ 01 43 26 46 47; tickets €4.20; ☼ 11am & 3.15pm Sat & Sun, 3.15pm Wed, school holidays daily; Ⓜ Luxembourg). There are also marionette shows at the **Parc du Champ de Mars** (Map pp40-1, D3; ☎ 01 48 56 01 44; tickets €3; ☼ 3.15pm & 4.15pm Wed & Fri-Sun; Ⓜ École Militaire).

Or you can buy your own puppets at the enchanting Clair de Rêve (p139).

◎ PANTHÉON

☎ 01 44 32 18 00; www.monum.fr; place du Panthéon; admission €7.50/4.80; ☼ 10am-6.30pm Apr-Sep, to 6.15pm Oct-Mar; Ⓜ Luxembourg

Commissioned by Louis XV as an abbey, this domed neoclassical building had the misfortune of reaching completion in 1789. Given the Revolutionary climate, it was converted into a mausoleum, housing leading lights including Victor Hugo, Voltaire, Louis Braille, Emile Zola among 80 or so others. Its first female resident, Marie Curie (accompanied by husband Pierre) only arrived in 1995.

◎ SORBONNE

☎ 01 40 46 20 25; www.sorbonne.fr in French; 12 rue de la Sorbonne, 5e; Ⓜ Luxembourg or Cluny–La Sorbonne

One of the world's most famous universities, 'La Sorbonne' was founded in 1253 by Robert de Sorbon as a theological college for just 16 pupils, going on to have its own government and laws. The main campus' imposing buildings, domed chapel and lime tree–shaded squares dominate the Latin Quarter, while its students dominate the local bars and cafés.

◎ TOUR MONTPARNASSE

☎ 01 45 38 52 56; www.tourmontparnasse56.com; rue de l'Arrivée, 15e; admission €9/6.50; ☼ 9.30am-11.30pm Apr-Sep, to 10.30pm Sun-Thu, to 11pm Fri & Sat Oct-Mar; Ⓜ Montparnasse Bienvenüe

In a built-up city, this early-'70s skyscraper would blend into the skyline, but in low-rise Paris it sticks out like a painfully sore thumb. On the upside, its 56th-floor exhibition centre and bar and 59th-floor terrace are about the only spots in Paris where visitors can't see this unsightly office block, and the panoramas absolve its architectural sins – almost.

WORTH THE TRIP

The residential southeast sector of Paris is an eclectic mix of quarters that makes for a fascinating half-day stroll if you've stood in one tourist queue too many. To help you to explore this part of Paris, pick up a free city-wide map from a branch of the Paris Convention & Visitors Bureau (see p220).

Cinephiles won't want to miss the **Cinémathèque Française** (☎ 01 71 19 33 33; www.cinemathequefrancaise.com in French; 51 rue de Bercy, enter via place Leonard Bernstein, 12e; permanent collection €4/2, temporary exhibitions €9/6; ☽ noon-7pm Mon, Wed & Fri, to 10pm Thu, to 8pm Sat & Sun; Ⓜ Bercy). Housed in stunning new Frank Gehry–designed premises, it showcases the history of French cinema as well as screening old black-and-white classics and edgy new films.

There are more cinemas at **Bercy Village** (☎ 01 40 02 90 80; www.bercyvillage.com in French; 28 rue François Truffaut; ☽ shops 11am-9pm, restaurants to 2am; Ⓜ Cour St-Émilion), converted from former wine stores, but the main reason to head here is the cobblestone strip of offbeat, *très* hip designer shops, bars and restaurants.

From Bercy, cross Paris' newest bridge, the steel-framed, oak-planked Pont Simone de Beauvoir (for pedestrians and cyclists only). The first of Paris' 37 bridges to be named after a woman, it leads, appropriately enough, to the **Bibliothèque Nationale de France** (National Library; ☎ 01 53 79 53 79, 01 53 79 40 41; www.bnf.fr; 11 quai François Mauriac, 13e; temporary exhibitions from €5/3.50, library €3.30; ☽ 10am-7pm Tue-Sat, 1-7pm Sun; Ⓜ Bibliothèque). The flaws of France's national library are well documented: books bake in the sun (or did until ultra-expensive shutters had to be fitted), while users read by artificial light, and the state-of-the-art automated stacks rarely work. But it's a work of art, with four glass towers shaped like open books and subterranean reading rooms wrap-

🛍 SHOP

Books and antiques are this area's mainstays, along with fashion, which tends to include many international luxe labels (Prada, Gucci and so on) as well as individual specialist shops and a couple of flagship stores such as Cacharel and Sonia Rykiel. Blvd St-Michel and its side streets have

some great secondhand record and CD shops. And, being Paris, you'll also find plenty of markets here.

🛍 ABBEY BOOKSHOP *Books*

www.abbeybookshop.net; 29 rue de la Parcheminerie, 5e; ☽ **10am-7pm Mon-Sat;** Ⓜ **St-Michel or Cluny–La Sorbonne**
More like a book-lined private lounge, this heritage-listed

ping around a rainforest, and it hosts excellent exhibitions. On the river out front, a **floating swimming pool** (Piscine Flottante; ☎ 01 56 61 96 50) opens in the summer months. Two of Paris' best floating nightclubs are also here: **Le Batofar** (☎ 01 56 29 10 33; www .batofar.net in French; opposite 11 quai François Mauriac, 13e; admission free–€15; ⏱ 9pm-midnight Mon & Tue, 9pm or 10pm to 4am, 5am or 6am Wed-Sun; Ⓜ Quai de la Gare or Bibliothèque), a tugboat with a bar on its upper deck and an electro-oriented club beneath; and **La Guinguette Pirate** (☎ 01 53 61 08 49; opposite 11 quai François Mauriac, 13e; admission €6-12; ⏱ 7pm-2am Tue-Sat, 5pm-midnight Sun; Ⓜ Quai de la Gare or Bibliothèque), aboard a three-mast Chinese junk.

Southeast of the Bibliothèque (and southeast of 2007's new metro station, Olympiades) is Paris' largest Chinatown, which, with its high-rises and malls, feels for all the world like another continent. Marvel over the array of Asian products jamming the shelves of supermarkets such as **Tang Frères** (☎ 01 49 60 56 78; 48 av d'Ivry, 13e; ⏱ Tue-Sun; Ⓜ Tolbiac or Porte d'Ivry), or twirl a pair of chopsticks in a bowl of noodles at **My-Canh** (☎ 01 45 70 87 36; 84 rue Baudricourt, 13e; mains €8-13; ⏱ lunch & dinner Tue-Sun; Ⓜ Tolbiac or Porte d'Ivry).

Otherwise, deviate a few blocks west to the café-clad rue de la Butte aux Cailles for a slice of Paris sans tourists. **Le Temps des Cérises** (☎ 01 45 89 69 48; 18-20 rue de la Butte aux Cailles, 13e; ⏱ lunch Mon-Fri, dinner Mon-Sat; Ⓜ Corvisart or Place d'Italie) hits the spot for hearty local fare and down-to-earth prices. Or meander north to place d'Italie for Christophe Beaufront's renowned classically inspired contemporary cuisine at **L'Avant-Goût** (☎ 01 53 80 24 00; 26 rue Bobillot, 13e; ⏱ lunch & dinner Tue-Fri; Ⓜ Place d'Italie).

townhouse-turned-bookshop has more than 18,000 new and used books (slide the shelves aside to see more books hidden behind). Canadian owner Brian Spence serves continuous free tea and coffee (with maple syrup), and organises weekend hikes around Paris as well as literary events where wine and conversation flow in equal measure.

⬜ ALEXANDRA SOJFER
Accessories
☎ 01 42 22 17 02; www.alexandrasojfer .fr; 218 blvd St-Germain; ⏱ 9.30am-7pm Mon-Sat; Ⓜ St-Germain des Prés
Parapluies and *ombrelles* (parasols and umbrellas) just don't come more elegant than these crea-tions handmade by Alexandra Sojfer, whose blvd St-Germain

> ## CARRÉE RIVE GAUCHE
> Art and antiques gather under the umbrella of **Carrée Rive Gauche** (☎ 01 42 60 70 10; www.carrerivegauche .com; Ⓜ Rue du Bac or Solférino), just east of the Musée d'Orsay, bounded by quai Voltaire, rue de l'Université, rue des St-Pères & rue du Bac. Within this 'Left Bank Square' are more than 120 highly specialised merchants, along with half a dozen restaurants. Antiques fairs (usually held in spring) trigger a flurry of professional buyers, and a program of exhibitions (such as an exhibition on masks: carnival masks, Australian Aboriginal and Native American masks and so on) unfolds during the year.

shop is devoted exclusively to them. If nothing on display catches your fancy, you can have one custom-made.

☐ CACHAREL
Fashion, Accessories & Perfume
☎ 01 40 46 00 45; 64 rue Bonaparte, 6e; Ⓨ 10am-7pm Mon-Sat; Ⓜ St-Sulpice
Another mid-20th-century label undergoing a revival, Cacharel (named for a bird from Provence's Camargue region) was founded in 1960 and unlike many fashion houses, it still remains a private company. It's best known for its floral-printed silk georgette dresses and signature perfumes such as the airy orange blossom-, rose-, lily- and jasmine-scented Anaïs Anaïs.

☐ LA GRANDE ÉPICERIE DE PARIS *Food & Drink*
☎ 01 44 39 81 00; www.lagrande epicerie.fr; 36 rue de Sèvres, 7e; Ⓨ 8.30am-9pm Mon-Sat; Ⓜ Sèvres Babylone
The exquisitely presented chocolates, pastries, tins of biscuits, fruit and vegetables, seafood, cheeses, wines and other luxury goods in this glorious grocery store, attached to Le Bon Marché (below), all appear far too beautiful to eat. The displays are a sight to behold even if you're not here to buy.

☐ LE BON MARCHÉ
Department Store
☎ 01 44 39 80 00; www.bonmarche.fr; 24 rue de Sèvres, 7e; Ⓨ 9.30am-7pm Mon-Wed & Fri, 10am-9pm Thu, 9.30am-8pm Sat; Ⓜ Sèvres Babylone
The name's actually a misnomer – *bon marché* is French for 'bargain', and this beautifully laid-out store isn't that, by any stretch of the imagination. But it is a Paris institution, built by Gustave Eiffel in 1852 as the city's first department store, and features designer salons and a fantastical food hall, La Grande Épicerie de Paris (above).

Marion Mille,
Fashion Designer

What do you design? I design for women: a lot of knitwear and jersey and accessories too – jewels and detached collars – clothes that are feminine and wearable and comfortable (see www.marionmille.com). **What's 'Parisian style'?** A typical Parisian woman knows what she wants and doesn't follow trends like a fashion victim; it's a personal style. She'll mix designer with vintage with pieces from H&M. **How important are Paris' fashion shows?** It's the consecration of a collection, and a lot of buyers come. But there's a big difference between shows and the real collection, it's very different. The shows are more to express the spirit; to see *l'air du temps* (the spirit of the times). **Favourite place to shop?** Le Bon Marché (opposite). There's a good selection of designers, but not too many, so I can concentrate my shopping.

🏠 LIBRAIRIE GOURMANDE
Books

☎ 01 43 54 37 27; www.librairie-gour
mande.fr in French; 4 rue Dante, 5e;
🕙 10am-7pm Mon-Sat; Ⓜ Maubert-
Mutualité

All the classic texts of the culinary
arts are here at this food bookshop, along with new collections of recipes accompanied by
mouthwatering photography.

🏠 MARCHÉ AUX PUCES DE LA
PORTE DE VANVES *Market*

🕙 7am-6pm Sat & Sun; av Georges
Lafenestre & av Marc Sangnier, 14e;
Ⓜ Porte de Vanves

Paris' smallest flea market is
nonetheless worth scouting out
for original retro homewares such
as '60s cocktail shakers and '70s
lamps, as well as new clothes,
leather boots, handbags and
wallets. The market is located
about 2.5km southwest of the
Catacombs.

🏠 SHAKESPEARE & COMPANY
Books

☎ 01 43 26 96 50; http://shakespeareco
.org; 37 rue de la Bûcherie, 5e; 🕙 noon-
midnight; Ⓜ St-Michel

Fossicking through this 'wonder-
land of books' (as Henry Miller
described it) unearths bargains,
but Shakespeare & Co is best
known for nurturing writers (see
p12). Its legendary open-invitation

tea parties are held at 4pm most
Sundays, and readings at 7pm
most Mondays. Legends-in-the-
making include travel writing
workshops and an open-to-all-
comers writers' group at 3pm on
Saturday afternoons.

🏠 SONIA RYKIEL *Fashion*

☎ 01 49 54 60 60; www.soniarykiel
.com; 175 blvd St-Germain, 6e; 🕙 11am-
7pm Mon-Sat; Ⓜ St-Germain des Prés

In the heady days of May 1968,
amid Paris' student uprisings,
Sonia Rykiel opened her inaugural
boutique here; she went on to
revolutionise garments with her
inverted seams, 'no hems' and
'no lining'. Her diffusion labels
are housed in separate boutiques
nearby.

🏠 VILLAGE VOICE *Books*

☎ 01 46 33 36 47; www.villagevoice
bookshop.com; 6 rue Princesse, 6e; 🕙 2-
8pm Mon, 10am-8pm Tue-Sat, 2-6pm
Sun; Ⓜ Mabillon

Situated on a quaint left bank
backstreet, this English-language
bookshop specialises in North
American literature (great for
picking up obscure Hemingway
novellas), and has an excellent
range of French literature in
translation. Good-natured staff
are well-read and helpful, and the
shop hosts lots of readings and
literary events.

Sylvia Whitman,
Manager, Shakespeare & Company

Favourite book about Paris There are so many! For the moment I am enjoying *Paris Stories* by Mavis Gallant. She is a wonderful writer who really captures the atmosphere of Paris. Another captivating read is *True Pleasures: A Memoir of Women in Paris* by Lucinda Holdforth; from Colette to Nancy Mitford. **Favourite Café** Any of the great cafés on rue de Bretagne (Map pp116–17, D1) in the 3e. **Best place for writers to get inspiration** The Château Rouge quarter (Map p89, D3) or the parc des Buttes Chaumont (Map pp104–5, E3). **Most requested book** *A Moveable Feast* by Ernest Hemingway. It's a classic. **Number of books written at Shakespeare & Co** About 50 books have been researched and written at the shop: for example Burroughs worked on *Naked Lunch* upstairs in the library.

🍴 EAT

🍴 CHEZ NICOS *Crêperie* €

44 rue Mouffetard, 5e; 🕐 **11am-1am;**
Ⓜ **Censier Daubenton**

The blackboard outside crêpe artist Nicos' unassuming little shop chalks up an overwhelming variety of fillings, but ask by name for his 'La Crêpe du Chef', which is stuffed with aubergines, feta, mozzarella, lettuce, tomatoes and onions (€4.50). There's a handful of tables inside; otherwise head to a nearby park.

🍴 GODJO *Ethiopian* €€

☎ **01 40 46 82 21; www.godjo.com;
8 rue de l'École Polytechnique, 5e;**
🕐 **noon-2am;** Ⓜ **Cardinal Lemoine**

Although its name means 'humble farmer's house', the woven wall-hangings, carved timber artefacts and paintings at this Ethiopian restaurant make eating here something like dining in an art gallery (but a buzzy, informal one). It's a great option for vegetarians, with a slew of meatless dishes to choose from.

🍴 LA PETIT LÉGUME

Vegetarian €

☎ **01 40 46 06 85; 36 rue des Boulangers, 5e;** 🕐 **lunch & dinner Mon-Sat;**
Ⓜ **Cardinal Lemoine;** Ⓥ

Yay, a vegetarian restaurant in Paris – and it serves organic wine! Salads are also a speciality, and *menus* are good value at both lunch and dinner.

🍴 LA TOUR D'ARGENT

Gastronomic €€€€

☎ **01 43 54 23 31; www.latourdargent
.com; 15 quai de la Tournelle, 5e;**
🕐 **lunch Wed-Sun, dinner Tue-Sun;**
Ⓜ **Cardinal Lemoine or Pont Marie**

L'Atelier de Joël Robouchon

In its four-and-a-quarter centuries (it opened in 1582), the 'silver tower' has refined every facet of fine dining. Its signature *quenelles de brochet* (pike-perch dumplings) and pressed duck continues to mesmerise diners, as do its glimmering views over Notre Dame and the Seine.

¶¶ L'ATELIER DE JOËL ROBOUCHON

International   €€€€

☎ 01 42 22 56 56; www.hotel-pont-royal.com; 5 rue de Montalembert, 7e; 🕐 lunch & dinner; Ⓜ Rue du Bac

The legendary Robouchon serves inspired cuisine at long bars rather than separate tables, reflecting the increasing numbers of Parisians dining alone who still want to eat *very* well. Bar Signature (p164) is also here.

¶¶ LE DÔME *Seafood*   €€€

☎ 01 43 35 25 81; 108 blvd du Montparnasse, 14e; 🕐 lunch & dinner to 12.30am; Ⓜ Vavin

So the stories go, it was here in this magnificent brasserie that Gertrude Stein allegedly convinced Henri Matisse to open his artists' academy – only for Matisse to add his voice to the *Testimony against Gertrude Stein* over her 1933 *Autobiography of Alice B Toklas*. Le Dôme is still one of the swishest places around for a seafood extravaganza.

Le Dôme

QUARTERS

LATIN QUARTER, ST-GERMAIN DES PRÉS & MONTPARNASSE

QUARTERS

LATIN QUARTER, ST-GERMAIN DES PRÉS & MONTPARNASSE

🍴 LE ZIRYAB *Arabian* €€
☎ 01 53 10 10 16; www.imarabe.org;
place Mohammed V; 🕑 restaurant lunch
Tue-Sun, dinner by reservation only,
tearoom 3-6pm Tue-Sun; Ⓜ Cardinal
Lemoine or Jussieu

You can visit the 9th floor of the
Institute du Monde Arab (p147)
for free to take in the incredible
views stretching across the Seine
and Notre Dame as far as Sacré-
Cœur, but better yet you can
savour them while also enjoying
the delicious flavours of the Arab
world. Or just head to the outdoor
terrace for a refreshing mint tea.

🍴 LES DIX VINS *French* €€
☎ 01 43 20 91 77; 57 rue Falguière, 15e;
🕑 lunch & dinner Mon-Fri; Ⓜ Pasteur

It's worth the trek to Montparnasse's outer flanks to get to this
chic little place, which serves
set *menus* of innovative, often
game-oriented cuisine and – as
the name implies – topnotch
hand-picked wines.

🍴 MARCHÉ BRANCUSI
Market €
place Constantin Brancusi, 14e; 🕑 9am-
2pm Sat; Ⓜ Gaîté

Overdose on organic produce at
this weekly open-air market.

🍴 MARCHÉ MAUBERT
Market €
place Maubert, 5e; 🕑 7am-2.30pm
Tue & Thu, to 3pm Sat; Ⓜ Maubert
Mutualité

St-Germain's bohemian soul lives
on at this colourful market.

🍴 MARCHÉ MONGE *Market* €
place Monge, 5e; 🕑 7am-2pm Wed & Fri,
to 2.30pm Sun; Ⓜ Place Monge

This open-air market is laden with
wonderful cheeses, baked goods
and a host of other tempting treats.

🍴 MARCHÉ RASPAIL *Market* €
blvd Raspail btwn rue de Rennes & rue
du Cherche Midi, 6e; 🕑 regular market
7am-2.30pm Tue & Fri, organic market
9am-2am Sun; Ⓜ Rennes

RUE MOUFFETARD

This narrow, sloping cobblestone street (F4) is one of Paris' most ancient, beginning its life
as a Roman road to Rome via Lyon. It acquired its current name in the 18th century, when
the then-nearby River Bievre (now piped underground) became the communal waste-
disposal for local tanners and wood-pulpers. The resulting odours gave rise to the name
Moffettes (French for 'skunk'), which was transmuted over the years to Mouffetard.

Nicknamed 'La Mouffe', the street is lined with ancient shopfronts housing cheap,
student-oriented cafés and bars, as well as a **market** (🕑 8am-7.30pm Tue-Sat, to noon
Sun; Ⓜ Censier Daubenton).

Market stalls, rue Mouffetard

A traditional open-air market on Tuesday and Friday, Marché Raspail is especially popular on Sundays when it's filled with organic produce.

🍴 PHO 67 RESTAURANT VIETNAM *Vietnamese* €
☎ 01 43 25 56 69; 59 rue Galande, 5e; ⏲ lunch & dinner; Ⓜ Maubert Mutualité

Tuck into Vietnamese dishes such as fried boned eel, crusty lacquered duck, rare tender goat with ginger and North Vietnamese soup amid the burgundy walls and suspended rattan lamps of this unpretentious gem. Pho's hidden in a little backstreet of the Latin Quarter, but is fortunately away from the over-touristy little maze of restaurants surrounding rue de la Huchette.

QUARTERS

LATIN QUARTER, ST-GERMAIN DES PRÉS & MONTPARNASSE

MONTPARNASSE

It might not be immediately apparent today, but Montparnasse (C5) was once at the centre of Paris' artistic endeavours. Creators including Chagall, Modigliani, Léger, Soutine, Miró, Kandinsky, Picasso, Stravinsky, Cocteau, Hemingway and Pound, and political exiles Lenin and Trotsky, all congregated here at some point. The Nazi occupation of Paris quashed Montparnasse's cultural life, and unlike Montmartre and the Latin Quarter, 20th-century developments such as the Gare Montparnasse complex have altered the landscape irrevocably. But reminders of Montparnasse's heyday are found in the surviving cafés, and backstreets such as rue Daguerre (B6), while the area around rue de la Gaîtié (B4) buzzes with newfound fervour.

▯ RESTAURANT HÉLÈNE DARROZE *French* €€€€
☎ 01 42 22 00 11; 4 rue d'Assas, 6e; ⏰ lunch & dinner Tue-Sat; Ⓜ Sèvres Babylone

Paris has very few female star chefs, but Hélène Darroze is a stellar exception. Her premises house the twin Michelin-starred restaurant upstairs, and the relaxed salon, Le Salon d'Hélène, renowned for its multicourse tasting menus, downstairs. Dishes lean towards Darroze's native southwestern France, such as wood-grilled foie gras.

▯ DRINK
▯ BAR SIGNATURE *Bar*
☎ 01 42 22 56 56; www.hotel-pont-royal.com; 5 rue de Montalembert, 7e; ⏰ daily; Ⓜ Rue du Bac

Under the same roof at the Hôtel Pont Royal as L'Atelier de Joël Robouchon (p161), this bar once the hangout of Aldous Huxley, Henry Miller, Truman Capote and TS Eliot.

▯ BISTRO DES AUGUSTINS *Bar*
☎ 01 43 54 04 41; 39 quai des Grands Augustins, 6e; ⏰ 11am-10pm Mon-Sat; Ⓜ St-Michel

Squeezed in among this quay's Irish pubs, Canadian bars and generic watering holes, this authentic left bank place, plastered with old advertising posters from the *bouquiniste* (booksellers) stalls opposite, is a cosy spot for a glass of red or for a light meal.

▯ BRASSERIE LIPP *Brasserie*
☎ 01 45 48 53 91; www.brasserie-lipp.fr; 151 blvd St-Germain, 6e; ⏰ 10am-1am; Ⓜ St-Germain des Prés

Of all the historic haunts, this is our favourite for its elegantly poured beers in long glasses, served by waiters wearing black waistcoats and long white aprons. Hemingway sang its praises in *A Moveable Feast* and today its faded glamour is neither too faded nor too glamorous but simply perfect. Stellar brasserie fare such as pork knuckle, too.

⅂ CAFÉ DE FLORE *Café*
☎ 01 45 48 55 26; www.café-de-flore .com; 172 blvd St-Germain, 6e; ⏱ 7.30-1.30am; Ⓜ St-Germain des Prés

This fêted 1880s café is where Sartre and de Beauvoir essentially set up office, writing in its warmth during the Nazi occupation. It's actually less touristy than neighbouring Les Deux Magots (p166), but alas, its prices are just as lofty.

Brasserie Lipp

QUARTERS

LATIN QUARTER, ST-GERMAIN DES PRÉS & MONTPARNASSE

☟ CAFÉ PANIS *Café*
☎ 01 43 54 19 71; 21 quai de Montebello, 5e; ☽ 7am-2am Mon-Fri, 8am-2am Sat & Sun; Ⓜ St-Michel

This rather elegant-looking café might seem an unlikely spot for the dishevelled studenty-types you see scribbling in notebooks here, but it's close to Shakespeare & Co (p158), and waiters benevolently let impoverished writers – who might just be future Hemingways – sit on a coffee for an hour or two. It's also a good spot for a salad or warming soup.

☟ LA CLOSERIE DES LILAS
Brasserie
☎ 01 40 51 34 50; 171 blvd du Montparnasse, 6e; ☽ noon-1.30am; Ⓜ Port Royal

With a legacy stretching back to Baudelaire, 'the Lilac Enclosure' is where Hemingway wrote much of *The Sun Also Rises* while he was living around the corner. Brass plaques tell you where he and luminaries such as Picasso, Apollinaire, Man Ray, Jean-Paul Sartre and Samuel Beckett imbibed. There's a lovely terrace and an upmarket restaurant.

☟ LA PALETTE *Café*
☎ 01 43 26 68 15; 43 rue de Seine, 6e; ☽ 8am-2am Mon-Sat; Ⓜ Mabillon

One of Henry Miller's faves, this mirrorlined café was also a haunt of Cézanne and Braque, and these days is popular with art dealers.

☟ LE SELECT *Café*
☎ 01 42 22 65 27; 99 blvd du Montparnasse, 6e; ☽ 7.30-2.30am; Ⓜ Vavin

No mention of Montparnasse would be complete without Le Select. Opened in the mid-1920s, it was the first of the area's *grande dame* cafés to open late into the night and still draws everyone from beer-swigging students to whisky-swilling politicians.

☟ LE VIEUX CHÊNE *Bar*
☎ 01 43 37 71 51; 69 rue Mouffetard, 5e; ☽ 4pm-2am Sun-Thu, to 5am Fri & Sat; Ⓜ Place Monge

Situated on ancient rue Mouffetard (see the boxed text, p162), this is thought to be Paris' oldest bar. It housed Revolutionary meetings in 1848 and was a dancing club during the *belle époque,* and today has a buzzing student crowd and live music on weekends. Like many of the surrounding bars, happy hour kicks off from 4pm once lectures let out.

☟ LES DEUX MAGOTS *Café*
☎ 01 45 48 55 25; 170 blvd St-Germain, 6e; ☽ 7am-1am; Ⓜ St-Germain des Prés

If ever there were a café that summed up St-Germain des Prés' early-20th-century literary scene, it's this former hangout of anyone

Les Deux Magots

who was anyone. You will spend *beaucoup* to sip a coffee at a wicker chair on the terrace shaded by dark-green awnings and geraniums spilling from window boxes, but it's an undeniable piece of Parisian history.

▼ LES ÉDITEURS *Café*
☎ 01 43 26 67 76; 4 carrefour de l'Odéon, 6e; 🕑 8am-2am; Ⓜ Odéon
This writerly café with a library of books (or is that a library of books with a writerly café?) does a terrific Sunday brunch and is great for sitting by the windows drawing inspiration from this buzzing quarter.

▼ STUDENT BAR & CIE *Bar*
38 rue Mouffetard; 🕑 4pm-2am; Ⓜ Censier Daubenton
This funky little space, with burgundy banquettes, a small timber

bar glowing with tealight candles, and silver fans keeping things cool, is an especially good bet if you're on your own, thanks to its welcoming staff and regulars. There's more seating downstairs in the cosy basement.

⭐ PLAY
⬚ LA COUPOLE *Club*
☎ 01 43 27 56 00; 102 blvd du Montparnasse, 14e; entry from €12; 🕑 club 9.30pm-3am Thu, 11.30pm-5.30am Fri, 10pm-5am Sat, brasserie 8.30am-1am Sun-Thu, 8am-1.30am Fri & Sat; Ⓜ Vavin
Since the roaring twenties, this showpiece has set Paris' trends (it heralded electronica and salsa), and now hosts diverse genres including reggae and funk. Its brasserie, with muraled columns painted by artists including Chagall,

Le Caveau de la Huchette

is favoured by young, serious French writers drawing inspiration from de Beauvoir, who worked on *L'Invitée* (*The Guest*) here in 1940.

⭐ LE CAVEAU DE LA HUCHETTE *Jazz*

☎ 01 43 26 65 05; www.caveaudelahuchette.fr; 5 rue de la Huchette, 5e; adult €11-13, student €9; 🕐 9.30pm-2.30am Sun-Thu, 9pm-4am Fri-Sat; Ⓜ St-Michel
Count Basie, Memphis Slim and Sacha Distel are among those who've played at this jazz club housed in former medieval cellars (later French Revolution torture chambers). Nowadays Le Caveau focuses on retrospectives, such as its swing show featuring Glenn Miller Dixieland and memories of Django Reinhardt, and the Philippe Lucas Jazz Band's homage to Sinatra.

⭐ LE CHAMPO *Cinema*

☎ 01 43 54 51 60; www.lechampo.com in French; 51 rue des Écoles, 5e; Ⓜ St-Michel or Cluny–La Sorbonne
The place to catch retrospectives of Hitchcock and Woody Allen as well as French actors and directors, this Latin Quarter cinema has two screens, one of which has wheelchair access.

⭐ THÉÂTRE DU VIEUX COLOMBIER *Theatre*

rue du Vieux Colombier, 6e
This theatre is one of the three venues of Comédie Française (p85).

Gardens, Maison de Claude Monet (p172)

VERSAILLES

When it comes to over-the-top opulence, the **Château de Versailles** is in a class of its own, even for France.

Set in the leafy, very bourgeois suburb of Versailles, this Baroque palace was the kingdom's political capital and the seat of the royal court from 1682 up until the fateful events of 1789. In that year, revolutionaries massacred the palace guard and dragged Louis XVI and Marie Antoinette back to Paris, where they were ingloriously guillotined.

Louis XIV (1643–1715) transformed his father's hunting lodge into the colossal Château de Versailles in the mid-17th century. The palace, set on 900 hectares of fountain-graced gardens, pond-filled parks and woods, boasted 700 rooms, 2153 windows, 352 chimneys and 28 acres of roof. It housed the entire court of 6000 (plus an additional 5000 servants), and emblemised the power of the French monarchy – as well as Louis XIV's appetite for decadence and self-glorification. The grandstanding king hired the finest talent of the day, including architects Louis Le Vau and later Jules Hardouin-Mansart; the landscape artist André Le Nôtre; and the painter/decorator Charles Le Brun, who, with his hundreds of artisans, ostentatiously adorned every interior moulding, cornice, ceiling and doorway with some 6300 paintings, 2000 sculptures and statues, 15,000 engravings, and 5000 fantastical furnishings and *objets d'art*.

Interior highlights include the **Grand Appartement du Roi** (King's Suite), with rooms dedicated to Hercules, Venus, Diana, Mars and Mercury; and the *pièce de résistance*, the **Galerie des Glaces** (Hall of Mirrors), a 75m-long ballroom with 17 massive mirrors, facing an equal number of windows looking out on the luxuriant gardens.

INFORMATION
Location 21km southwest of Paris
Getting there The RER line C5 (€2.55) from Paris' Left Bank RER stations to Versailles-Rive Gauche station is only 700m southeast of the chateau; there are up to 70 trains a day (half that number on Sunday), and the trip takes 35 minutes
Contact www.chateauversailles.fr
Costs Admission from €10 to €25 depending on day/access; skip queues by purchasing your ticket ahead of time from ticket agency Fnac, or a combined train/palace *Forfait Loisirs Château de Versailles* SNCF pass from train station ticket windows (€21.15)
When to go 9am-6.30pm Tue-Sun Apr-Oct, to 5.30pm Nov-Mar

Left *Gaulois Mourant* (Dying Gaul), Château de Versailles **Above** Gardens, Château de Versailles

GIVERNY

After viewing Monet's variegated gardens and floating water lilies in Paris' galleries, you can see them in living colour in the flourishing gardens of his former home in the village of Giverny.

The 'Painter of Light' and his family lived at the **Maison de Claude Monet** from 1883 to 1926, during which time he dug a pool, planted a seasonally blooming garden, and constructed the Japanese bridge recreated in many of his paintings (it has since been rebuilt). Entwined with purple wisteria, the footbridge blends into the asymmetrical foreground and background, creating the intimate atmosphere for which Monet was famous.

Yellow daffodils and a rainbow of tulips, rhododendrons, wisteria, irises, poppies and lilies create a spectacle in spring. Nasturtiums, roses and sweet peas blossom in summer, while dahlias, sunflowers and hollyhocks flower in autumn.

The northern part of the property shelters Monet's famous pastel pink-and-green house and the **Atelier des Nymphéas** (Waterlilies Studio), now the home's entrance hall, hung with precise reproductions of his works (though you'll have to head back to Paris to see any originals).

Just 100m northwest of the Maison de Claude Monet, the modern **Musée d'Art Américain** (American Art Museum; www.maag.org; admission €5.50 🕒 10am-6pm, closed Mon Nov-Mar) contains works by many of the American impressionist painters who flocked to France in the late 19th and early 20th centuries.

INFORMATION
Location 76km northwest of Paris
Getting there From Paris' Gare St-Lazare there are two early-morning trains to Vernon (€11.30) from where Transport Val de Seine buses (☎ 02 32 71 06 39; €2.10) depart for Giverny, 7km to the northwest; there's roughly one train an hour back to Paris from 5pm to 9pm
Contact www.fondation-monet.com
Costs Admission €5.50
When to go 🕒 9.30am-6pm Tue-Sun Apr-Oct

CHAMPAGNE

Popping over to the stately city of **Reims**, in the vineyard-ribboned Champagne region, makes a refreshing change from Paris' prevailing day-tripper destinations (Paris Disney, Parc Astérix; and Chartres, Chantilly, Fontainebleau et al).

Easily accessible from Paris thanks to the new TGV, Reims was the site of jubilant celebrations when WWII ended in Europe here. This city of 215,000 residents is graced with pedestrianised streets; illuminating museums including the exceptional Musée des Beaux-Arts; and a stained-glass Gothic cathedral, Cathédrale Notre Dame, whose roof can be climbed.

Moreover, it's where you'll find the region's eponymous sparkling wines. According to French law, only bubbly from the region – grown in designated areas, then aged and bottled in accordance with exacting standards – can be labelled as true champagne.

Eight of Reims' champagne houses and their cellars can be visited on guided tours. Among them are **Mumm** (☎ 03 26 49 59 70; www.mumm.com; 34 rue du Champ de Mars); **Pommery** (☎ 03 26 61 62 55; www.pommery.fr; 5 place du Général Gouraud); and **Taittinger** (☎ 03 26 85 84 33; www.taittinger.com; 9 place St-Niçaise), which occupies 4th-century stone quarries, with sections added in the 13th century by Benedictine monks. Most tours cost about €8 and end, *naturellement,* with a tasting.

INFORMATION

Location 144km northeast of Paris
Getting there From June 2007, the TGV Est Européen line (with fruity-coloured carriage interiors conceived by Christian Lacroix) whisks you to/from Paris's Gare de l'Est in 45 minutes eight times daily; check www.sncf.com or www.tgvesteuropeen.com for times and ticket prices; once in Reims, you can walk to most sights, including champagne houses
Contact www.reims-tourisme.com
Costs Champagne house tours cost about €8
When to go Champagne houses are open year-round, but you need to reserve ahead for tours

Paris' reputation precedes it when it comes to café culture, art and literary scenes, culinary traditions, and classic and cutting-edge fashion. But there's also a host of lesser-known facets of Parisian life to experience. This chapter spotlights Paris' diversity to allow you to tailor your trip to your interests.

> Accommodation	176
> Artistic Paris	178
> Food	180
> Literary Paris	182
> Markets	184
> Panoramas	186
> Romantic Paris	188
> Shopping	190
> Walking	192
> Classical Music & Theatre	194
> Drinking	195
> Gay & Lesbian	196
> Jazz, Chansons & Cabarets	197
> Mondial Paris	198

Place du Tertre (p90), Montmartre

SNAPSHOTS

ACCOMMODATION

The world's most visited city has an extensive array of sleeping options – in theory. In practice, although Paris counts no fewer than 75,000 beds in 1450 establishments, they're often *complet* (full) well in advance. Reservations are recommended at any time of year, and are essential during the high season (Easter to October) and the fashion shows (January to March). If you get stuck, the tourist office (p220) can help find you a room.

Accommodation outside central Paris is marginally cheaper than within the city itself, but it's almost always a false economy. Travelling into the city will eat up precious time and can be expensive. And should there be a transport strike during your trip, you will be hamstrung. Your best bet is to choose somewhere within Paris' 20 arrondissements, where you can experience Parisian life the moment you step out the door.

If you're coming to Paris to kick up your heels, the Marais and Bastille, Montmartre and its surrounds, the Latin Quarter, St-Germain des Prés and Montparnasse, and the Louvre and Les Halles are all in the heart of the action. And if you're coming to shop, you won't go wrong in either these areas or the glamorous Arc de Triomphe, Champs-Élysées and Grands Boulevards precinct. Consider the Invalides and Eiffel Tower area or the Île St-Louis if you're seeking a bit more serenity.

Whichever area you stay in, the city's premium on space and its antiquated – though enchanting – architecture means many Parisian hotel rooms resemble dolls' houses in size.

haystack.lonelyplanet.com

Need a place to stay? Find and book it at lonelyplanet .com. More than 60 properties are featured for Paris – each personally visited, thoroughly reviewed and happily recommended by a Lonely Planet author. From family-run *chambres d'hôtes* (B&Bs) to minimalist design hotels, we've hunted out the places that will bring you unique and special experiences. Read independent reviews by authors and other travel aficionados like you, and get practical information including amenities, maps and photos. Then reserve your room simply and securely via Haystack – our online booking service. It's all at www.lonelyplanet.com/accommodation.

Paris does not have a strong hostelling scene, especially compared with other major European capitals. Info on Paris' HI (Hostelling International) hostels is online at www.fuaj.org; staying at one of these hostels requires a membership card. Under 35s can also try two central hostels run by the **Bureau des Voyages de la Jeunesse** (Youth Travel Bureau; www.bvjhotel .com) near the Louvre and the Latin Quarter.

Websites with online booking services include www.gomio.com, specialising in budget accommodation, and www.hotels-paris.fr. For short-stay apartments, try www.parisattitude.com.

BEST BACKPACKER BEDS
> Young & Happy Hostel (www .youngandhappy.fr)
> Caulaincourt Square Hostel (www .caulaincourt.com)
> Le Montclair Hostel (www.montclair -hostel.com)

BEST SPOTS TO RUB SHOULDERS WITH STARS
> Hôtel Costes (www.hotelcostes.com)
> Hôtel Ritz Paris (www.ritzparis.com)
> Hôtel Bourg Tibourg (www.hotel bourgtibourg.com)
> L'Hôtel (www.l-hotel.com)

BEST DESIGNER DIGS
> Murano Urban Resort (www .muranoresort.com)
> Hôtel du Petit Moulin (www.paris -hotel-petitmoulin.com)
> Hôtel Le A (www.paris-hotel-a.com)
> Kube (www.kubehotel.com)
> Pavillon de Paris (www.pavillonde paris.com)

BEST ISLAND HIDEAWAYS
> Hôtel Henri IV (☎ 01 43 54 44 53)
> Hôtel des Deux Îles (www.deuxiles -paris-hotel.com)
> Hôtel Île St-Louis (www.hotelsaint louis.com)
> Hôtel du Jeu de Paume (www.jeude paumehotel.com)

MOST MAGNIFICENT PALACES
> Fouquet's Barrière Champs-Élysées (www.fouquets-barriere.com)
> Hôtel de Crillon (www.crillon .com)
> Hôtel Plaza Athénée (www.plaza-ath enee-paris.com)

BEST BUDGET BARGAINS
> Hôtel Esmeralda (☎ 01 43 54 19 20)
> Hôtel La Marmotte (☎ 01 40 26 26 54)
> Grand Hôtel du Loiret (hotelduloiret@ hotmail.com)
> Hôtel Eldorado (www.eldorado hotel.fr)

ARTISTIC PARIS

Paris is one of the great art capitals of the world, harbouring treasures from throughout the ages.

An integral part of Parisians' leisure activities is viewing art, and it's something that's fostered by all levels of government. Permanent collections are free at 11 of the 15 *musées municipaux* (city-run museums), though there's a fee for temporary or special exhibitions; see www.paris .fr for details. On top of that, the *musées nationaux* (national museums) are free on the first Sunday of every month, although temporary or special exhibitions also incur a fee; see www.rmn.fr for further info. This commitment to culture ensures art's place in the hearts, minds and eyes of Parisians from childhood onwards, and is one of the underlying reasons for Parisians' appreciation of aesthetics (see p204).

Just as Parisians love art, artists have long loved Paris. A roll call of masters – whose works are displayed in the museums – have painted the City of Light over the centuries.

Art is everywhere in Paris. Parks and public spaces are filled with sculptures. A month-long festival focuses on photography (p28). Metro stations act as de facto galleries. And the lavish *haute couture* shows presented twice yearly by the glamorous fashion houses are arguably more about art than garments.

A thriving artistic culture exists in Montmartre (p88), where artists still set up their easels in squares, and in the ateliers of Belleville and its surrounds (p108). Workshops housing tapestry repairers, engravers and other artisan crafts are found throughout the city, such as in the Viaduc des Arts (p125), while multimedia exhibitions are held at cutting-edge venues. The government has even protected some artist squats, guaranteeing their future as creative spaces – the website www.kisinis.ch/squats has info. And where else but Paris would you find inconceivably specialised museums like the Musée de d'Érotisme (p91), including works by Degas, which elevates erotica to an art form?

See p215 for information on museum passes.

BEST IMPRESSIONIST COLLECTIONS
> Musée de l'Orangerie (p14)
> Musée d'Orsay (p43)
> Musée Marmottan (p55)
> Musée d'Art Américain (p172)

MOST ARTISTIC METRO STATIONS
> Abbesses (Map p89, C4)
> Arts et Métiers (Map pp116–17, C1)
> Bastille (Map pp116–17, E4)
> Louvre Rivoli (Map pp74–5, E5)
> Palais Royal–Musée du Louvre (Map pp74–5, D4)

BEST MODERN & CONTEMPORARY COLLECTIONS
> Musée Picasso (p121)
> Musée National d'Art Moderne (p73)
> Musée d'Art Moderne de la Ville de Paris (p54)
> Dalí Espace Montmartre (p91)

BEST SPECIALITY MUSEUMS
> Musée du Parfum (p55)
> Musée de la Poste (p150)
> Musée de la Publicité (p79)
> Musée du Stylo et de l'Écriture (p55)
> Musée de la Contrefaçon (p55)

Top left Statue and the Eiffel Tower (p39) **Above** Musée Picasso (p121)

SNAPSHOTS

FOOD

Parisians relish talking about, shopping for, preparing and, above all, enjoying food. The city doesn't have its own local cuisine per se, but is the crossroads for the regional produce and flavours of France.
As one of the great gastronomic capitals, Paris creates endless discussion among foodies worldwide.

Paris' latest culinary trends include *bistronomique* (pared-down regional fare by name chefs with pared-down prices), as well as *le fooding*. Combining 'food' and 'feeling' (décor and ambience), this movement has become a thermometer gauging the hottest places to be seen. *Le fooding* has also wittily been referred to as 'con fusion' – *con* being French for a 'fool', to put it politely. However, *le fooding*'s focus on food and atmosphere often results in memorable meals, and it has a strong following among Parisian hipsters.

For the vast majority of Parisians, the skilful combination of fresh ingredients is more important than fads. A meal in Paris is something to be savoured, whether it's *haute cuisine* or a picnic built from the markets. In addition to classical French fare, also look out for cuisines from around the globe (see p198).

Breakfast isn't a priority in Paris – most locals take a chunk of baguette with butter and jam (croissants are usually weekend treats), accompanied by strong black coffee (served espresso-style in a short cup unless you specify otherwise). It's seen as a mere precursor to lunch, which remains the traditional main meal; smaller shops and businesses often close for a couple of hours at this time. Lunch generally starts around 12.30pm with an aperitif, and is almost always washed down with wine.

Restaurants usually serve a plat du jour (dish of the day) or *formule* (fixed main course plus starter or dessert) at lunch (and occasionally at dinner), as well as three- and four-course *menus* (fixed-price meals). The latter offer infinitely better value than ordering à la carte; most include an entrée, *plat* (main course), and *fromage* (cheese) or dessert or both. Many top-end restaurants serve an *amuse-bouche* (complimentary morsel of something very delicious) between the starter and main; some also serve a sweet equivalent before dessert, plus petit fours (bite-sized biscuits or cakes) with coffee.

The North American convention of diners taking away a doggy bag of leftovers is nonexistent here – even if portion sizes permitted it, local culture doesn't.

Most restaurants open for dinner about 7pm or 7.30pm, but don't really get busy until an hour or two later; many serve late into the night. Note that high-end restaurants often close on weekends (unthinkable but true – see p206), and many close during the busy tourist month of August.

Booking ahead (which may just mean popping in to a place that looks appealing as you pass by at lunchtime to make your dinner reservations) is usually a good idea. Popular places, such as *haute cuisine* establishments, should be booked as far ahead as possible – anything from a couple of weeks up to a couple of months.

Good resources for gourmet travellers include specialist bookshop Librairie Gourmande (p158), which stocks a fantastic array of cookbooks. **Edible Paris** (www.edible-paris.com) creates personalised 'food itineraries' and has links for wine courses. For a mouthwatering read, check out the blog *Chocolate & Zucchini* (http://chocolateandzucchini.com).

See p46 for vegetarian info, and p84 for information about dining with kids.

BEST LOCAL BISTROS
> Le Roi du Pot au Feu (p65)
> Le Relais Gascon (p95)
> Le Chansonnier (p109)
> Le Coude Fou (p128)

BEST FINE-DINING EXTRAVAGANZAS
> L'Arpège (p45)
> Alain Ducasse au Plaza Athénée (p63)
> Guy Savoy (p64)
> Pierre Gagnaire (p65)
> Le Grand Véfour (p83)

Top left Marché Belleville (p110)

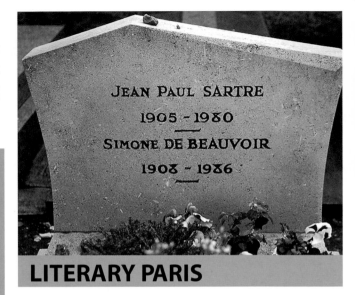

JEAN PAUL SARTRE

1905 ~ 1980

SIMONE DE BEAUVOIR

1908 ~ 1986

LITERARY PARIS

A quick flick through the Parisian street directory reveals that this is a city that takes its literary history seriously. In its index you'll find listings like place Colette, square Charles Dickens, avs Marcel Proust and Emile Zola, and rues Balzac, George-Sand, George Bernard Shaw and Ernest Hemingway. The city has nurtured countless French writers over the centuries, and expat writers who've made the pilgrimage have sealed Paris' literary reputation.

You can leaf through Paris' literary heritage in atmospheric bookshops and libraries, and haggle for bargains at the open-air *bouquiniste* (booksellers) stalls lining the banks of the Seine (see the boxed text, p139). You can hang out in cafés and bars frequented by literary luminaries, visit their former-homes-turned-museums (check www.paris.fr for info), or sleep in hotels where they holed up, such as the Relais Hôtel du Vieux Paris (p177), where William Burroughs and Allen Ginsberg compiled *Naked Lunch*, or L'Hôtel (p177) where Oscar Wilde fought a duel to the death with his wallpaper. And you can pay your respects to Wilde and other departed writers at the city's cemeteries (p146, p90, p20). And we could go on. But as Hemingway wrote in *A Moveable Feast*, 'There is never any ending to Paris.'

Our pick of Paris' English-language bookshops (below) all have details of literary events throughout the year, many of which held at the shops themselves). They also sell stacks of books on Paris' literary connections, including walking tour guides such as Noël Riley Fitch's *Walks in Hemingway's Paris: A Guide to Paris for the Literary Traveler* (1990).

For a reading list of books set in Paris, see p207.

BEST BOOKSHOPS
> Shakespeare & Co (p12)
> Abbey Bookshop (p154)
> Red Wheelbarrow Bookstore (p125)
> Village Voice (p158)

MOST HISTORIC LITERARY CAFÉS
> Les Deux Magots (p166)
> Brasserie Lipp (p164)
> Café de Flore (p165)
> La Closerie des Lilas (p166)

BEST SPOTS TO WORK ON YOUR NOVEL
> Café Panis (p166)
> Le Progrès (p131)
> Le Loir dans la Theiere (p129)

SWISHEST LITERARY BARS
> Bar Hemingway (p66)
> Bar Signature (p164)

Top left Cimetière du Montparnasse (p146) **Above** Secondhand bookshop

MARKETS

Nowhere encapsulates Paris' village atmosphere more than its markets. Nearly every little quarter has its own street market at least once a week, with long trestle tables groaning under the weight of whole roasted chickens, geese and ducks; seafood on beds of crushed ice; freshly killed meat; huge cheese wheels; boiled sweets; whole cakes; sun-ripened fruit and vegetables; and all sorts of other delicacies. Many markets also sell clothes, shoes, baskets and homewares. The markets are more than just places to shop – they're social gatherings for the entire neighbourhood, where residents toting those quintessentially Parisian canvas shopping bags on wheels chat with stallholders and pick up culinary tips.

Marchés biologiques (organic markets) are also sprouting up all over Paris, selling chemical-free produce at its freshest and healthiest, while in the city's more multicultural neighbourhoods, particularly in the northeastern part of the city, market stalls brim with an amazing array of ethnic goods, including exotic fruits and vegetables, and imported herbs and spices (p198).

The website of the Mairie de Paris, www.paris.fr, lists every market in Paris, including opening hours, and you can search the list by arrondissement. The same site also maintains a separate list of Paris' speciality markets, which include bird markets, a stamp market, craft markets, and flower markets filled with buckets of blooms.

Antiques, vintage and retro clothing, jewellery, bric-a-brac, racks of cheap brand-name jeans, denim and leather jackets, footwear, African carvings, woven Rastafarian caps, CDs and electronic items are laid out at the city's fabulous flea markets, which are always buzzing with activity. They're also buzzing with pickpockets – stay alert. It's a good idea to use cash rather than credit cards at the flea markets, as scams are not uncommon. In any case, cash is your best bet for haggling, which is encouraged by flea-market stallholders; there are some genuine bargains to be had.

BEST OPEN-AIR MARKETS
> Marché Bastille (p129)
> Marché Maubert (p162)
> Marché Monge (p162)

BEST COVERED MARKETS
> Marché St-Quentin (p110)
> Marché aux Enfants Rouges (p129)

BEST ORGANIC MARKETS
> Marché Batignolles-Clichy (p96)
> Marché Brancusi (p162)
> Marché Raspail (p162)

BEST FLEA MARKETS
> Marché aux Puces d'Aligre (p124)
> Marché aux Puces de St-Ouen (p92)

SNAPSHOTS

PANORAMAS

Paris is a photographer's dream. Capturing the city on camera is only limited to the size of your memory card or the number of rolls of film in your bags. Along with close-up shots of local street life, there are spectacular vantage points where you can snap vistas of the city – from the top of monuments, on hilltops, in vast squares and on bridges. Even if you don't have a camera, the views are unforgettable.

We've listed our top viewing spots here and throughout this book, but there are many more, and as you stroll around you'll no doubt find your favourite panoramas of Paris.

BEST BUILDINGS WITH A VIEW
> Eiffel Tower (p39)
> Tour Montparnasse (p153)
> Arc de Triomphe (p52)
> Grande Arche (p53)
> Centre Pompidou (p22)

MOST ICONIC CHURCHES WITH A VIEW
> Basilique du Sacré-Cœur (p90)
> Cathédrale de Notre Dame de Paris (p135)
> Église de la Madeleine (p53)

BEST BRIDGES WITH A VIEW
> Pont Neuf (Map pp136–7, B1)
> Pont St-Louis (Map pp136–7, F4)
> Pont des Arts (Map p75, D6)
> Pont Simone de Beauvoir (p154)

BEST PARK WITH A VIEW
> Parc de Belleville (p106)

BEST BALLOON WITH A VIEW
> Ballon Eutelsat (p39)

BEST SQUARE WITH A VIEW
> Place de la Concorde (p56)

BEST TRANSPORT WITH A VIEW
> Boat ride on the Seine (p17)
> Boat trip on the canals (p218)
> Cross-town bus (p214)

BEST DINING ROOMS WITH A VIEW
> Les Ombres (p46)
> La Tour d'Argent (p160)
> Georges (p83)
> Café des Hauteurs (p47)
> Le Jules Verne (p46)

Top left Paris from the Eiffel Tower (p39) **Above** Ballon Eutelsat (p39)

ROMANTIC PARIS

People sometimes wonder if it's worth visiting Paris solo, saying 'But don't you have to be madly in love? Isn't it the perfect setting for romance?'

Paris is so seductive that if you're single or travelling here sans partner, you still can't help but be smitten by the city. Even if you're falling madly *out* of love with someone, it's one of the most memorable places to do it. (Only Paris could make breaking up feel romantic.)

But yes, if you are here and in love, it is the perfect setting. Strolling over the bridges at dusk as the wrought-iron lamps cast a yellow glow on the darkened water, drinking champagne in centuries-old hotel bars or cheap wine in parks and gardens, and dining in bistros with flickering candles will make you feel as if you've stepped into a giant film set, with nonchalant waiters the supporting actors and buskers providing the soundtrack.

Lovers come to Paris for all sorts of reasons, not the least of which is to propose. Proposing in Paris is almost a cliché but, like all good clichés, there's a reason it became a cliché in the first place. Standing in the queue to climb the Eiffel Tower (p10), you'll instantly spot the nervous-looking couples who are likely to come down engaged (unless you're too busy nervously planning or awaiting your own proposal). It has to be said the top viewing platform is tiny and teeming with visitors, making it pretty public if the proposal doesn't go well; if it does, though, you'll have no problems finding someone to take your photo. But even though it's probably more romantic in retrospect than at the time, the iconic tower has an undeniable allure and a proposal here is something you'll never forget.

The best part of Paris' seductiveness is that it isn't contrived – the authenticity of this 'capital of romance' keeps its spark alive. And after your trip's over, you'll always have Paris. Clichéd but true.

BEST PLACES TO PROPOSE (EIFFEL TOWER ASIDE)
> Cathédrale de Notre Dame de Paris (p135)
> Promenade Plantée (p15)
> Arc de Triomphe (p52)
> Jardin des Tuileries (p73)
> Musée Rodin rose garden (p44)

MOST ROMANTIC PLACE TO WATCH THE SUNSET
> Pont St-Louis (Map pp136–7, F4)

BEST ANTIDOTES TO ROMANCE
> Spa treatment at Guerlain (p60)
> *Baba rhum* (rum-drenched brioche) from Stohrer (p84)
> Shopping spree in the Triangle d'Or (p63)

MOST ROMANTIC PLACE TO WATCH THE SUNRISE
> Steps of Basilique du Sacré-Cœur (p90)

Top left Jardin des Tuileries (p73) **Above** Busker on Pont St-Louis

SHOPPING

Paris, like anywhere, has its international chains, but what sets the city apart is its incredible array of specialist shops.

Instead of stocking up at a supermarket, Parisians will buy their bread at a *boulangerie,* their cheese at a *fromagerie,* their meat at a *charcuterie,* and fruit and vegetables at the street-market stalls (p184). It takes longer, but the food is better and fresher, and the social interaction between shopkeepers and regulars helps give Paris its village feel.

It's not only food shops that are specialised. There are shops that sell just hats, others that sell just umbrellas. Even Paris' pampered pooches are in on the act, given that there are shops sell nothing but dog outfits and accessories.

Fashion shopping is Paris' forte. The many luxe labels that originated here are anchored by flagship stores, particularly in the 8e's Triangle d'Or (Golden Triangle), which is bordered by avs Georges V, Champs-Élysées and Montaigne (see p63). Edgier, experimental designers are also a fashion force; rue Étienne Marcel in the 2e (Map pp74–5, G4) and Canal St-Martin (see the boxed text, p103) are fertile ground for up-and-coming talent. Vintage items can be found at Paris' flea markets (p184). Paris' covered arcades are treasure chests of small, exquisite boutiques. These sublime passages – marble-floored, glass-roofed shopping corridors streaming with natural light – were the elegant forerunners to department stores and malls (see p192). The *grande dame* department stores are filled with specialist sections, and are beautiful to wander around.

If you're watching your *centimes*, **Monoprix** (www.monoprix.fr in French) has branches around town selling well-made clothes at low prices and affordable gourmet goods.

Because of Paris' villagelike layout, shopping spreads throughout the city's quarters, and Parisians will cross town for a *bonne adresse* (good address). A number of enticing streets specialise almost exclusively in just one product. Head to rue des Sts-Pères (Map pp144–5, C1) for silk and lace underwear; rue de Paradis (Map pp104–5, B3) for crystal, glass and tableware; rue Drouot (Map pp50–1, H3) for collectable postage stamps; rue du Pont Louis Phillipe (Map pp116–17, C3) for stationery and fine paper; and rue Keller (Map pp116–17, F4) for comic books, mangas and DVDs. Similarly, rue Martel (Map pp104–5, B4) specialises in sewing machines and rue Victor Massé (Map p89, C5) specialises in musical instruments.

What's somewhat ironic for a city so dedicated to shopping is that Paris doesn't have a consumer culture as such. Shopping here is about quality, first and foremost, rather than status or acquisition. Coupled with the fact that almost all shops close at least one or two days a week, shopping itself is a luxury.

MOST LAVISH DEPARTMENT STORES
> Le Bon Marché (p156)
> Galeries Lafayette (p60)
> Le Printemps (p62)

BEST BOUTIQUES
> Colette (p79)
> Antoine et Lili (p122)
> Les Belles Images (p124)
> Shine (p125)

Top left Window display at Le Printemps (p62) **Above** Antoine et Lili (p122)

WALKING

The single-best way to acquaint yourself with any city is walking, or in Paris' case, *flâneurie*. Writer Charles Baudelaire (1821–67) came up with the whimsical term *flâneur* to describe a 'gentleman stroller of city streets' or a 'detached pedestrian observer of a metropolis' (the metropolis being Baudelaire's native Paris). The word is now widely used, especially in the context of architecture and town planning, but Paris, with its backstreets, riverbank paths, green spaces and ornate arcades, remains the ultimate place for a *flâneur* to meander without any particular destination in mind.

The arcades first appeared in the 1820s, numbering 150 by the mid-19th century. Walter Benjamin scrutinised the passages as he walked them from 1927 to 1940. In his resulting work *The Arcades Project,* which is tied to the concept of *flâneurie,* he reflects on these exquisite 'cities in miniature' to critique everyday Parisian life, including cafés, collecting, commodity fetishism, fashion, window displays, advertising, architecture, photography, panoramas, prostitution and progress. (You shudder to think what Benjamin would have made of the Forum des Halles.) Today, the 18 remaining passages provide a fascinating history lesson, as well as unique shopping.

Paris' elegantly laid-out gardens are idyllic for strolling, with plenty of benches as well as kiosks and cafés. Recent innovations include the fantastical Parc de la Villette (p107) and the disused-railway-viaduct-turned-walking-path, the Promenade Plantée (p15). Further out, the

Bois de Boulogne (p57), on the western edge of Paris, and the Bois de Vincennes (p122), on the eastern edge, are easily reached by metro. Or you can amble in the hi-tech urban environment of La Défense (p53), which incorporates walking paths, sculptures and art.

And the quarters' backstreets are enthralling to explore for as little or as much time as you have.

See p219 for organised walking tours of the city.

BEST COVERED PASSAGES
> Galerie Vivienne (p61)
> Passage des Panoramas (p61)
> Passage du Grand Cerf (p61)
> Passage Jouffroy and Passage Verdeau (p61)
> Galerie Véro Dodat (p80)

BEST QUARTERS TO GET LOST IN
> Montmartre (p88)
> Marais and Bastille (p114)
> Latin Quarter, St-Germain des Prés and Montparnasse (p142)

Top left Street scene, Marais (p114) **Above** Galerie Véro Dodat (p80)

SNAPSHOTS

CLASSICAL MUSIC & THEATRE

With performances by the world's finest artists and boasting historic – even legendary – venues, Paris is an absolute treat for concert and theatre audiences.

Paris is the premier place to catch world-class French and international opera and ballet companies in some virtuoso venues, while (if your French is up to it) there's also a host of theatre productions playing throughout the year around town.

In addition to the classics, Paris is a hotbed of creativity and fringe art, and on any given day there are innumerable local performances and productions, which are often very avant-garde. Paris' centuries-old stone churches have magnificent acoustics and are a compelling setting to take in a classical concert. Posters outside churches advertise upcoming events with ticket information, or you can check www.ampconcerts.com.

The 'What's On' section of www.parisinfo.com is searchable by date and is a good source of info when you're planning your trip. See p23 for details of listings publications available for sale in Paris. See p215 for ticket outlets.

TOP OPERA VENUES
> Palais Garnier (pictured right; p71)
> Opéra Bastille (p133)

MOST ATMOSPHERIC CHURCHES FOR CLASSICAL CONCERTS
> Ste-Chapelle (p139)
> Église de la Madeleine (p53)

DRINKING

Paris' atmospheric cafés are the city's communal lounge rooms: places to meet friends, read, write, philosophise, flirt and fall in love. As such, they've played a central role in the city's history over the centuries, particularly its philosophy and literature. See p183 for some of the most celebrated literary haunts.

For the French, drinking and eating go together like wine and cheese, and the line between what constitutes a café, a bistro, a brasserie and a bar is blurred. Watering holes come in all shapes and sizes, from lavish establishments inside palatial hotels (with prices to match) to supersleek holes-in-the-wall. All usually serve at least light meals (sometimes full menus), and it's fine to order a coffee or alcohol if you're not dining.

If you're craving a cuppa, there are also some charming *salons de thé* (tearooms) that serve hot chocolate and cakes as well as tea, a beverage that is gaining ground in this city of coffee drinkers. For a mint tea and Turkish water pipe, the mosaic-tiled courtyard of the Mosquée (pictured below; p149) is sheer bliss.

Many of Paris' drinking establishments have a tiered pricing structure that depends on where you sit, with the coveted seats on the terraces more expensive than perching at the counter.

Websites such as www.paris-on-line.com and www.parispubs.com list drinking venues citywide.

BEST LOCAL CAFÉS
> Le Tambour (p85)
> Les Deux Moulins (p97)
> Café Le Refuge (p96)
> Drôle d'Endroit pour une Rencontre (p97)
> L'Atmosphère (p111)

SLICKEST BARS
> Kong (p84)
> Andy Wahloo (p130)
> Curieux Spaghetti Bar (p130)
> China Club (p133)
> Le Bastille (p133)

V

SNAPSHOTS

GAY & LESBIAN

The city known as 'gay Paree' lives up to its name. Paris became the first European capital to vote in an openly gay mayor when Bertrand Delanoë was elected in 2001, and the city itself is very open – it's common to see same-sex couples displaying affection publicly. Gay couples are also unlikely to experience any problems when checking into a double hotel room.

In fact, Paris is so open that there's less of a defined 'scene' here than in cities where it is more underground. As one traveller told us after his recent trip: 'It was hard to tell where gay Paris ended and straight Paris started – everyone's so stylish and sexy. I found a gay café which was packed and had devastatingly cute staff. But once again, I could be mistaken – it might not actually be gay at all.'

The Marais (pictured below; p114) – particularly around the intersection of rue Ste-Croix de la Bretonnerie and rue des Archives, and eastwards to rue Vieille du Temple – is the mainstay of gay and lesbian Parisian nightlife. But you'll find venues right throughout the city, which all increasingly attract a mixed straight and gay crowd.

Gay pride peaks during the city's annual Gay Pride March (p25), which has over-the-top floats, costumes and festivities.

Check out www.actupparis.org, www.petitfute.com/petitfutegay (in French), www.tetu.com (in French) and www.cglparis.org for gay and lesbian internet resources.

BEST GAY & LESBIAN BOOKSHOP
> Le Mots à la Bouche (p124)

BEST GAY BARS & CLUBS
> Le Quetzal (p131)
> Open Café (p132)
> Le Queen (p70)

BEST LESBIAN BARS & CLUBS
> Le Pulp (p70)
> 3W Kafé (p130)

JAZZ, CHANSONS & CABARETS

Catching a jazz or *chanson* session or a show-stopping cabaret will leave you in little doubt that you're in Paris.

Paris has some fantastically atmospheric jazz clubs. Though habitually dark and smoky, by law all will soon be smoke free (p219). Jazz greats have long flocked here, playing alongside local musos, and the city remains a standout on the international scene. During June and July, free jazz concerts are held on Saturday and Sunday in parks across the city during the Paris Jazz Festival; see www.parcfloraldeparis.com for further details.

While *chanson* literally means 'song' in French, it also specifically refers to a style of heartfelt, lyric-driven music typified by Édith Piaf, Maurice Chevalier, Charles Aznavour et al. You'll come across some stirring live covers of their most famous songs, plus contemporary twists on the genre such as the fusion of dance beats with traditional *chanson* melodies.

The cabarets' whirling lines of feather boa–clad, high-kicking dancers are a quintessential fixture on Paris' entertainment scene – for everyone but Parisians. Still, the dazzling sets, costumes and dancing (and champagne) guarantee an entertaining evening. The most legendary, especially since its big-screen revival (see p208), is the can-can creator, the Moulin Rouge (p101). Cabaret tickets start from €40 for a performance, or from €100 with dinner.

For info on tickets, see p215.

BEST JAZZ CLUBS
> Le Duc des Lombards (p87)
> Sunset & Sunside (p87)
> New Morning (p113)

BEST CHANSONS VENUES
> Chez Louisette (p99)
> Le Vieux Belleville (p113)
> Au Lapin Agile (p99)
> Le Limonaire (p69)

MONDIAL PARIS

Paris might be very French, but these days that definition incorporates the myriad nationalities that call this cosmopolitan city home.

Unlike France's second-largest metropolis, Marseille, where residents of all backgrounds mix throughout the entire city, Paris has specific quarters that are vibrant hubs of cultural life. Visiting the grocery stores, delis, markets, shops and places of worship in these areas is like taking a mini world tour.

Around metro stations La Chapelle (Map pp104–5, C2) and Château d'Eau (Map pp104–5, C4) in the 10e you'll find a concentration of Indian, Pakistani and Turkish communities. The largest Chinatown district (p154) is in the 13e, with an amazing array of establishments including vast supermarkets selling goods from Thailand, Vietnam, Japan and more, in addition to products from China. In the Marais, the area around rue des Rosiers (Map pp116–17, C3) is the heart of Jewish life in central Paris. North African–Jewish restaurants and Sephardic kosher shops also cluster just south of the Cadet metro stop (Map p89, D6) in the 9e. And the area around metro stations Château Rouge and Barbès Rochechouart (Map pp104–5, B2) in the 18e is the colourful North African quarter.

See p206 for background info on Paris' multicultural make up.

BEST MULTICULTURAL MARKETS
> Marché Belleville (p110)
> Marché Beauvau (p129)
> Marché aux Enfants Rouges (p129)

BEST MONDIAL MUSEUMS
> Musée du Quai Branly (p44)
> Institut du Monde Arabe (p147)
> Musée d'Art et d'Histoire du Judaïsme(p120)

Place de la Concorde (p56)

BACKGROUND

HISTORY

Several influential eras are woven into Paris' contemporary fabric: magnificent stained-glass cathedrals and palaces were created from the 11th century onwards; Baron Haussmann's 'renovation' of the medieval city's disease-ridden streets in the late 19th century demolished more than 20,000 homes, making way for wide boulevards lined by over 40,000 new apartments; and the turn of the 20th century ushered in many of the city's signature sights, including the ornate art nouveau brasseries and wrought-iron metro signs. Through it all, political rebellion has remained a constant theme.

Paris' history is unravelled at the Musée Carnavalet (p119).

PRE-20TH CENTURY HISTORY

Paris was born in the 3rd century BC, when a tribe of Celtic Gauls known as the Parisii settled on what is now the Île de la Cité. Centuries of conflict between the Gauls and Romans ended in 52 BC, when Julius Caesar's legions crushed a Celtic revolt. Christianity was introduced in the 2nd century AD, and Roman rule ended in the 5th century with the arrival of the Germanic Franks. In 508 Frankish king Clovis I united Gaul and made Paris his seat.

France's west coast was beset in the 9th century by Scandinavian Vikings (also known as Norsemen and, later, as Normans) who, three centuries later, started pushing towards Paris, which had risen rapidly in importance; construction began on the cathedral of Notre Dame in the 12th century, the Louvre began life as a riverside fortress around 1200, the beautiful Ste-Chapelle was consecrated in 1248 and the Sorbonne opened its doors in 1253. The Vikings' incursions heralded the Hundred Years' War between Norman England and Paris' Capetian dynasty, bringing the French defeat at Agincourt in 1415 and English control of the capital in 1420. In 1429 the 17-year-old Jeanne d'Arc (Joan of Arc) rallied the French troops to defeat the English at Orléans. With the exception of Calais, the English were eventually expelled from France in 1453.

The Renaissance helped Paris get back on its feet at the end of the 15th century. Less than a century later, however, Paris was again in turmoil, as clashes between Huguenot (Protestant) and Catholic groups increased, culminating in the St Bartholomew's Day massacre in 1572, in which 3000 Huguenots died.

A five-year-old Louis XIV ascended the throne in 1643 and ruled until 1715, virtually emptying the national coffers with his ambitious battling and building, including his extravagant palace at Versailles (p170). The excesses of the grandiose king and his heirs helped lead to an uprising of Parisians on 14 July 1789, kick-starting the French Revolution. Within four years, the so-called Reign of Terror was in full swing.

The unstable postrevolutionary government was consolidated in 1799 under Napoleon Bonaparte, who declared himself first consul. In 1804 he had the Pope crown him emperor of the French, going on to conquer most of Europe before he was eventually defeated at Waterloo in Belgium in 1815. He was exiled and died in 1821.

France struggled under a string of mostly inept rulers until a coup d'état in 1851 brought Emperor Napoleon III to power. At his behest, Baron Haussmann modernised Paris, razing whole tracts of the city and replacing them with sculptured parks, a hygienic sewer system and – strategically – boulevards too broad for rebels to barricade. Napoleon III embroiled France in a costly war with Prussia in 1870, which ended within months with the defeat of the French army and the capture of the emperor. When the masses in Paris heard the news, they took to the streets, demanding that a republic be declared.

Despite its bloody beginnings, the Third Republic gave rise to the glittering creative period known as the *belle époque* (beautiful era), celebrated for its graceful art nouveau architecture and the advances made in the arts and sciences.

MODERN HISTORY

Out of WWI's conflict came increased industrialisation, confirming Paris' place as a major commercial centre; its *belle époque*–inspired arts scene likewise endured. By the 1930s Paris had become a centre for the artistic avant-garde and had established its reputation among freethinking intellectuals. This was halted by WWII and the Nazi occupation of 1940; Paris would remain under direct German rule until 25 August 1944. After the war, Paris regained its position as a creative centre and nurtured a revitalised liberalism that reached a climax with the student-led uprisings of May 1968 – the Sorbonne was occupied, the Latin Quarter blockaded, and some nine million people nationwide joined a general strike that paralysed the country.

Avant-garde additions to the city's architecture in the latter half of the 20th century came as the result of French presidents' bold *grands projets* or *grands travaux* (great projects or works). President Georges Pompidou's Centre Pompidou, constructed between 1971 and 1977, caused an outcry when it was unveiled, while during the 1980s, President François Mitterrand oversaw a slew of *projets*, all of them costly and most with at least some teething problems. In mid-1995, the presidential baton passed to the right wing with the election of President Jacques Chirac; his pet *projet,* the Musée Quai Branly, opened in June 2006.

The late 1990s saw Paris seize the international spotlight with the rumour-plagued death of Princess Di in 1997, and France's first-ever World Cup victory in July 1998. (Fast-forwarding to 2006, France loses the World Cup final to Italy on penalties after French captain Zinadine Zidane is sent off in the dying moments of the match for head-butting Italian Marco Materazzi.)

In 1997, Chirac's political party lost the parliamentary elections to a coalition of Socialists, Communists and Greens headed by Lionel Jospin, forcing Chirac to work with an opposition prime minister and cabinet. In the 2002 presidential elections, far-right leader Jean-Marie Le Pen was highly successful in the first round of the elections, knocking Jospin out of the race due to a low voter turnout. Extensive protests ensued, with scores of thousands of Parisians marching through the Marais to the Bastille. But ironically, with the left-wing Jospin out of the running, socialist voters who 'forgot' to vote now faced a choice between the right-wing Chirac and the extreme-right-wing Le Pen. A subsequent strong show of support for Chirac gave him a landslide victory.

In May 2001 Bertrand Delanoë, a Socialist with support from the Green Party, was elected mayor. He has enjoyed widespread popularity, particularly for his efforts to make Paris more liveable through better infrastructure and more green spaces.

RECENT HISTORY

Chirac named Dominique de Villepin (a Moroccan-born, South American–raised career diplomat and published poet) as prime minister in May 2005, following the resignation of Jean-Pierre Raffarin from the post. In October the same year, the deaths of two teenagers who were accidentally electrocuted while allegedly hiding from police in an electricity substation in Clichy-sous-Bois sparked riots that quickly spread across other regions of Paris, and then across France.

Consequently, the government promised to address the disenfranchisement felt by large numbers of unemployed French youth, but one of Villepin's first efforts – the introduction of two-year work contracts for workers under 26 years of age – was met by street protests of up to three million people and transport strikes by sympathetic unions around the country, sparking comparisons with May '68. This crippling crisis was averted when Chirac (backed by a reputed 70% of the French public) overrode Villepin, denouncing the controversial plan and scrapping the week-old law.

This left Villepin on shaky ground in the run-up to the presidential elections. At the time of writing, with Chirac expected to retire, he remains a contender; though he faces stiff opposition from other key political figures.

Parisian history seems set to remain colourful. Stay tuned...

LIFE AS A PARISIAN

A fresh-off-the-plane traveller once exclaimed to us, with a startling lack of irony, 'Wow – Paris is so French!'

But the thing is, he's right. It is.

Paris is defined by its walls (that is, the *Périphérique*, or ring road), the interior of which spans 105 sq metres. *Intra-muros* (Latin for 'within the walls'), the city has a population of 2.144 million, while the greater metropolitan area – the Île de France *région,* encircled by rivers – has 11.3 million inhabitants, or about 18.5% of France's total population of 60.7 million. This makes Paris – the capital of both the *région* and the country – in effect an 'island within an island' (or, as residents of other regions might say, a bubble).

In this highly centralised country, Paris is the principal place where the national identity is defined and embraced.

VILLAGE LIVING

Paris' large inner-city population is a defining feature of the city. Paris is not merely a place of business and commerce; instead, its shops, street markets, parks and other facets of day-to-day living evoke a village atmosphere, and its lack of high-rises gives it a human scale.

France's bureau of statistics places single-occupant dwellings at more than half of the total number of households in central Paris. On top of this, residential apartments are often tiny. As a result, communal spaces such as parks, cafés and restaurants are the living and dining rooms and backyards of many Parisians. Most residents shop at a series of small neighbourhood shops, each with its own speciality (see p190), and this ritual is an important part of Parisians daily life.

The high concentration of city dwellers means that most bars and cafés close around 2am, due to noise restrictions, and nightclubs in the inner city are few.

It also explains why so many domestic dogs (some 200,000) live in Paris – and why there's so much dirt on the streets. However, the days when dog owners wouldn't deign to clean up are fading into the past (boosted by the introduction of hefty fines), and the pavements are the cleanest they've ever been. Still, watch your step.

WALKING THE WALK

Parisians have a highly developed sense of aesthetics, and take immeasurable care in the presentation of everything from food to fashion to their private and public domains. This extends to personal presentation on the streets – you will never see a Parisian leave their apartment with just-out-of-the-shower wet hair or wearing running shoes with a business suit. Rarely will you see a Parisian in shorts (save for on a football pitch). For both men and women, wearing shorts or tying a jumper around the waist (rather than the shoulders) mark the wearer out as a tourist as surely as an unfolded map and a camera.

There is an underpinning sense of obligation to look good out of respect for fellow city-dwellers and the city's overall aesthetics. Sarah Turnbull's bestseller *Almost French* (p207) describes her French husband-to-be's horror as she's about to nip out for a baguette in her *pantalons de jogging* (tracksuit pants); he tells her 'But it's not nice for the baker!' And as one international photographer commented when asked how she managed to find the time to dress fashionably while living out of suitcases on shoots, 'I'm Parisian – I *make* the time.'

Smart casual is a fail-safe form of dress, but it's nearly impossible to overdress in this fashion-conscious city, which at times looks and feels like a giant catwalk.

TALKING THE TALK

Etiquette – itself a French word – is extremely important in Paris, which is central to understanding how the city and its residents operate.

It's customary to greet anyone you interact with, such as a shopkeeper, with '*Bonjour Madame/Monsieur*'. Substitute *bonjour* (good day) for *bonsoir* (good evening) once the sun goes down. Similarly, when leaving, conclude with '*Au revoir Madame/Monsieur*' (increasingly, though, *bonjour/au revoir* alone suffices). Particularly in smaller shops, shopkeepers may not appreciate you touching the merchandise until they invite you to do so.

People who know each other well greet one another with *bises* (kisses on the cheek). The usual ritual is one glancing peck on each cheek (starting with the left), but some people go for three or even four kisses. Parisians who don't kiss each other will almost always shake hands when meeting. People always stand up when meeting one another for the first time, including women with women.

An important distinction is made in French between *tu* and *vous,* which both mean 'you'. *Tu* is only used when addressing people you know very well, children or animals. When addressing an adult who is not a personal friend, *vous* should always be used until the person invites you to use *tu*. In general, younger people insist less on this distinction, and they may use *tu* from the beginning of an acquaintance (but never with an elder). If this sounds confusing, take heart that French people can often find it hard to distinguish when to use *tu* and *vous,* too. In fact, it is even more confusing in today's society as communication becomes more informal overall. If in doubt, use *vous*.

Conversations between locals often revolve around philosophy, art and other intellectual and artistic pursuits, as well as sports such as rugby, football, cycling and tennis. Talking about money (salaries, for example) is generally avoided in public.

Although English is increasingly spoken in Paris, and non-French speakers will have few-to-no problems (see the boxed text, below), you will earn infinitely greater respect by addressing locals in French, even if the only thing you muster up is '*Parlez-vous anglais*?' (Do you speak English?).

PARLEZ-VOUS FRANÇAIS?

Parisians have long had a reputation for being unable or unwilling to speak English, but this has changed dramatically in recent years, particularly since the internet became commonplace. Street signs, menus, establishment names (such as Spoon, Food & Wine) and buzz words (such as *le fooding;* see p180) incorporate ever more English. Indeed, if you've come here to practise your French, you may find little opportunity to use it. On detecting an accent, Parisians will often automatically switch to English to facilitate conversation. Feel free to say if you prefer to converse in French.

Think of it the same way as you would a stranger addressing you in a foreign language in your home country. Many times, what is mistaken for (mythical) Parisian arrogance is the result of foreigners bypassing this basic courtesy.

WORKING TO LIVE
By and large, the French work to live rather than live to work.

In January 2000 a 35-hour working week became part of French law. It was introduced with the aim of creating jobs and lowering unemployment, and its success or otherwise is the subject of much debate, but it is also a key part of the Parisian tempo. Hence, many businesses will shut the doors on the dot of closing time, if not a few minutes before.

Les anglais (the French term for anyone from the English-speaking world, including the United States, Australia and so on) are often shocked to find that most shops and services shut on Sundays (some on Saturday afternoons, too). The upside is that without the impetus to make and spend money 24/7/365, friends, family and leisure activities are all much more important than in many other Western countries. If you're here on a Sunday, you won't find yourself short of things to do, with museums, galleries and markets attracting plenty of Parisians and visitors alike (see p33).

In addition to weekly closures and long annual leave (which for Parisians might be anything up to nine weeks), France is blessed with a *lot* of public holidays, when shops and services generally shut (see p216).

MULTICULTURAL PARIS
The city is an exhilarating mix of dozens of different ethnicities. France has experienced waves of immigration for centuries and, in particular, has received a large number of immigrants from its former colonies since the middle of last century. The number of official immigrants in central Paris is just under 400,000 or 18.5% of the city's population; the figure would be much higher – possibly four times that number – if the number of those living clandestinely and in the greater metropolitan region was known. Of these official immigrants, 29% come from a North African country, 28% come from EU countries, 15% from Sub-Saharan Africa, 17% from Asia and 7% from other countries.

This influx of immigrants over the years has changed Parisian's tastes in many things – in recent years ethnic food has become as Parisian as onion soup.

Like anywhere, unfortunately, racism does rear its ugly head, and the incidences of racist acts of violence have been high in recent years, particularly in the crowded suburbs. The news is not all bleak though. As one French-Tunisian web designer pointed out, '...then you see the French team in the World Cup – it's multicoloured and it advanced a lot more because of that, more than if there had been only been one ethnic community of French people playing.'

To discover multicultural Paris, see p198.

FURTHER READING

This capital of romance and culture has inspired endless literature over the centuries.

A Moveable Feast (Ernest Hemingway; 1964) Witty, wry work recalling the author's early writing career in 1920s Paris – a lifestyle that expat writers continue to emulate.

Almost French: A New Life in Paris (Sarah Turnbull; 2003) An unpretentious insight into the Parisian psyche. Australian journalist Turnbull meets and marries a Parisian and struggles over the course of eight years to adapt to the city's unwritten social rules.

Down and Out in Paris and London (George Orwell; 1933) Eric Blair's (aka Orwell) first published book is a gloriously gritty account of early-20th-century Paris; it recounts his days as a downtrodden dishwasher in the bowels of a Parisian hotel.

The Flâneur: A Stroll Through the Paradoxes of Paris (Edmund White; 2001) A small, absorbing collection of random observations from American novelist White as he ambles Paris' quarters, musing on the city's Jewish history, gay community, literary luminaries and jazz heritage.

Les Misérables (Victor Hugo; 1862) Epic novel adapted to the stage and screen that traces 20 years in the life of convict Jean Valjean through the battles and barricades of early-19th-century Paris.

Life: A User's Manual (Georges Perec; 1978) Intricately structured novel by French writer Perec distilling Parisian life through the parade of characters inhabiting a 10-storey apartment block between 1833 and 1975.

Perfume: The Story of a Murderer (Patrick Süskind; 1985) Protagonist Jean-Baptiste Grenouille is born in the fish-market filth of 18th-century Paris with an uncanny olfactory gift, and goes on to become a macabre perfume creator. *Perfume* was made into a film in 2006.

The Phantom of the Opera (Gaston Leroux; 1910) The basis for the longest-running Broadway musical in history, this dark novel evokes the ghostlike figure who lurks in the Garnier opera house.

Satori in Paris (Jack Kerouac; 1966) Frenetic novella based on Kerouac's whirlwind foray to France to discover his roots and the source of his *satori* (sudden awakening).

This is Paris (Miroslav Sasek; 1959) A delight for nostalgia buffs, this iconic 'children's guidebook' was re-released in 2004 with its illustrations and text intact, and a little list of updates at the back.

FILMS

Paris is at least as much a star as the actors who compete with it on the big screen.

À Bout de Souffle (Breathless; 1960) Filmed with hand-held cameras, this new wave film about a car thief who kills a policeman revolutionised cinema in its day.

Before Sunset (2004) This arthouse Academy Award–nominated sequel to 1995's *Before Sunrise* was cowritten by leads Ethan Hawke and Julie Delpy, and follows the star-crossed lovers on a stroll around Paris. See p132 for shooting locations.

The Bourne Identity (2002) Featuring Matt Damon as an amnesiac government-agent-turned-target, this fast-moving action flick twists and turns against a fabulous Parisian backdrop.

The Da Vinci Code (2006) There's no avoiding da code (unfortunately), but the Parisian setting is the sole redeeming aspect of this blockbuster based on Dan Brown's ubiquitous novel of the same name.

Frantic (1988) Stylish thriller set in and around the city's seedier quarters. It sees Harrison Ford enlist the help of a feisty Emmanuelle Seigner to help him track down his kidnapped wife.

Last Tango in Paris (1972) Marlon Brando steams up the screen as a US businessman embroiled in a sordid, sexually charged affair with a young Parisian woman.

Le Fabuleux Destin d'Amélie Poulain (*Amélie;* 2001) Quirky contemporary fable about a Montmartre café waitress (Audrey Tautou); director Jean-Pierre Jeunet saturates the film with the colours red and green to create a dreamlike quality, enhanced by an emotive soundtrack.

Les Amants du Pont-Neuf (1991) Haunting romance between two young homeless Parisians, set against the backdrop of the city's oldest bridge.

Moulin Rouge (2001) Although shot at Fox's Sydney studios, this all-singing, all-dancing spectacular starring Nicole Kidman and Ewan McGregor epitomises Toulouse-Lautrec's turn-of-the-20th-century Montmartre.

Paris je t'aime (2006) A roll call of the film industry contributes to this ensemble of 18 five-minute films about finding love in Paris' *arrondissements* (all 20 *arrondissements* were originally slated to appear). Wes Craven, the Cohen brothers and Gus Van Sant are among the directors who team with actors including Elijah Wood, Natalie Portman, Nick Nolte, Gérard Depardieu, Willem Dafoe, Juliette Binoche and Miranda Richardson.

DIRECTORY
TRANSPORT
ARRIVAL & DEPARTURE
AIR

Almost all international airlines call into Paris. The Aéroports de Paris website (www.adp.fr) has information on flights, routes and carriers.

Paris' two major international airports, Aéroport Roissy Charles de Gaulle and the smaller Aéroport d'Orly, both have numerous options for travelling to/from central Paris; we've listed the most expedient.

Further out, Paris-Beauvais handles charter and budget carriers including Ryanair, and is served by buses.

Aéroport Roissy Charles de Gaulle

Paris' largest international airport, **Charles de Gaulle** (☎ 01 48 62 22 80 in English; www.adp.fr), is 30km northeast of the city centre in the suburb of Roissy. A free *navette* (shuttle bus) runs every six minutes between its two main terminals, CDG1 and CDG2.

Train

Both terminals are served by Rois-syRail on RER line B3. Trains leave every 15 minutes from 5.30am to midnight (€8.10 one way) and take 40 minutes to the centre of Paris.

Bus

Air France bus (☎ 08 92 35 08 20; www .cars-airfrance.com in French) Runs services to several locations in central Paris.
Noctilien Night bus (☎ 08 92 68 77 14, 08 92 68 41 14 in English; tickets €7) Buses run every hour from 12.30am to 5.30am; Bus 121 goes to Montparnasse, Châtelet, Gare du Nord; Bus 140 goes to Gare du Nord and Gare de l'Est.
Roissybus (☎ 08 92 68 77 14; one-way €8.40) Links the airport with rue Scribe, Place de l'Opéra (Map pp50–1, G3). Buses take 45 minutes and run from 5.45am to 11pm.

CLIMATE CHANGE & TRAVEL

Travel – especially air travel – is a significant contributor to global climate change. At Lonely Planet, we believe that all who travel have a responsibility to limit their personal impact. As a result, we have teamed with Rough Guides and other concerned industry partners to support Climate Care, which allows people to offset the greenhouse gases they are responsible for with contributions to energy-saving projects and other climate-friendly initiatives in the developing world. Lonely Planet offsets all staff and author travel.

For more information, turn to the responsible travel pages on www.lonelyplanet .com. For details on offsetting your carbon emissions and a carbon calculator, go to www .climatecare.org.

Shuttle Bus

Prebook for private door-to-door shuttles such as **Paris Airports Service** (☎ 01 49 62 78 78; single/2-plus passengers per person €26/17); allow time for numerous pick-ups and drop-offs.

Taxi

The tariff to the city is €40 to €55. The journey takes 30 to 50 minutes, depending on traffic.

Aéroport d'Orly

Situated 18km south of the city centre, **Orly** (☎ 01 49 75 15 15; www .adp.fr) has two terminals – Ouest (West; mainly domestic flights) and Sud (South; mainly international flights), linked by the free Orlyval shuttle train.

Train

The **Orlyval shuttle train** (☎ 08 92 68 77 14; one-way €9.05) links Orly with RER line B at Antony (eight minutes), at least every seven minutes from 6am to 11pm. From Antony it's a 35-minute trip to central Paris.

Bus

Noctilien Night bus (☎ 08 92 68 77 14, 08 92 68 41 14 in English; tickets €5.60) Bus 31 runs every hour from 12.30am to 5.30am, linking Gare de Lyon, Place d'Italie and Gare d'Austerlitz with Orly-Sud.
Orlybus (☎ 08 92 68 77 14; one-way €5.80) Links Place Denfert Rochereau, 14e with the airport. Buses take 30 minutes; buses run every 15 to 20 minutes from 6am to 11.30pm from

Orly to the airport, from 5.35am to 11pm from the airport to Orly.

Shuttle Bus

Take **Air France Bus No 1** (☎ 08 92 35 08 20; one-way/return €8/12) from the airport to the eastern side of Gare Montparnasse (Map pp144–5, B5), and Aérogare des Invalides (Map pp40–1, F1). Buses takes 30 to 45 minutes, and run every 15 minutes from 6am to 11pm.

See left for details of door-to-door services.

Taxi

The tariff to the city is €40 to €45 (depending on time of day). The journey takes upwards of 30 minutes.

Aéroport Paris-Beauvais

Located 80km north of Paris, **Paris-Beauvais** (☎ 03 44 11 46 86, general inquiries 08 92 68 20 64; www.aeroport beauvais.com) is used by charter companies and Ryanair.

Bus

Express services leave the airport about 20 to 30 minutes after each flight arrival, from 5.45am to 7.15pm, and drop passengers on Paris' place de la Porte Maillot (Map pp50–1, A2). Buses leave Paris for the airport three hours and 15 minutes before flight departure at **Parking Pershing** (Map pp50-1, A1; 1 blvd Pershing, 17e; Ⓜ Porte Maillot).

AIR TRAVEL ALTERNATIVES

To save the environment (and, often, save time and/or costs too), alternatives to air travel include the following:

Bus See right for international bus information.

Ferry Boats to/from destinations including Ireland and England serve the French coast, from where you can connect to Paris; info-packed www.seat61 .com has ferry info.

Train The Eurostar (right) is a stellar option for crossing the Channel. Within mainland Europe, long-haul trains converge on Paris. Check www.seat61 .com for advice.

Tickets for the 75-minute trip (€13 one way) can be purchased (cash only) from **Ryanair** (☎ 03 44 11 41 41) at the airport or a kiosk in the parking lot; or online at ticket .aeroportbeauvais.com.

Taxi

Between the city and Beauvais, taxis cost from €110 (day) and €150 (night and all day Sunday) – probably more than the cost of your flight.

TRAIN

Paris has six stations for long-distance trains, each with its own metro station: Gare d'Austerlitz (Map pp144–5, H5), Gare de l'Est (Map pp104–5, C3), Gare de Lyon

(Map pp116–17, F6), Gare du Nord (Map pp104–5, C3), Gare Montparnasse (Map pp144–5, B5) and Gare St-Lazare (Map pp50–1, F2). Contact **SNCF** (Société Nationale des Chemins de Fer; ☎ 08 92 35 35 35; www.sncf.com) for information.

The highly civilised **Eurostar** (☎ 08 36 35 35 39, UK 09 90 186 186; www.eurostar.com) whisks you between Paris' Gare du Nord and London's Waterloo Station in two hours, 35 minutes.

Thalys (www.thalys.com) links Paris' Gare du Nord to Brussels-Midi, Amsterdam CS and Cologne's Hauptbahnhof.

BUS

Eurolines (Map pp144-5, E3; ☎ 01 43 54 11 99, 08 92 89 90 91; www.eurolines .com; 55 rue St-Jacques, 5e; **M** Cluny–La Sorbonne) has services throughout Europe. The **Gare Routière Internationale de Paris-Galliéni** (Map pp104-5, H5; ☎ 08 92 89 90 91; 28 av du Général de Gaulle; **M** Gallieni), the city's international bus terminal, is in the inner suburb of Bagnolet.

GETTING AROUND

Walking is the best way to see Paris, but the city also has a fast, efficient and safe public transit system operated by **RATP** (Régie Autonome des Transports Parisians; www .ratp.fr). This book notes the nearest metro station after the **M** in each listing.

Recommended Modes of Transport

	Eiffel Tower	Arc de Triomphe	Louvre	Sacré-Cœur
Eiffel Tower	n/a	metro 25min	metro 35min	metro/funicular 40min
Arc de Triomphe	metro 25min	n/a	metro 20min	metro/funicular 25min
Louvre	metro 35min	metro 20min	n/a	metro/funicular 35min
Sacré-Coeur	metro/funicular 40min	metro/funicular 25min	metro/funicular 35min	n/a
Père Lachaise	metro 50min	metro 35min	metro 30min	metro/funicular 30min
place de la Bastille	metro 40min	metro 25min	metro 20min	metro/funicular 35min
Notre Dame	metro 30min	metro 25min	metro 20min	metro/funicular 30min
Église St-Germain des Prés	metro 30min	metro 30min	metro 25min	metro/funicular 30min

TRAVEL PASSES

The Mobilis and Paris Visite passes are valid on the metro, RER, SNCF's suburban lines, buses, night buses, trams and the Montmartre funicular railway.

The Mobilis card coupon allows unlimited travel for one day in two to eight zones (from €5.50 for zone 1–2). It is available at all metro, RER and SNCF stations in the Paris region.

Paris Visite (www.parisvisite.com) gives users unlimited travel, as well as discounted entry to certain museums, and other discounts and bonuses. Passes are valid for either three, five or eight zones. The zone 1–3 pass costs €8.35/13.70/18.25/26.65 for one/two/three/five days. A zone 1–5 pass (including travel to/from the two main airports) costs €16.75/26.65/37.35/45.70. Passes are sold at larger metro and RER stations, SNCF offices in Paris, and the airports.

METRO, RER & TRAM

Paris' underground rail network is the fastest way of getting around the city. It has two separate but linked systems: the metro, which has 14 lines and several hundred

Père Lachaise	place de la Bastille	Notre Dame	Église St-Germain des Prés
metro 50min	metro 40min	metro 30min	metro 30min
metro 35min	metro 25min	metro 25min	metro 30min
metro 30min	metro 20min	metro 20min	metro 25min
metro/funicular 30min	metro/funicular 35min	metro/funicular 30min	metro/funicular 30min
n/a	metro 25min	metro 30min	metro 35min
metro 25min	n/a	metro 15min	metro 20min
metro 30min	metro 15min	n/a	metro 15min
metro 35min	metro 20min	metro 15min	n/a

stations; and the RER (Réseau Express Régional), a network of five suburban services (designated A to E) that pass through the city centre.

Each metro line is marked by a number, colour and final destination, and has its own schedule. Most services begin about 5.30am with the last train starting between 12.35am and 1am. Services run to 2.15am on Saturday nights and the night before every public holiday.

Paris has three tram lines, two which go to the suburbs, and the new T3, which connects the 13e, 14e and 15e south of the Seine.

For transport information, contact **RATP** (☎ 08 92 68 77 14 in French, 08 92 68 41 14 in English; www.ratp.fr; 🕑 6am-9pm). Tram information is available at www.tramway.paris.fr.

Tickets for travel within the Paris city limits cost €1.40, or €10.90 for a *carnet* (book) of 10.

One ticket allows you to travel between any two metro stations for a period of two hours, no matter how many transfers are required. You can also use a ticket on the RER for travel within zone 1; on the bus; or on the tram (but you cannot transfer between them).

Keep your ticket until you exit the station or you risk a fine.

BUS

Frequent bus services run from
5.45am to 8.30pm, but the
number of routes is reduced at
night and on Sundays. Timetables
and route information is available
from RATP (p213).

Noctilien (www.noctilien.fr) night
buses operate after the metro
closes; the website has information and maps. The service's 27
routes cover most of the city.
Tickets cost the same as one metro
ticket for short journeys; longer
journeys require two tickets.

TAXI

You'll find taxis at ranks around
major intersections, or you can
hail them in the street. The *prise en
charge* (flag fall) is €2. Within the
city, it costs €0.77 per km for travel
between 7am and 7pm Monday
to Saturday (*Tarif A;* white light
on meter), and €1.09 per km from
7pm to 7am, all day Sunday and
public holidays (*Tarif B;* orange
light on meter). Travel in the suburbs *(Tarif C)* is €1.31 per km.

There's a €2.60 surcharge for
taking a fourth passenger, but
most drivers refuse to accept more
than three people for insurance
reasons. Each luggage item over
5kg costs €1, as do pick-ups from
SNCF mainline stations.

Radio-dispatched taxi companies, on call 24 hours, include the
following ones.

Alpha Taxis (☎ 01 45 85 85 85)
Taxis Bleus (☎ 01 49 36 10 10)
Taxis-Radio Étoile (☎ 01 42 70 41 41)

PRACTICALITIES
BUSINESS HOURS

Opening hours fluctuate con-
stantly – it's always safest to call
ahead. In general, shops and
business close on Sunday and
either Monday or Tuesday; many
also close for lunch (12.30pm to
2.30pm), and some also close
on Saturday afternoons. Shops
often open to 10pm once a week,
usually Thursday. Most banks are
open from 9am to 4pm (some
close for lunch).

Restaurants generally open
for lunch from noon to 3pm and
dinner from 7pm or 7.30pm until
at least 9.30pm. Restaurants that
vary from these times by more
than an hour have been noted in
the relevant reviews.

Final entry to attractions such
as monuments, museums and galleries is generally half an hour to
an hour before the official closing
times, including those listed in
this book.

DISCOUNTS

Concessions (usually 30% to 50%)
abound for youth, students and
seniors on everything from transport to museums. Bring whatever
concession ID you have from

home and flash it every time you pull out your wallet.

If you plan to visit a lot of museums, your best bet is a **Paris Museum Pass** (www.parismuseumpass.fr), available for two, four or six days (€30/45/60). It gives you entry to more than 60 museums and allows you to skip the queues and head straight in. Pick it up from tourist offices, participating museums and monuments, or branches of Fnac.

See right for ways to save on theatre tickets.

ELECTRICITY

Plugs in France have two round pins. Voltage is 220V AC, 50Hz. Appliances rated US 110V need a transformer to work safely. Transformers and adaptors can be bought at shops including Fnac in Forum des Halles (p80) and BHV (p123).

EMERGENCIES

Pickpockets prey on busy places; stay alert to the possibility of someone surreptitiously reaching for your pockets or bags.

Many locals find the park above the Forum des Halles (p80) dodgy, especially at night.

The metro is safe to use until it closes, including for women travelling alone, but stations best avoided late at night include the long passageways of Châtelet–

Les Halles and Montparnasse Bienvenüe, as well as Château Rouge, Gare du Nord, Strasbourg St-Denis, Réaumur-Sébastopol and Stalingrad. *Bornes d'alarme* (alarm boxes) are located in the centre of each metro/RER platform and in some station corridors.

Emergency phone numbers:
Ambulance (☎ 15)
Fire Brigade (☎ 18)
Police (☎ 17)
Rape Crisis Hotline (☎ 08 00 05 95 95)
SOS Helpline (☎ 01 47 23 80 80)

ENTERTAINMENT BOOKING AGENCIES

Tickets to concerts, theatre performances and sporting events are available from **Fnac** (www.fnac.fr in French), including its large branch in the Forum des Halles (p80). **Virgin Megastore** (www.virginmega.fr in French), including its late-opening Champs Élysées store (p63), also sells tickets. Otherwise try **Agence Perrossier & SOS Théâtres** (Map pp50-1, F4; ☎ 01 42 60 58 31, 01 44 77 88 55; www.agencedetheatresdeparis.fr; 6 place de la Madeleine, 8e; 🕑 10am-7pm Mon-Fri, to 5.30pm Sat; Ⓜ Madeleine).

If you haven't prebooked your theatre tickets, on the day of the performance theatres across town make unsold tickets available to plays, concerts, operas, ballets and other events at half price (plus commission of about €2.50). The two main discount ticket outlets:

Kiosque Théâtre Madeleine (Map pp50-1, F3; opposite 15 place de la Madeleine, 8e; ⏰ 12.30-7.45pm Tue-Sat, 12.30-3.45pm Sun; Ⓜ Madeleine)
Montparnasse Kiosque Théâtre (Map pp144-5, B5; parvis Montparnasse, 15e; ⏰ 12.30-7.45pm Tue-Sat, 12.30-3.45pm Sun; Ⓜ Montparnasse Bienvenüe) which keeps the same hours.

Websites www.billetreduc.com and www.ticketac.com (both in French) sell discounted tickets online.

HOLIDAYS

New Year's Day *(Jour de l'An)* 1 January
Easter Sunday *(Pâques)* late March/April
Easter Monday *(Lundi de Pâques)* late March/April
May Day *(Fête du Travail)* 1 May
Victoire 1945 (Victory in Europe Day) 8 May
Ascension Thursday *(L'Ascension)* May
Whit Sunday/Whit Monday *(Pentecôte/ Lundi de Pentecôte)* May/June
Bastille Day *(Fête Nationale)* 14 July
Assumption Day *(L'Assomption)* 15 August
All Saints' Day *(La Toussaint)* 1 November
Armistice Day *(Le Onze Novembre)* 11 November
Christmas Day *(Noël)* 25 December

INTERNET

You'll find phonecard-operated internet terminals called **Netanoo** (www.netanoo.com in French) in certain phone boxes throughout Paris. A €7.50 *télécarte* gives about 50 minutes online. Some metro and RER stations offer free internet access and 50-odd post offices have internet stations called **Cyberposte** (www.laposte.net in French). Many hotels and some cafés offer wi-fi.

Internet cafés are prevalent throughout Paris; prices start at around €3 per hour.

Useful websites include the following:
Lonely Planet (www.lonelyplanet.com) Information, links and resources.
MA Shuman (http://mashumin.com) Short documentaries in English on little-known aspects of Paris by a Chinese-Parisian filmmaker.
Paris DJs (www.parisdjs.com) Groove around town with free weekly podcast compilations by northern *arrondissement* DJs.
Paris Notes (www.parisnotes.com) Paid subscription for in-depth newsletters, as well as lots of handy info online for free.
Paris Tourist Office (www.parisinfo.com) Official tourism website with stacks of info in multiple languages.
Secrets of Paris (www.secretsofparis.com) Despite its author's likeness to Mona Lisa, this terrific website and free newsletter are chock-full of up-to-date city info.

LANGUAGE
BASICS

Hello.	*Bonjour.*
Good evening.	*Bonsoir.*
Goodbye.	*Au revoir.*
How are you?	*Comment allez-vous?*
I'm fine.	*Bien, merci.*
Please.	*S'il vous plaît.*
Thank you.	*Merci.*

Yes.	Oui.
No.	Non.
Excuse me/ Sorry.	Excusez-moi/ Pardon.
I (don't) understand	Je (ne) comprends (pas).
Do you speak English?	Parlez-vous anglais?

EATING & DRINKING

That was delicious!	C'était délicieux!
I'm a vegetarian.	Je suis végétarien/ végétarienne. (m/f)
The bill, please.	L'addition, s'il vous plaît.

SHOPPING

How much is it?	C'est combien?
It's too expensive.	C'est trop cher.

EMERGENCIES

I'm sick.	Je suis malade.
Help!	Au secours!
Call the police!	Appelez la police!
Call a doctor!	Appelez un médecin!
Call an ambulance.	Appelez un ambulance!

DAYS & NUMBERS

today	aujourd'hui
tomorrow	demain
yesterday	hier

0	zéro
1	un
2	deux
3	trois
4	quatre
5	cinq
6	six
7	sept
8	huit
9	neuf
10	dix
11	onze
12	douze
13	treize
14	quatorze
15	quinze
16	seize
17	dix-sept
18	dix-huit
19	dix-neuf
20	vingt
21	vingt et un
22	vingt-deux
30	trente
40	quarante
50	cinquante
60	soixante
70	soixante-dix
80	quatre-vingts
90	quatre-vingt-dix
100	cent
1000	mille

MONEY

When you hear Londoners and New Yorkers lament how expensive Paris is, you know its bohemian days are well and truly past. Count on spending around €85 to €150 per person, per day on top of your hotel bill (much more if you're planning on *haute cuisine* dining or hitting the ritzy boutiques or both). Savvy budget travellers might get by on around €50 in addition to accommodation expenses.

For currency exchange rates, see the inside front cover.

ATMS

Many ATMs won't accept PIN codes with more than four digits – ask your bank for advice before you leave.

CHANGING MONEY & TRAVELLERS CHEQUES

Ever-fewer establishments accept travellers cheques. Since the advent of the euro, there are also fewer *bureaux de change* – though they offer a better rate for travellers cheques (6% to just under 10% plus €3) than for cash (6% and 13% plus €3 or €4).

The most flexible travellers cheques are issued by Amex and Visa, as they can often (but not always) be changed at post offices.

CREDIT CARDS

Visa is the most widely accepted credit card, followed by Master-Card. American Express and Diners Club cards are only accepted at the more exclusive establishments. Some restaurants still don't accept credit cards. A computer-chip credit card is required for many automated services, such as ticket machines.

NEWSPAPERS
Paris' main daily newspapers are the conservative *Le Figaro,* the sombre, centre-left *Le Monde,* and the arty, left-leaning *Libération*.

ORGANISED TOURS
BICYCLE & SEGWAY TOURS
Fat Tire Bike Tours (Map pp40-1, D3; ☎ 01 56 58 10 54; www.fattirebiketours paris.com; 24 rue Edgar Faure, 15e; ⏰ office 9am-7pm; Ⓜ La Motte-Picquet Grenelle) Popular day- and night-time city tours by bicycle from March to November; prices start from €24. The same company runs fun 'segway' tours on gyroscopic two-wheeled contraptions between mid-February and mid-December, starting from €70.

BOAT TOURS
Numerous companies cruise on *la ligne de vie de Paris* (the lifeline of Paris, aka the Seine) and Paris' charming canals.

Canal Cruises
Canauxrama (☎ 01 42 39 15 00; www .canauxrama.com; Mon-Fri €14/8, after noon Sat & Sun €14; ⏰ Mar-Nov; Ⓜ Jaurès or Bastille) Barges travel between Port de Plaisance de Paris-Arsenal, 12e, opposite 50 blvd de la Bastille, and the Parc de la Villette, 19e, along Canal St-Martin and Canal de l'Ourcq, including an illuminated underground section. Departures are at 9.45am and 2.30pm from Port de Plaisance de Paris-Arsenal (Map pp116–17, E5) throughout the season and, in July and August, at 9.45am and 2.45pm from Bassin de la Villette (pull-out map, N3).

Paris Canal Croisières (☎ 01 42 40 96 97; www.pariscanal.com; Bassin de la Villette, 19-21 quai de la Loire, 19e; cruises €16/9; ☼ mid-Mar–mid-Nov; Ⓜ Jaurès or Assemblée Nationale) Daily 2½-hour cruises depart from quai Anatole France (Map pp40–1, H1), just northwest of the Musée d'Orsay at 9.30am and depart from Bassin de la Villette (Map pp116–17, E5) for the return trip at 2.30pm.

River Cruises

Bateaux-Mouches (Map pp50-1, D5; ☎ 01 42 25 96 10; www.bateaux mouches.com in French; Port de la Conférence, 8e; tickets €8/4; ☼ every 30 min 10am-11pm Apr-Sep, every 45 min 11am-9pm Oct-Mar; Ⓜ Alma-Marceau) A 70-minute cruise with multilanguage commentary.

Bateaux Parisiens (Map pp40-1, C2; ☎ 01 46 99 43 13; www.bateauxparis iens.com; Port de la Bourdonnais, 7e; tickets €9.50/4.50; Ⓜ Alma-Marceau) One-hour river circuits with commentary in 13 languages; cruises run every 30 minutes from 10am to 10.30pm from April to September, and every hour from 10am to 10pm from October to March.

Batobus (☎ 08 25 05 01 01; www .batobus.com; day pass €11/5) Hop-on, hop-off waterbus making eight stops between the Eiffel Tower and the Jardin des Plantes; boats leave every 25 to 30 minutes from 10am; no boats run from early January to early February.

WALKING TOURS

Locals lead walks through the Belleville area; see p103.

Paris Walks (☎ 01 48 09 21 40; www .paris-walks.com; walks from €10/5) Entertaining and informative tours in English focussing on various quarters/themes.

SMOKING

As of 1 February 2007, smoking is forbidden in all public places throughout France; with restaurants and bars following within a year at the latest.

TELEPHONE

France uses the GSM 900/1800 cellular system, compatible with phones from the UK, Australia and most of Asia (and all tri-band phones), but not GSM 1900 phones from North America (GSM 1900/900 phones are OK), or the separate Japanese system.

Public telephones require a phonecard *(télécarte)*, which can be purchased at post offices, *tabacs*, supermarkets, SNCF ticket windows, metro stations and anywhere displaying a blue sticker with *'télécarte en vente ici'* (phonecards sold here). Cards start from €7.50.

COUNTRY & CITY CODES

France's country code is ☎ 33. There are no area codes – you always dial the full 10-digit number. Paris numbers start with ☎ 01 (drop the 0 if calling from abroad). To call abroad from France, dial ☎ 00 before the country code.

USEFUL NUMBERS
International directory assistance
(☎ 32 12)
Local directory assistance (☎ 11 87 10)
Full list at www.allo118.com.

TIPPING
French law requires that restaurant, café and hotel bills include a *service compris* (service charge), usually 15%, so a tip is neither necessary nor expected, although people sometimes leave a euro or two in restaurants.

TOURIST INFORMATION
The main branch of the **Paris Convention & Visitors Bureau** (Office de Tourisme et de Congrès de Paris; Map pp50-1, G4; ☎ 08 92 68 30 00; www .parisinfo.com; 25-27 rue des Pyramides, 1er; ⏱ 9am-7.30pm Jun-Oct, 10am-7pm Mon-Sat & 11am-7pm Sun Nov-May; Ⓜ Pyramides) is about 500m northwest of the Louvre.

The tourist bureau also maintains six centres (telephone numbers and websites are the same as for the main office) elsewhere in Paris.

Anvers (Map p89, D4; opposite 72 blvd Rochechouart, 18e; ⏱ 10am-6pm; Ⓜ Anvers)

Eiffel Tower (Map pp40-1, C2; btwn Piliers Nord and Est, Parc du Champ de Mars, 7e; ⏱ 11am-6.40pm 25 Mar-Oct; Ⓜ Champ de Mars-Tour Eiffel) Kiosk located between the Nord and East Pillars beneath the Eiffel Tower.

Gare de Lyon (Map pp116-17, F6; Arrivals hall, 20 blvd Diderot, 12; ⏱ 8am-6pm Mon-Sat; Ⓜ Gare de Lyon) In the arrivals hall for mainline trains.

Gare du Nord (Map pp104-5, C3;18 rue de Dunkerque, 10e; ⏱ 8am-6pm; Ⓜ Gare du Nord) At the station's eastern end.

Opéra-Grands Magasins (Map pp50-1, G3; 11 rue Scribe, 9e; ⏱ 9am-6.30pm Mon-Sat; Ⓜ Auber or Opéra)

Syndicate d'Initiative de Montmartre (Map p89, C4; 21 place du Tertre, 18e; ⏱ 10am-7pm; Ⓜ Abbesses)

TRAVELLERS WITH DISABILITIES
Paris' antiquated architecture, including much of the metro, means unfortunately that wheelchair access is severely limited throughout the city and ramps are rare – though newer hotels, museums and public facilities must by law have *fauteuil roulent* (wheelchair) access. In this book, we've used the symbol ♿ to denote sites that are wheelchair accessible, but check ahead regarding specific requirements. Many restaurants may only have partial access and restaurant bathrooms may not accommodate wheelchairs or provide rails – ask ahead when you book.

INFORMATION & ORGANISATIONS
The tourist office website (www .parisinfo.com) has excellent

information for travellers with disabilities, and lists organisations, as well as some establishments with facilities for travellers with physical, mental, visual and hearing disabilities. Access-Able Travel Source (www.access-able.com) also has some good links for organisations that can provide advice about wheelchair access in Paris.

For information on wheelchair accessibility for all forms of public transport, the *Guide Practique à l'Usage des Personnes à Mobilité Réduite* from the **Syndicat des Transports d'Île de France** (☎ 01 47 53 28 00; www.stif-idf.fr) is indispensable.

>INDEX

See also separate indexes for See (p228), Shop (p229), Eat (p230), Drink (p231) and Play (p232).

1968 uprising 201

A
accommodation 176-7
air travel 209-11
ambulance 215
Aquarium Tropical 122
Arc de Triomphe 52
Arc de Triomphe area
  48-71, **50-1**
Arc de Triomphe du
  Carrousel 73
arcades 192, *see also* Shop
  and Eat *subindexes*
architecture
  Art Deco 15, 65, 95,
    131, 149
  Art Nouveau 39, 47,
    63-4, 83, 119, 126,
    201
  Gothic 135, 173
  Islamic 147-8
  medieval 151
  neoclassical 153
art 178-9,
  Arabian 147-8
  Art Nouveau 43, 119
  contemporary 22, 54,
    73
  cubism 22, 54, 73,
    121

000 map pages

impressionism 14, 43,
  55, 172
surrealism 54, 91
ATMs 218

B
ballet 194, *see also* Play
  subindex
Ballon Eutelsat 39
Balzac, Honoré de 54
Banlieues Bleues 24
bars, *see* Drink *subindex*
Basilique du Sacré-Cœur 90
Bastille 114-33, **116-17**
Bastille Day 26
Beach, Sylvia 12
Before Sunset (film) 132,
  208
belle époque period 201
Belleville 102-13, **104-5**
Bercy Village 154
Bibliothèque Nationale de
  France 154
Bibliothèque Publique
  d'Information 22
bicycle tours 218
boat tours 17, 218-19
Bois de Boulogne 57
Bois de Vincennes 122
Bonaparte, Napoleon
  43, 201
books 207
bouquinistes 139

bridges 138, 187
brunch 129
bus travel 211, 214
business hours 206, 214,
  see also inside front cover

C
Ça Se Visite! Belleville
  Walking Tours 103
cabarets 197, *see also* Play
  subindex
cafés, *see* Drink *subindex*
canal cruises 17, 218-19
Canal St-Martin 103
Carrée Rive Gauche 156
Catacombes 146
Cathédrale de Notre Dame
  de Paris 135
cathedrals, *see* See *subindex*
cell phones 219
cemeteries, *see* See
  subindex
Centre Pompidou 22, 73
Champagne region 173
Champs-Élysées 52
Champs-Élysées area 48-71,
  50-1
chansons 99, 197, *see
  also* Play *subindex*
Château de Bagatelle 57
Château de Versailles 170-1
Château de Vincennes 122
children's meals 84

Chinatown 155
Chinese New Year 24
Chirac, Jacques 202-3
churches, *see* See *subindex*
Cimetière de Montmartre 90
Cimetière du Montparnasse 146
Cimetière du Père Lachaise 20-1, 103
cinema, *see* film
cinemas, *see* Play *subindex*
Cité des Sciences et de l'Industrie 103
climate change 209
clubbing 68, 71, *see also* Play *subindex*
coffee 111
comedy 85-6
Conciergerie 138
costs 217-18, *see also inside front cover*
    discount cards 214-15
credit cards 218
cruises 17, 218-19

D
Da Vinci Code, The (film) 18, 208
Dalí Espace Montmartre 91
dangers 215
Delanoë, Bertrand 202
disabilities, travellers with 220-1
discount cards 214-15

000 map pages

drinking 195, *see also* Drink *subindex*
    Arc de Triomphe area 66-8
    Bastille 130-2
    Belleville 111
    Champs-Élysées area 66-8
    Eiffel Tower area 47
    Grands Boulevards area 66-8
    Invalides 47
    Latin Quarter 164-7
    Les Halles 84-5
    Louvre area 84-5
    Marais 130-2
    Montmartre 96-7
    Montparnasse 164-7
    St-Germain des Prés 164-7

E
economy 206
Église de la Madeleine 53
Église du Dôme 43
Église St-Germain des Prés 146-7
Église St-Sulpice 147
Eiffel Tower 10-11, 39, 42, 43
Eiffel Tower area 38-47, **40-1**
electricity 215
emergencies 215
entertainment booking agencies 215-16
Espace Histoire 53
ethnicity 198, 206-7
etiquette 204-5
European Heritage Days 27

events 23-8
exchange rates, *see inside front cover*

F
fashion 190-1, *see also* Shop *subindex*
    festivals 24
    museums 55
Festival d'Automne 27
festivals 23-8, 108
Fête des Vendages de Montmartre 27
Fête du Beaujolais 28
film 208
    festivals 27
fire services 215
Foire du Trône 25
Foire Internationale d'Art Contemporain 27
Fondation Cartier Pour l'Art Contemporain 147
food 180-1, *see also* Eat *subindex*
    Arc de Triomphe area 63-6
    Bastille 126-30
    Belleville 108-10
    brunch 129
    Champs-Élysées area 63-6
    children's meals 84
    costs, *see inside front cover*
    Eiffel Tower area 45-7
    Grands Boulevards area 63-6
    Île de la Cité 141
    Île St-Louis 141
    Invalides 45-7

Latin Quarter 160-4
Les Halles 81-4
Louvre area 81-4
Marais 126-30
Montmartre 93-9
Montparnasse 160-4
St-Germain des Prés 160-4
vegetarian travellers 46
football 202
French Revolution 201

G
Gainsbourg, Serge 147
Galerie d'Anatomie Comparée et de Paléontologie 150
Galerie de Minéralogie et de Géologie 150
Galerie Musée Baccarat 53
Galeries du Panthéon Bouddhique du Japon et de la Chine 56
galleries 178, see also See subindex
gardens, see See subindex
gay & lesbian travellers 196, see also Drink and Play subindexes
festivals 25
Gay Pride March 25
Giverny 172
Grande Arche 53
Grande Galerie de l'Évolution 150
Grande Parade de Paris 24
Grands Boulevards area 48-71, **50-1**
Guimard synagogue 119

H
hamams 150
Haussmann, Baron Georges-Eugène 48, 201
Hemingway, Ernest 66, 166, 183, 207
history 200-3
holidays 216
horse racing 57
Hôtel de Sully 115
Hôtel de Ville 118
Hôtel des Invalides 43

I
ice cream 140, see also Eat subindex
ice skating 28
Île de la Cité 134-41, **136-7**
Île St-Louis 134-41, **136-7**
immigration 206-7
Institut du Monde Arabe 147-8
Internationaux de France de Tennis 25
internet access 216
internet resources 216
food 181
gay & lesbian travellers 196
markets 185
theatre 194, 216
Invalides 38-47, **40-1**
islands 134-41, **136-7**
itineraries 29-33

J
Jardin d'Acclimatation 57
Jardin des Plantes 148

Jardin des Tuileries 73
Jardin du Luxembourg 13, 149
Jardin du Palais Royal 76
Jardins du Trocadéro 54
jazz 87, 112, 197, see also Play subindex
Jeu de Paume 76
Joan of Arc 200

K
Kerouac, Jack 207

L
La Course des Garçons de Café 25
La Défense 53
La Goutte d'Or en Fête 26
language 111, 204-6, 216-17
Latin Quarter 142-68, **144-5**
Le Pen, Jean-Marie 202
Les Halles 72-87, **74-5**
lesbian travellers, see gay & lesbian travellers
libraries, see See subindex
literature, see books
Louis XIV 170, 201
Louvre, the 18-19, 77, 78
Louvre area 72-87, **74-5**

M
Maison de Balzac 54
Maison de Claude Monet 172
Maison de l'Air 106
Maison de Victor Hugo 118
Maison Européenne de la Photographie 119

INDEX

Marais 114-33, **116-17**
Marathon International de Paris 25
marionettes 153
markets 184, *see also* Shop and Eat *subindexes*
Ménagerie du Jardin des Plantes 149
metro 46, 212-13
    safety 215
    tours 121
mobile phones 219
Mois de la Photo 28
Mona Lisa 18, 79
Monet, Claude 14, 55, 76, 172
money 217-18, *see also* costs
Montmartre 16, 88-101, **89**
Montparnasse 142-68, **144-5**
Morrison, Jim 20
Mosquée de Paris 149, 150
Moulin Rouge 101
Mumm 173
Musée Carnavalet 119
Musée Cognacq-Jay 119
Musée d'Art Américain 172
Musée d'Art et d'Histoire du Judaïsme 120
Musée d'Art Moderne de la Ville de Paris 54
Musée de la Contrefaçon 55
Musée de la Marine 56
Musée de la Mode et du Textile 79

Musée de la Poste 150
Musée de la Publicité 79
Musée de l'Armée 43
Musée de l'Érotisme 91
Musée de l'Homme 56
Musée de l'Orangerie 14, 76
Musée de Montmartre 91-2
Musée des Arts Décoratifs 79
Musée des Arts et Métiers 120
Musée des Égouts de Paris 43
Musée d'Orsay 43-4
Musée du Louvre 18-19, 77, 78
Musée du Luxembourg 150
Musée du Parfum 55
Musée du Quai Branly 44
Musée du Stylo et de l'Écriture 55
Musée Édith Piaf 106
Musée Galliera de la Mode de la Ville de Paris 55
Musée Grévin 55-6
Musée Guimet des Arts Asiatiques 56
Musée Marmottan 55
Musée National d'Art Moderne 22, 73
Musée National d'Histoire Naturelle 150
Musée National du Moyen Age 151
Musée National Eugène Delacroix 151
Musée Picasso 121
Musée Rodin 44-5
museums & galleries 178-9, *see also* See *subindex*
    discount cards 215

music 194, *see also* Play *subindex*
    chansons 99, 197
    festivals 24, 25, 26
    jazz 87, 112, 197
    opera 194

N
Napoleon III, Emperor 201
New Year's Eve 28
newspapers 218
nightlife, *see* Play *subindex*
Noir, Victor 20
Nouvel, Jean 149
Nuit Blanche 27

O
opera 194, *see also* Play *subindex*

P
Palais de Chaillot 56
Palais de Tokyo 56
Panthéon 153
Parc de Bagatelle 57
Parc de Belleville 106
Parc de la Villette 107
Parc du Champ de Mars 153
Parc Floral de Paris 122
Paris, Capitale de la Creation 24
Paris Cinéma 27
Paris Jazz Festival 25
Paris Plage 26
Paris Zoo 122
parks, *see* See *subindex*
Passage Brady 110
Patinoire de l'Hôtel de Ville 28
Périphérique 203

000 map pages

Piaf, Édith 20, 106
Picasso, Pablo 121
place de la Bastille 121
place de la Concorde 56
place de la Madeleine 59
place des Vosges 125
place du Tertre 90
place Vendôme 56, 58
planning 33, 214
Pletzl 119
police 215
politics 202-3
Pommery 173
Pont Neuf 138
population 203
Portes Ouvertes des Ateliers
    d'artistes de Belleville
    108
Portes Ouvertes des Ateliers
    de Ménilmontant 108
Promenade Plantée 15, 121

R
Reims 173
restaurants, see Eat
    subindex
ring road 203
river cruises 17, 219
Rodin, Auguste 44-5
romance 188
Romans 200
rue Cler 45
rue Montorgueil 81
rue Mouffetard 162

S
St-Germain des Prés
    142-68, 144-5
Ste-Chapelle 139

Salman, Yvan 20
Seine 17
Shakespeare & Company
    12, 158, 159
shopping 190-1, see
    also Shop subindex
    Bastille 122-6
    Belleville 108
    Eiffel Tower area 45
    Île de Cité 139-41
    Île St-Louis 139-41
    Invalides 45
    Latin Quarter 154-9
    Les Halles 79-81
    Louvre area 79-81
    Marais 122-6
    Montmartre 92-3
    Montparnasse 154-9
    St-Germain des Prés
        154-9
smoking 219
soccer 202
Sorbonne 153
sporting events
    Internationaux de France
        de Tennis 25
    Marathon International
        de Paris 25
    Tour de France 26
sporting venues, see Play
    subindex
Stade de France 101

T
Taittinger 173
taxis 214
telephone services 219-20
Tenniseum-Musée de
    Roland Garros 57

theatre 194, 215-16, see
    also Play subindex
Théâtre-Musée des
    Capucines 55
Thinker, The 44-5
tipping 220
Tombeau de Napoléon 1er 43
Tour de France 26
Tour Montparnasse 153
Tour St-Jacques 73
tourist information 220
tours 218-19
    bicycle 218
    boat 17, 218-19
    metro 121
    walking 103, 219
train travel 211, 212-13
trams 212-13
travel passes 212
travellers cheques 218

V
vacations 216
vegetarian travellers 46, see
    also Eat subindex
Versailles 170-1
views 186-7
Vikings 200
Villepin, Dominique de
    202-3

W
walks 103, 192-3, 219
Waterlilies 14, 55, 76
Wilde, Oscar 20
wine
    festivals 27, 28
    museums 65
WWII 201

SEE

Aquariums
Aquarium Tropical 122

Bridges
Pont Neuf 138

Canals
Canal St-Martin 103

Cemeteries & Memorials
Catacombes 146
Cimetière de Montmartre 90
Cimetière du Montparnasse 146
Cimetière du Père Lachaise 20-1, 103
Tombeau de Napoléon 1er 43

Champagne Houses
Mumm 173
Pommery 173
Taittinger 173

Châteaus & Palaces
Château de Bagatelle 57
Château de Versailles 170-1
Château de Vincennes 122
Conciergerie 138
Palais de Chaillot 56
Palais de Tokyo 56

Churches & Cathedrals
Basilique du Sacré-Cœur 90
Cathédrale de Notre Dame de Paris 135
Église de la Madeleine 53

Église du Dôme 43
Église St-Germain des Prés 146-7
Église St-Sulpice 147
Ste-Chapelle 139

Libraries
Bibliothèque Nationale de France 154
Bibliothèque Publique d'Information 22

Mosques
Mosquée de Paris 149, 150

Museums & Galleries
Centre Pompidou 22, 73
Cité des Sciences et de l'Industrie 103
Dalí Espace Montmartre 91
Espace Histoire 53
Fondation Cartier Pour l'Art Contemporain 147
Galerie d'Anatomie Comparée et de Paléontologie 150
Galerie de Minéralogie et de Géologie 150
Galerie Musée Baccarat 53
Galeries du Panthéon Bouddhique du Japon et de la Chine 56
Grande Galerie de l'Évolution 150
Hôtel de Sully 115
Hôtel de Ville 118
Institut du Monde Arabe 147-8
Jeu de Paume 76
Maison de Balzac 54

Maison de Claude Monet 172
Maison de l'Air 106
Maison de Victor Hugo 118
Maison Européenne de la Photographie 119
Musée Carnavalet 119
Musée Cognacq-Jay 119
Musée d'Art Américain 172
Musée d'Art et d'Histoire du Judaïsme 120
Musée d'Art Moderne de la Ville de Paris 54
Musée de la Contrefaçon 55
Musée de la Marine 56
Musée de la Mode et du Textile 79
Musée de la Poste 150
Musée de la Publicité 79
Musée de l'Armée 43
Musée de l'Érotisme 91
Musée de l'Homme 56
Musée de l'Orangerie 14, 76
Musée de Montmartre 91-2
Musée des Arts Décoratifs 79
Musée des Arts et Métiers 120
Musée des Égouts de Paris 43
Musée d'Orsay 43-4
Musée du Louvre 18-19, 77, 78
Musée du Luxembourg 150
Musée du Parfum 55
Musée du Quai Branly 44
Musée du Stylo et de l'Écriture 55
Musée Édith Piaf 106
Musée Galliera de la Mode de la Ville de Paris 55
Musée Grévin 55-6

000 map pages

Musée Guimet des Arts Asiatiques 56
Musée Marmottan 55
Musée National d'Art Moderne 22, 73
Musée National d'Histoire Naturelle 150
Musée National du Moyen Age 151
Musée National Eugène Delacroix 151
Musée Picasso 121
Musée Rodin 44-5
Palais de Chaillot 56
Palais de Tokyo 56
Tenniseum-Musée de Roland Garros 57
Théâtre-Musée des Capucines 55

Notable Buildings & Structures
Arc de Triomphe 52
Arc de Triomphe du Carrousel 73
Ballon Eutelsat 39
Centre Pompidou 22, 73
Eiffel Tower 10-11, 39, 42, 43
Grande Arche 53
Hôtel de Sully 115
Hôtel de Ville 118
Hôtel des Invalides 43
Musée du Louvre 18-19, 77, 78
Panthéon 153
Sorbonne 153
Tour Montparnasse 153
Tour St-Jacques 73

Notable Streets & Places
Champs-Élysées 52
place de la Bastille 121
place de la Concorde 56
place du Tertre 90
place Vendôme 56, 58

Parks & Gardens
Jardin d'Acclimatation 57
Jardin des Plantes 148
Jardin des Tuileries 73
Jardin du Luxembourg 13, 149
Jardin du Palais Royal 76
Jardins du Trocadéro 54
Parc de Bagatelle 57
Parc de Belleville 106
Parc de la Villette 107
Parc du Champ de Mars 153
Parc Floral de Paris 122
Promenade Plantée 15, 121

Synagogues
Guimard synagogue 119

Walks
Ça Se Visite! Belleville Walking Tours 103

Zoos
Ménagerie du Jardin des Plantes 149
Paris Zoo 122

SHOP
Accessories
Alexandra Sojfer 155
Cacharel 156
Lancel 61

Antiques
Zut! 92

Arcades
Galerie Véro Dodat 80
Galerie Vivienne 61
Passage des Panoramas 61
Passage du Grand Cerf 61
Passage Jouffroy 61
Passage Verdeau 61
Viaduc des Arts 125

Arts & Crafts
Boutique Paris-Musées 124
Viaduc des Arts 125

Books
Abbey Bookshop 154
Le Mots à La Bouche 124
Librairie Gourmande 158
Librairie Ulysse 139
Red Wheelbarrow Bookstore 125
Shakespeare & Company 12, 158, 159
Village Voice 158

Department Stores
Bazar de l'Hôtel de Ville (BHV) 123
Drugstore Publicis 59
Galeries Lafayette 60
Le Bon Marché 156
Le Printemp 62-3
Tati 92

Fashion
agnès b 79
Antoine et Lili 122
Azzedine Alaïa 123

Cacharel 156
Chanel 63
Chloé 58
Christian Dior 63
Christian Lacroix 63
Colette 79-80
Commes des Garçons 63
Eres 59
Givenchy 63
Hermès 63
Jean-Paul Gaultier 63
Kenzo 81
Lanvin 61-2
Les Belles Images 124
Louis Vuitton 63
Shine 125
Sonia Rykiel 158
Un Chien dans le
    Marais 125
Thierry Mugler 63
Yves Saint Laurent 63

Food & Drink
Fauchon 59
Fromagerie Alléosse
    59-60
La Grande Épicerie de
    Paris 156
La Maison de la Truffe 61
La Maison du Miel 61
La Petite Scierie 139
O&Co 141

Homewares
Antoine et Lili 122
Vache & Cow 81

Markets
Marché aux Fleurs 140
Marché aux Puces d'Aligre
    124
Marché aux Puces de la
    Porte de Vanves 158
Marché aux Puces de
    Montreuil 108
Marché aux Puces de
    St-Ouen 92

Music
Virgin Megastore 63

Notable Places &
Squares
Carrée Rive Gauche 156
place de la Madeleine 59
place des Vosges 125

Perfume
Cacharel 156
Guerlain 60-1
Kenzo 81
Lanvin 61-2
Séphora 63

Sex Shops
Rebecca Rils 92

Shopping Centres & Malls
Carrousel du Louvre 79
Forum des Halles 80

Toys
Clair de Rêve 139

EAT
Arabian
Le Ziryab 162

Brasseries
Brasserie Bofinger 126
Brasserie de l'Île
    St-Louis 141
Le Relais Gascon 95
Restaurant Musée
    d'Orsay 47

Breton
Crêperie Bretonne 126

Caféterias
Bazar de l'Hôtel de Ville
    (BHV) Cafétéria 126
Le Loir dans la Theiere 129

Crêperies
Chez Nicos 160
Crêperie Bretonne 126

Ethiopian
Godjo 160

French
À la Cloche d'Or 94
Au Pied de Cochon 81
Aux Négociants 94
Café Marly 82
Chez Marie 95
Chez Toinette 95
La Maison Rose 95
Le Chansonnier 109
Le Clown Bar 128
Le Coude Fou 128
Le Petit Bofinger 128
Le Roi du Pot au Feu 65
Le Train Bleu 128
Le Villaret 110
Les Dix Vins 162
L'Escargot 84

000 map pages

Restaurant Hélène Darroze
164
Ripaille 96

Fusion
Spoon, Food & Wine 66

Gastronomic
Alain Ducasse au Plaza
Athénée 63
Altitude 95 46
Comptoir de la
Gastronomie 83
Guy Savoy 64
La Tour d'Argent 160
L'Arpège 45-6
L'Avant-Goût 155
Le Bistrot du Sommelier 64-5
Le Cristal Room 65
Le Grand Véfour 83
Le Jules Verne 46
Les Ombres 46-7
Maison Prunier 65
Musée du Vin restaurant 65
Pierre Gagnaire 65
Taillevent 66

Ice Cream
Café le Flore en l'Île 140
Esterina 140
Maison Berthillon 140
Pozzetto 129-30

Indian
Bistro Indien 110

International
Georges 83
L'Atelier de Joël Robouchon
161

Kosher
Chez Marianne 126
La Boutique Jeune 127
L'As de Felafel 127

Lyonais
Aux Lyonnais 63-4

Markets
Marché aux Enfants Rouges
129
Marché Bastille 129
Marché Batignolles-Clichy 96
Marché Beauvau 129
Marché Belleville 110
Marché Brancusi 162
Marché Maubert 162
Marché Monge 162
Marché Raspail 162
Marché St-Quentin 110
rue Cler 45

**Notable Streets &
Arcades**
Passage Brady 110
rue Cler 45
rue Montorgueil 81
rue Mouffetard 162

Patisseries
Stohrer 84

Salons de Thé
Les Deux Abeilles 46

Seafood
Au Rocher de Cancale 82
Charlot, Roi des
Coquillages 95
Le Dôme 161

Senegalese
Au Village 108

Supermarkets
Tang Frères 155

Thai
Le Krung Thep 110

Tratiurs
Stohrer 84

Vegetarian
Grand Apétit 126
La Petit Légume 160

Vietnamese
My-Canh 155
Pho 67 Restaurant
Vietnam 163

DRINK
Bars
Andy Wahloo 130
Bar Hemingway 66
Bar Signature 164
Bistro des Augustins 164
Café Baroc 130
Café Chéri(e) 111
Curieux Spaghetti Bar 130
Harry's New York Bar 67
Kong 84-5
Le Tambour 85, 86
Le Vieux Chêne 166
Student Bar & Cie 167
Taverne Henri IV 141

Brasseries
Brasserie Lipp 164
La Closerie des Lilas 166

Cafés
Café Branly 47
Café Charbon 111
Café de Flore 165
Café des Hauteurs 47
Café des Phares 130
Café Le Refuge 96
Café Panis 166
Chez Prune 111
Drôle d'Endroit pour une
 Rencontre 97
La Palette 166
L'Atmosphere 111
L'Autre Café 111
Le Progrès 131
Le Pure Café 131
Le Select 166
Le Viaduc Café 132
Les Deux Magots 166
Les Deux Moulins 97
Les Éditeurs 167

Gay & Lesbian Venues
3W Kafé 130
Le Quetzal 131
Open Café 132

Salons de Thé
Angélina 84
Café Branly 47
Hédiard 67-8
La Charlotte en l'Île
 141
Ladurée 68
Mariage Frères 132

PLAY

Ballet
Ballet de l'Opéra National
 de Paris 68

Cabarets
Au Lapin Agile 99
Crazy Horse 68
Folies-Bergère 99
Le Lido 69
Moulin Rouge 101

Chansons
Chez Louisette 99
Le Limonaire 69
Le Vieux Belleville 113

Cinemas
Cinémathèque Française 154
Forum des Images 87
La Pagode 47
Le Champo 168

Clubs
Bistrot Latin 132
La Coupole 167
La Guinguette Pirate 155
Le Balajo 133
Le Batofar 155
Le Baron 68-9
Le Bastille 133
Triptique 71

Gay & Lesbian Venues
Le Pulp 70
Le Queen 70

Jazz Venues
China Club 133
Le Baiser Salé 87
Le Caveau de la Huchette 168
Le Duc des Lombards 87
New Morning 113
Sunset & Sunside 87

Live Music
La Cigale 100
La Java 113
Le Nouveau Casino 113
L'Élysée-Montmartre 100
L'Olympia 70

Opera Houses
Opéra Bastille 133
Palais Garnier 71

Pool Halls
Académie de Billard 99

Salsa Bars
Barrio Latino 132

Sporting Venues
Piscine Flottante 155
Stade de France 101

Theatres
Comédie Française Salle
 Richelieu 87
Comédie Française Studio
 Théâtre 87
Théâtre du Luxembourg 153
Théâtre du Vieux Colombie
 168

000 map pages